Death, Resurrection, and Transporter Beams

Death, Resurrection, and Transporter Beams

An Introduction to Five Christian Views on Life after Death

Silas N. Langley

WIPF & STOCK · Eugene, Oregon

DEATH, RESURRECTION, AND TRANSPORTER BEAMS
An Introduction to Five Christian Views on Life after Death

Copyright © 2014 Silas N. Langley. All rights reserved. Except for brief quotations in critical publications or reviews, no part of this book may be reproduced in any manner without prior written permission from the publisher. Write: Permissions. Wipf and Stock Publishers, 199 W. 8th Ave., Suite 3, Eugene, OR 97401.

Wipf and Stock
An Imprint of Wipf and Stock Publishers
199 W. 8th Ave., Suite 3
Eugene, OR 97401

www.wipfandstock.com

ISBN 13: 978-1-62564-176-2

Manufactured in the U.S.A.   08/15/2014

Unless otherwise indicated, Scripture quotations are from the New Revised Standard Version of the Bible, copyright 1989, Division of Christian Education of the National Council of Churches of Christ in the United States of America. Used by permission. All rights reserved.

Scripture quotations labeled NIV are from THE HOLY BIBLE, NEW INTERNATIONAL VERSION®, NIV® Copyright © 1973, 1978, 1984, 2011 by Biblica, Inc.® Used by permission. All rights reserved worldwide.

Scripture quotations labeled REB are taken from the Revised English Bible, copyright © Cambridge University Press and Oxford University Press 1989. All rights reserved.

This book is dedicated to my family,
Rhonda, Peter, and Joseph.

May you know the joys of this life and the next.

Contents

Introducing the Puzzle of Life after Death

   1. Death, Resurrection, and Transporter Beams | 3

   2. Thinking about Death and How We Survive It | 7

Framing the Puzzle: Guidelines for Choosing

   3. The Outer Frame: What Does the Bible Say? | 17

   4. The Middle Frame: What Does Science Say? | 30

   5. The Inner Frame: What Does Philosophy Say? | 38

Filling In the Puzzle: Five Ways to Die and Live Again

   6. Soul-Flight, Part 1 | 51

   7. Soul-Flight, Part 2 | 66

   8. Particle Beam: Resurrection as Reassembly | 77

   9. Data Stream: Resurrection as Re-creation | 89

   10. Saved by the Soul: Resurrection as Re-formation | 107

   11. Surfing in Slipstream: Death and Other Dimensions | 127

Processing the Puzzle: Implications of the
Five Options for the Here and Now

   12. Dealing with Death: Remembering the Dead and Preparing for Death | 147

   13. Near-Death Experiences, Ghosts, and Speaking with the Dead | 157

   14. Inward or Outward? On Saving, Healing, Caring, and Communing | 166

   15. Animals and the Earth: Toto, Dirt, and Eternal Life | 178

Finishing the Puzzle: Final Reflections

   16. Conclusion: Thoughts on Making a Choice | 197

Appendices

   A. Death and Resurrection: The Options | 207
   B. Views of the Self | 211
   C. The Timing of the Resurrection | 214
   D. Glossary | 215

Bibliography | 219

Introducing the Puzzle of Life after Death

1

Death, Resurrection, and Transporter Beams

You are on a spaceship set to self-destruct in one minute. There is only one way off the ship and you are not sure that one way will work.

You look out the ship's window and see the ship's destination. It is a planet with blue oceans, lush continents, and white clouds drifting dreamily over its surface. The designer of the ship said that the planet is a paradise, with a mild climate, abundant food sources, and no dangerous predators. You need to get down to that planet. You have less than a minute to figure out how.

Next to you is a panel. On that panel are five buttons and some instructions. Above the buttons you read the following:

> ### Teleportation Device
>
> One and only one of these buttons will get you to the planet. You may press only one of them. Choose wisely.
> 1. Soul-Flight
> 2. Particle Beam
> 3. Data Stream
> 4. Saved by the Soul
> 5. Surfing in Slipstream

Each button has further instructions:

Soul-Flight

This button will separate your soul from your body, which will remain on the ship. It will then propel your soul to the planet, where it may join with a completely new body. You will enjoy the ride to the planet, because you will be conscious the whole time. You are your soul after all and your body is just a shell.

Particle Beam

This button will disassemble your body into its atoms. Then it will teleport your atoms to your destination. There, your body will be reassembled from the very atoms that made up your body at the moment that you pushed the button. Then you will exist again, for you are your body after all.

Data Stream

This button will scan your mind and body. It will record all your memories, character traits, likes, dislikes, bodily features, and such, and then upload that information onto a computer. The computer will then transmit your data to another computer on the planet. The planet's computer will use that data to completely reconstruct an exact replica of your current mind and body. Your new body will be mostly like the one you have now, except that it will no longer be subject to pain or disease. But once reconstructed, you will regain your consciousness, sense of self-identity, memories, and everything else that makes you you. You will cease to exist while your data is transferred. But don't worry, you will live again.

> ### Saved by the Soul
>
> Like the first button, this button will propel your soul to the planet and you will be conscious during the journey. Once on the planet below, your soul will gather around itself whatever matter is at hand and re-create your very same body. It will be your very same body because it is made by your very same soul. After all, your body is the perfect expression of your soul. You will live again because you will have the same soul and the same body.

> ### Surfing in Slipstream
>
> This button will temporarily shift you into another dimension, parallel universe, or other such unimaginable realm and leave your body behind on the ship. But you will soon shift back into this dimension, universe, or whatever and show up right on the planet below. You will have some kind of weird dimensional body during the journey, since you can't exist without one. But don't worry. You will get a better body when you shift back into this dimension.

The designer of the ship left a guidebook. The guidebook mostly describes the ship and your journey on it. But it also says a few things about the end of your journey on the ship and your new life on the planet below. You remember it says that you would have a body on that planet. You think it says you would have the same body you have now, but improved. You also think the book says that you would be separated from your body during your journey from the ship to the planet. In places, the book seems to suggest you would be conscious during that journey. But you are not sure if you understand the book correctly. Some of your shipmates said that the book actually teaches that you will die on the ship, but then reawaken on the planet below. Others said that the book did not teach that we will have the *same* bodies on the planet as we have now. Some even said that the book teaches that we will not have any bodies at all. "Body" is just a metaphor for a disembodied soul romping around the planet.

The guidebook has proved trustworthy so far. Surely it can help you choose which button to push. But you aren't sure how to interpret what the book says. Your shipmates have already chosen which buttons to push. You are the only one left on the ship.

The clock is ticking. You must push one of the buttons or abandon all hope of your future survival.

Life is like a spaceship set for self-destruct. It will come to an end. Our hearts will stop beating and our neurons will stop firing. Our bodies will become corpses. Yet we are not without hope, because we believe that there is a way to jump ship.

We also face a "panel of buttons." Each button represents different beliefs about how we might survive our deaths and corresponds to one of the options on the teleportation device.

Most Christians believe there is a guidebook, the Bible, that helps them choose which button to push. But we are not always sure what the guidebook teaches. Scholars interpret the Bible in different ways much like the travelers on the spaceship interpret the spaceship's guidebook in different ways.

The Bible speaks of a paradise, heaven, waiting for us after we die. It is a place without death, pain, or suffering. The Bible also says that God will raise our bodies from the dead so that we will live forever with them in heaven. But we are unsure what it means for our bodies to raise from the dead. Some Christians believe the resurrection of the body is a metaphor for something else—for our living on in the memories of others, or for our disembodied souls going directly to heaven. Some Christians believe that the resurrection of the body refers to the raising of the same bodies that we have now. Others believe that it refers to altogether new bodies. The Bible also seems to say that we will be separate from our bodies for a time between death and resurrection and that we will be conscious during that time. But others say that a closer look at the Bible shows that it does not really teach this. Thus, we sometimes do not know what to believe because we are not sure who has the right interpretation.

Our survival after death, however, does not depend on getting it right. God will get us to heaven even if we haven't a clue how he does it. But we still have an important choice about what we are going to believe—about which button to push. Our choice does not influence what will happen to us after we die. But it does influence our choices in this life and our ability to reassure the skeptics and the doubters. Thus, we need to choose a button. Otherwise, our unconscious will choose for us. It may not choose wisely.

2

Thinking about Death and How We Survive It

THIS BOOK TACKLES ONE of the most important questions that we face in our lives: What happens after we die? Yet it is a question that we avoid asking. Thinking about death reminds us that we too shall sometime die. We'd rather not have the reminder. Sometimes we would rather get on with living than worry about the dying that will come.

We also have deeply held beliefs about death and the afterlife that we do not want to question. We hope, sometimes more profoundly than we hope for anything else, that we will live on after we die. That hope helps us endure the hardships of life. It sustained the slaves of the American South who had no hope of freedom in this life. Many also take comfort in the belief that our dearly departed loved ones are in heaven looking down on us. But we fear that thinking too deeply about the afterlife might lead us to doubt such beliefs.

Some cultures discourage talking about death. Many say that this is true about American society. We in America are not around death as much as persons from other societies both past and present. Fewer die young and death usually occurs in hospitals rather than in homes. We have few rituals to help us mourn the dead and are discouraged from mourning in public. Death has replaced sex as the current conversational taboo. Think about how often you have had a conversation with another person about death and the afterlife. Probably not too often.

We are at a disadvantage when we have such conversations. Most of us have not thought much about what we think happens to us when we die. We have beliefs about it, many of which we have gotten from church, parents, books, or films. But we haven't thought carefully about how to connect all those beliefs together. Part of us believes that we become ghosts like in the movie *Ghost*. Another part of us believes we become angels like Clarence in the movie *It's a Wonderful Life*. Yet another part believes that we become reincarnated again in another body here on earth, as in the Robin Williams movie *What Dreams May Come?* Or perhaps instead we imagine that we simply step into a great Light like the one the characters walk into at the end of the television show *Lost*. Such beliefs are like different types of Legos stored in separate cupboards in our brains. We never take them out to see if they will all fit together.

On one Sunday, the pastor preaches that we are our souls and not our bodies and that our souls go to heaven when we die. On another Sunday, he preaches that we are our bodies and God will raise them from the dead at the Last Judgment. But these two beliefs are inconsistent. They are the Legos in the cupboard that do not fit together.

But why worry about inconsistency? "A foolish consistency," as Ralph Waldo Emerson says, "is the hobgoblin of little minds."[1] Christians might say that it is the bugbear of those with little faith. Let the preacher preach. If his message doesn't square, then perhaps his faith is all the greater. Never mind the mind. It only causes trouble.

But we'd better mind the mind. Inconsistency violates the law of non-contradiction, which is the fundamental rule of all our thinking: "No statement and its denial can both be affirmed as true at the same time and in the same respect." It is important that Christians accept this rule. It makes communication possible. If I tell my wife that I love her, she's got to be able to know that I don't also mean that I don't love her. Because if I am also meaning that I don't love her when I say that I love her, then my statement has no meaning and is nonsense. Likewise, none of our statements can have any meaning if we intend that their opposites are also true at the exact same time and in the exact same respect. If the preacher preaches an inconsistency, then we are obliged to correct him.

We are sometimes tempted to make an exception when it comes to God. God can do anything, can't he? Therefore, God can make the impossible possible. Thus, we do not need to worry about how we survive our deaths. God will get us to heaven no matter how many contradictions he must commit to do it.

But even God has his limits. He can't, for example, create a stone that he can't lift. An all-powerful being must by definition be able to lift any stone. If God could not lift some stone, then God would not be God.

---

1. Emerson, "Self-Reliance," 155.

Thus, God can't create such a stone. God can create a stone that Hercules can't lift, but not one that he himself can't lift.

It might seem that God can't be all-powerful if there is something that he can't do. But a stone that God can't lift is not a something. It is a nothing. It is nonsense. It is like a square circle. It just cannot be. Anyone who says otherwise is trying to sell you something.

We make the mistake of thinking that God must be able to create square circles and stones that he can't lift because we get the wrong idea about what it means to be omnipotent. Omnipotence means being able to do everything that isn't nonsense. Or, as philosophers would say, it means being able to do everything that is *logically possible*. As great Christian thinkers such as Thomas Aquinas and C. S. Lewis point out, omnipotence does not mean having the power to create a contradiction.[2] If life after death hinges on a contradiction, then there can be no life after death. We need to show that it doesn't. That's one reason why we need to think hard about it.

We also need to think about death and what comes after it, because belief in life after death has come on hard times. Ever since the rise of modern science, it has become more difficult to take seriously the idea that we will live on after we die. The astronomer Carolyn Porco sums up the rising secular attitude in one of her quotes that recently made the rounds on Facebook status updates: "All the atoms of our bodies will be blown into space in the disintegration of our solar system, to live on forever as mass or energy. That's what we should be teaching our children, not fairy tales about angels and seeing Grandma in heaven."[3]

Many people throughout history have placed their hope for life after death in the continuing existence of their souls after their bodies die. But science has not found the soul. Instead it has apparently explained away many of the functions that we used to associate with the soul. As a result, many now think that thinking happens only in the brain. Many, if not most, contemporary philosophers tell us that we have no souls, or if we do, they cannot survive the deaths of our bodies.

If we have no souls, then it seems that our hopes for heaven depend on the survival of our bodies. But we know that, at death, our bodies do not float to heaven. Nor do they conveniently disappear at death like the

2. See Aquinas, *Summa Theologica* 1a.25.3, 137–38, and Lewis, *Problem of Pain*, 26–28.

3. Quoted in Adler, "Atheists Discuss the Benefits of Faith."

bodies of Yoda or Obi-Wan Kenobi. Instead, they remain exactly where we left them when we died. And then they rot until they become compost. So if we are to continue to believe in a personal afterlife, then we need to show how such an afterlife is possible given what we know about how the world works—given what we know about how corpses rot and how thoughts link up with brains. We will need to show how belief in a personal afterlife does not demand that we check in our minds at the door. We will need to show that good scientists and good thinkers can believe in it. That does not mean that we need to prove that a personal afterlife exists. Religious thinkers of the past and present have tried to prove, for example, that we are immortal. Our task is humbler. We need only show that belief in an afterlife is plausible and possible.

Proof is probably the wrong way to go anyway because devising bad proofs does more damage than devising none at all. Too many bad proofs and no one wants to believe the idea anymore. That is one of the reasons why atheism became more popular in the modern world. There were so many bad proofs for God's existence that it became easy to give up on the idea of God altogether. Less ambitious goals can bear better fruit. The chance of success is higher and less fuel is fed to the skeptic's fire.

We need only give a compelling account of how we can survive our deaths. Such an account will need to meet a number of requirements. First, for most Christians, it will need to be biblical. That means that it will need to fit the biblical understanding of human nature—of who we are as human beings. It will need to fit what the Bible has to say about whether we are souls or bodies or both or neither.

It will also need to fit the various references to the afterlife that are scattered throughout Scripture. First and foremost, it will need to explain why the resurrection of the body is so important to the Bible's understanding of our survival after death. Paul is adamant about its importance, which is clear from even a cursory glance at 1 Corinthians 15. Somehow and for some reason our existence in eternity involves inhabiting a raised body. Any biblical account of life after death must come to terms with how and why such a body is raised.

Second, the Bible claims that life after death is God's doing. It isn't natural. It doesn't happen on its own in the way that a caterpillar transforms into a butterfly. Without God's intervention, we would have no hope for the afterlife. Death would be the end of us.

Third, the Bible suggests that the very same person who lives now will live again in heaven. *I* will be in the hereafter, not just a part of me or a copy of me. This seems obvious. It is not so obvious, however, when we consider that other views deny this. Some say that we each merge with the universe or some sort of Cosmic Mind when we die. But that is not what the Bible seems to teach. Others say that our hope lies in the survival of some of our memories and psychological traits. They will say that there will be a being in heaven that remembers fishing with my dad, pushing toy boats in Paris with my sons, and holding hands with my wife in Woodward Park. That being will also have some of my personality traits, like my love of food and philosophy. They will say that that is all that matters to us anyway. It does not matter that that being is no longer me. But the Bible seems to suggest that it does matter. *I* will survive. How else can *I* be judged and saved?

Any viable account of the afterlife will also need to fit the findings of science. While science is not 100 percent certain, we need to remember that little, if anything, is 100 percent certain. It is true that scientific theories are sometimes radically altered, or even overturned. Nonetheless, science is the most reliable method that we humans have for achieving knowledge about the world around us. Scientists, for the most part, proceed cautiously. Their research is tested and triple tested. If a near consensus of scientists agrees on some theory, then we need to heed them. We would be irrational not to. Therefore, we need, for example, to pay close attention to what neuroscientists are discovering about the brain.

Finally, any account of the afterlife will need to be philosophically viable. First and foremost, that means that it will need to be consistent. What it says about who we are, for example, must not contradict what it says about how we survive our deaths.

Any philosophically viable account will also need to have promising responses to any objections to it. Many Christians throughout history have believed that God will someday raise their very same bodies from the dead. But this belief faces a serious objection. How can your same body rise from the dead when it has decomposed into dirt? If this view is going to work then it will have to give a good response to this objection.

Any viable philosophical account will also need to explain what makes me me. If I am going to survive my death, then whatever makes me me will need to survive my death. I am still me if I lose my knee. But am I still me if I lose my entire body? I am still me if I lose my memory of getting left behind at a gas station in Nevada. But what if I lose all my memories? What if I forget who I am? Can I still be me? There must be something that I can't lose and still be me—something that has to be there for me to be there.

The first part of the book explores the biblical, scientific, and philosophical concerns that each theory of life after death will need to address. The second part explores the main theories of life after death and how well they address these concerns.

Thinking about death is also important because it influences the way that we think about life. Even TV's Jerry Seinfeld knows this:

> ELAINE: You know, funerals always make me think about my own mortality and how I'm going to die someday. Me, dead. Imagine that.
>
> GEORGE: They always make me take stock of my life and how I've pretty much wasted all of it, and how I plan to continue wasting it.
>
> JERRY: I know, and then you continue to say to yourself, "From this moment on, I'm not going to waste any more of it." But then you go, "How? What can I do that's not wasting it?"
>
> ELAINE: Is this a waste of time? What should we be doing? Can't you have coffee with people?[4]

Death reminds us to seize the day. But what does it mean to seize the day? What should we be doing, given that we will someday die? Jerry and Elaine do not know how to answer that question. For that, they need to think beyond death. They need to think about whether they survive it and if so, how. The way that we think we survive our deaths naturally leads to different conceptions of what it means to seize the day.

If we are to live life to the fullest, then we need to know what kind of life to live. One kind of life is more within and the other is more without. One is lived in the world of ideas, imagination, meditation, and prayer. The other is lived in the world of persons, places and things. One takes place in the soul. The other takes place on earth. We can focus our

---

4. "The Pony Remark," *YouTube* video, 5:54, posted May 11, 2011, from *Seinfeld*, http://www.youtube.com/watch?v=AzMlbDCNkdQ.

energies on either of these lives. We mostly pay attention to the world without. But we can always shut our eyes and get in touch with our inner selves. Some people focus more on their outward lives—careers, family, friends, gardening, eating, hiking, traveling. Others focus more on their inner lives—on connecting with God, training the mind, or thinking about ideas. Others seek to balance them both.

Life is a seesaw between the inner and the outer. And we, its players, must decide on which side to put the most weight. Believe that we are souls destined for heaven and we tip the balance toward the inner. Believe that we are bodily beings destined for a bodily heaven and we tip the balance toward the outer. And then yes, Elaine, we can have coffee with people. Believe that we are both soul and body and that both go to heaven and we strike an even balance. We frequent both the pub and the prayer chapel.

More importantly, living life to the fullest involves caring about other persons—something that Jerry, George, and Elaine don't often get. But we have limited time and energy. We must choose carefully how to spend it on others. If the afterlife is just a soul-ish thing, then better to invest our energies in saving souls. If it is just a bodied thing, then better to invest our energies in healing bodies.

If only souls have eternal value, then healing bodies is only important insofar as it helps the souls which they carry. Taken to extremes, this view can justify harming the body to save the soul, following the example of the Inquisitors who applied thumbscrews to get heretics to confess Christ. Fortunately, we now know better. But this view can have other implications. We sometimes, for example, give soup to the starving only if they will listen to a sermon.

But if, on the other hand, our bodies have eternal value, then we will tend to the physical needs of others for the sake of their bodies. This view inclines us to give the soup without the sermon. But then we might be tempted to neglect any need for spiritual healing and the soul's salvation.

Thinking about death is also important because it bears on other questions that we care about, such as:

1. What kind of rituals and emotions should we adopt when someone dies? Should we have a party to celebrate their life or a funeral that expresses grief over their death? Should we treat death as a natural passage to something better or a tragedy that cuts someone's life short? Should we bury or cremate?

2. Should we talk about the dead as if they are currently conscious and watching over us? Does it make sense to pray for the dead? Should we celebrate All Saint's Day as if the dead are awake and paying attention? Should we remind each other that Grandma is smiling at us from heaven?
3. How should we understand *near-death experiences,* in which revived patients claim to have left their bodies and experienced the afterlife when they were near death? Do they accurately portray what happens when we die? Or are they hallucinations? How as Christians should we talk about them?
4. Is it possible to speak with the dead, or to see ghosts?
5. Do animals go to heaven? Will I see my beloved Chihuahua again?

The last part of the book will explore these questions. It will show how the different theories about how we survive our deaths lead to different answers to them.

And finally, we should think about death because it is an extremely personal topic for all of us. Both because we will each die and because we will all lose loved ones. My father died when I was twelve years old. I have lost all my grandparents. I have known people who have committed suicide, one of whom was a beloved uncle and another was a dear friend to my family. I love all these people and I hope to see them again on the other side of death.

I have thought a lot about death. I wrote my doctoral dissertation on what St. Thomas Aquinas, the greatest of all Christian thinkers, thought about how we survive our deaths. I tend to emphasize death and the afterlife in many of the philosophy classes that I teach.

I have come to believe more strongly than ever that we will live again after we die. I don't mean this in the sense that we will be remembered by others. I mean that we ourselves—the individual persons that we are—will live again and live forever.

Has thinking deeply and philosophically about death and the afterlife hurt my beliefs? Far from it. Thinking hard about death has only increased my hope that it will not have the last word. I hope that it will do the same for you.

Framing the Puzzle: Guidelines for Choosing

3

The Outer Frame: What Does the Bible Say?

IN AN ACT OF desperation, you quickly flip through the pages of the ship's guidebook. You hope that it will tell you which of the five buttons to push. But you only find hints and clues. How do you piece them together? Meanwhile, the clock is ticking.

We often expect the Bible to tell us exactly how we can survive our deaths. We want it to tell us how it is possible that the Henry in heaven is the very same person as the Henry whose corpse lies in the casket. We want it to tell us which theory of life after death we should choose. But it doesn't. It does, however, say important things about death and the afterlife—things that help us assess which option we ought to choose.

The Bible's silence tempts us to read our own views into it. We must resist the temptation. Let the Bible say what it says and no more. We may wonder why the Bible does not give us the answers that we seek. For one thing, its purposes are different. It is more concerned with how we are saved and what God's kingdom is like. But perhaps God also wishes us to engage our minds and our imaginations. Perhaps he does not intend us to make of our minds a blank slate on which he will write in the answers to all our questions. The point is not for us to get our minds out of the way so that we can correctly hear what he has to say to us. The point is for our minds to actively inquire into what he has to say to us and to actively fill in the missing pieces. God values our input, for we are, after all, his good creation. His world is a far better place because there are saints, poets, philosophers, and everyday Bible readers, who put together the puzzles of the universe.

The purpose of this chapter is to put together the puzzle's frame. It does not show us what the picture will look like in the end. But, for those who believe the Bible is an authority, the pieces of that picture will need to fit into the frame—to connect with it. The frame consists of what the Bible says and implies about death and how we survive it.

Hebrew Holism

The first part of the frame consists of what the Bible says about who we are as persons and as human beings. We tend to think of ourselves as made up of parts. But not just the parts that make up our bodies, like hearts, lungs, livers, and brains. We often think of the whole body as itself a part that is joined to another part which we call the soul. The body is the part that is physical and that we can see and touch. The soul is that invisible part of us that is not physical. It is spiritual, like God or angels. The soul is the part of us that thinks about daisies, communes with God, and gets happy or sad. This view of who we are is called *dualism*. We could just as well call it two-ism, because it says that we are made of two parts. Most Christians throughout history have held this view. Many Christians, both now and in the past, take a further step and say that we are our souls and not our bodies. Our souls temporarily wear our bodies like a man wears his coat.

Others believe instead that we are made up of three parts: body, soul and spirit. This view is called *trichotomism*, which means "divided into three parts." The soul and the spirit are the two immaterial parts. But there are diverse understandings of how they are different from each other. The spirit is usually understand to be our most inward self—the part of us that is able to make contact with God. The soul is the part of us that we share with animals—the part that gives life to our bodies and is responsible for our desires and emotions. It is the connecting point between our spirits and our bodies.

But many biblical scholars believe that both *dualism* and *trichotomism* are more Greek than Hebrew. The ancient Greeks tended to divide things up into parts. That makes for a cleaner and more ordered world where everything can be put in its place. Many Greeks would like cubbies and cubicles. Not all Greeks thought this way, but it is a tendency in Greek thought.

Most scholars believe that the Hebrews of the Old Testament instead held a *holistic* view of the person.[1] According to that view, we are

---

1. See, e.g., Green, "Bodies," 158; Gundry, *Sōma in Biblical Theology*, 119; and

integrated wholes. What we think of as our parts are actually different dimensions or aspects of our single unified existence. We have a spiritual dimension, but the whole person is spiritual. We have a bodily dimension, but the whole person is bodily. The spirit refers to that dimension by which the person relates to God. The body refers to that dimension whereby the person relates to the physical world. But it is the whole person who relates to God and the whole person who relates to the physical world. The person's different dimensions are thus like the different ways that she relates to others and the world around her. So the Hebrews also have a more relational understanding of who we are. I am an integrated whole in relationship with God, others, and creation. Those relationships are fundamental to what I am.

Thus, according to these scholars, the ancient Hebrews did not think of the soul as a part of the person. Their word for "soul" refers to the whole living person. While the Greeks tended to think of the person as an embodied soul, the Hebrews tended to think of the person as a living body.

Older translations of the Bible mislead us. For example, the KJV translates Genesis 2:7 as "And the Lord God formed man of the dust of the ground and breathed into his nostril the breath of life and man became a *living soul.*" But more recent translations do not use the word soul. For example, the NIV translates it as "living being" instead of "living soul," and the REB translates it as "living creature." For example, the KJV translates Psalm 25:20 as "Oh keep my *soul* and deliver me." But the NIV translates it as "Guard my *life* and rescue me."

Many Hebrews became influenced by Greek ideas during New Testament times. One of the burning questions in biblical scholarship is whether the writers of the New Testament are more *dualist* or *holist*. Most contemporary scholars think the latter.[2] But some prominent scholars disagree.[3]

Dunn, *Theology of the Apostle Paul*, 54. Fuller Seminary professor Nancey Murphy provides a helpful discussion in *Bodies and Souls*, 17–22.

2. See Green, "Bodies," 173n64.

3. See Cooper, *Body, Soul, and Life Everlasting*, for a sustained argument that the Bible holds a *dualist* view, although with some *holistic* elements.

The Interim State

The debate continues because the Bible implies that the soul can exist without its body. Not just in the New Testament. The ancient Hebrews believed that at death, something of us lives on in a shadowy unpleasant place called *Sheol*. The Psalmist calls it the "Pit," and to earlier Hebrews, it was the pits, as we might phrase it today. Our best hope was a good life here and now, because nothing great awaits us after it. Later Hebrews believed that *Sheol* was divided into two regions: a gloomy region for the bad and a rosier region for the good. Belief in *Sheol* means that the ancient Hebrews did believe that a part of us, presumably the soul, survives the deaths of our bodies. The New Testament agrees, it seems.

Paul especially seems to believe that we live on after our bodies die, since he said, "Absent from the body . . . present with the Lord" (2 Cor 5:8 KJV). A better translation would be: "We would rather be away from the body and at home with the Lord" (NRSV). But how can we be somewhere that is "away" from our bodies unless we could exist without them? Some biblical scholars suggest that this verse refers to our existence after the resurrection of our bodies.[4] Our "home with the Lord" is in the kingdom that will come when we will have new bodies. On this interpretation, Paul is saying, "We would rather be away from our bodies *that we have now* and at home with the Lord *in our new bodies.*"

But Paul also says: "I know a person in Christ who fourteen years ago was caught up to the third heaven . . . And I know that such a person . . . was caught up into Paradise" (2 Cor 12:2–4). Most scholars believe that Paul is referring to himself.[5] In which case, Paul seems to claim that he left his body and temporarily went to paradise, the very place that Jesus said the thief would instantly go to when he died. Paul does, however, add that he does not know whether this man, presumably himself, was in the body or not: "whether in the body or out of the body, I do not know." At the very least, Paul seemed to believe in the possibility of an existence that was separate from his present body.

Some might think that Paul is the only biblical writer who teaches such "outdated" ideas about souls separating from bodies. They are the sorts who do not like Paul and point out that he believed in crazy ideas like women needing to cover their heads and slaves obeying their masters. But even those who dis Paul had better not assume that his belief

---

4. See, e.g., Harris, *Raised Immortal*, 99.
5. Dunn, *Theology of Paul*, 108n33.

about souls is as outdated as his views on women, because Jesus also seemed to believe that our souls, or some such part of us, live on between death and resurrection.

"Today you will be with me in Paradise," said Jesus to the thief on the cross (Luke 23:43). What could that mean but that the thief would be in paradise right after his body died on the cross? Jesus's words also suggest that at least some get to go to a happy place after they die. Not everyone is destined for the pit.

Jesus also told the story about a rich man and a beggar named Lazarus. Lazarus begged for crumbs at the rich man's table and received none. They both died. Lazarus went to the happy place of "Abraham's Bosom." The rich man went to hades. He cried out to Abraham and asked him to send Lazarus to him to cool his tongue because of the flames of hades. He also asked that Abraham warn his still living brothers of hades. But Abraham replied that none can cross the great gulf between the "bosom" and hades and that his brothers wouldn't listen to him anyway. This story only makes sense if Lazarus and the rich man survive their deaths while their bodies remain on earth dead and buried. So Jesus assumes that they survive their deaths and so assumes the existence of something like the soul that lives on.

Jesus may not intend this story to illustrate what actually happens to us after we die. Its importance may lie more in its message about life than about death. In *this* life, one should heed the Law and the Prophets and show compassion for the poor. Those who live high while others die will someday be judged. We do need to keep our focus on the story's message whether or not we also believe that it tells us something about the state of the dead.

The Christian tradition has interpreted such passages to mean that we survive our deaths, and like Lazarus and the thief, go to a heavenly place where we await the resurrection of our bodies. That tradition holds that we will be conscious and aware, just as Lazarus is in Jesus's story. It also holds that our departed loved ones, assuming they are saved, are aware of the goings on of earth.

This state between death and resurrection is called the *interim state*. The Christian tradition teaches it. The Bible seems to teach it. Most Christians throughout history have taken comfort in it. So there is good reason to find an after-death scenario that includes it.

Resurrection Hope

The *interim state* is pleasant. But whatever Paul believes about the *interim state*, he does not believe that it is what we hope for after we die. He places our hope in the future resurrection of our bodies. "But in fact Christ has been raised from the dead, the first fruits of those who have died. For since death came through a human being, the resurrection of the dead has also come through a human being; for as all die in Adam, so all will be made alive in Christ" (1 Cor 15:20–22). And if Christ did not rise again from the dead, then neither will we, and all hope is lost (1 Cor 15:18–19).

If there is an *interim state*, then our resurrected bodies offer something that the *interim state* does not. If we want to imagine the happiness of heaven, then we will need to imagine bodies—our bodies. We do not look forward to being spirits roaming around a spirit world. We do not look forward to just *spiritually* communing with God and our loved ones. We do such things in the interim state. But what we really look forward to, what really gives us hope, is romping through a meadow without needing to sneeze, or hugging the mother that we dearly miss, or *seeing* Jesus *face* to *face*. We look forward to dancing without getting tired, listening to the music of the spheres, and feeling the cool wind on our face without its frosty bite. We do not look forward so much to voiceless thoughts and faceless feelings. We look forward to faces and voices and the love that they convey. I think that most of us, if we really thought about it, would agree with Paul that our hope lies in new bodies, not in free-floating spirits.

For some people, the resurrection of the body is bad news. They may hate their bodies and long to be rid of them. They may feel like they do not match their bodies. But it is important to remember that the Bible does not teach that our resurrected bodies will be just like our bodies are now. It is safe to assume that the Bible implies that whatever our resurrected bodies will be like, they will be bodies that we like and will feel at home in. They will feel like the bodies we were always meant to have.

The General Resurrection and the Renewing of Creation

The most straightforward reading of the Bible suggests that we will all be raised at the same time when the trumpet sounds at the Last Judgment. Paul writes: "For the trumpet will sound, and the dead will be raised imperishable, and we will all be changed" (1 Cor 15:52b). Again, he writes: "For the Lord himself, with a cry of command, with the archangel's call and with the sound of God's trumpet, will descend from heaven, and the dead in Christ will rise first" (1 Thess 4:16). The Christian tradition has, for the most part, agreed that we will all rise together and calls it the *general resurrection*.

The *general resurrection* has important implications. For one thing, the idea that we are all raised together emphasizes the importance of community. Our salvation is not just an individual affair, although it is that too. We reach our eternal destiny *together*. We obtain our incorruptible and imperishable bodies together and thus become whole *together*. We face the Last Judgment *together*.

The *general resurrection* occurs in what Revelation calls "the new heavens and the *new earth*." Some might take this to mean a completely new earth created from scratch in some other plane of existence. But some theologians today suggest that it refers instead to the restoration, renewal, and perfection of this earth.[6] Did not Jesus himself encourage us to pray, "Your kingdom come . . . *on earth*, as it is in heaven?" (Matt 6:10). Paul also suggests that creation will ultimately be healed:

> For the creation waits with eager longing for the revealing of the children of God...in hope that the creation itself will be set free from its bondage to decay and will obtain the freedom of the glory of the children of God. We know that the whole creation has been groaning in labor pains until now; and not only creation, but we ourselves, who have the first fruits of the Spirit, groan inwardly while we wait for adoption, the redemption of our bodies." (Rom 8:19–23)

This passage suggests that we are healed right along with creation. The *general resurrection* of our bodies coincides with the renewal of the earth. Creation is not scrapped like an old Dodge Colt and replaced by a brand new Toyota Prius. It is transformed into that Prius. Even better, it is transformed into an electric run Nissan Leaf with a battery that never wears out and never needs recharging.

Finally, the *general resurrection*, as Scripture and the Christian tradition suggest, is also in the future of *this* world. That does not mean that time will function the same way in the *new earth* as it does in the old one. But it does mean that the new time of the *new earth* arises out of the old

---

6. See, e.g., Polkinghorne, *God of Hope*, 113, and Wright, *Surprised by Hope*, 162.

time of the old earth so that the history of the *new earth* is a continuation of the history of the old earth.

But Some Christian scholars believe instead that our future resurrection happens right after we die. This is called *immediate resurrection*. When Jesus says to the thief that he will be in paradise that very day, he means that the thief's resurrection will occur right after he dies.

At one point, Paul seems to suggest that resurrection happens right after death. He writes:

> For in this tent we groan, longing to be clothed with our heavenly dwelling—if indeed, when we have taken it off we will not be found naked. For while we are still in this tent, we groan under our burden, because we wish not to be unclothed but to be further clothed, so that what is mortal may be swallowed up by life. (2 Cor 5:2–4)

Paul is not talking about living in tents while yearning for the comforts of a home, as many homeless persons might do. Instead, he uses a metaphor from his experience as a tentmaker. Our current bodies are like tents—rough, uncomfortable, fragile, impermanent. We long for the better bodies that we will have in heaven. Then Paul switches metaphors. Our bodies, our tents, are like clothes. We are naked without them. But we do not wish to be naked. We want more comfortable clothes. We do want bodies of some kind. Living as souls without bodies is no hope at all. Our hope is in better bodies, not no bodies.

Verse 3 is the key: "if indeed, when we have taken it off, we will not be found naked." It suggests that there is no time in which we are naked—no time in which we do not have a body. The implication is that at death, we immediately get new bodies, or that our old bodies are further clothed with heavenly features. No waiting around as souls in heaven until the Last Judgment when we get our bodies back. No *interim state*.

Immediate resurrection appeals to those who believe that we cannot exist without bodies but who wish to also take seriously those biblical passages that suggest an *interim state*. The thief will be in paradise today because he will be resurrected today, not because his soul will immediately go there. Lazarus and the rich man are fully conscious after death because they have already been raised from the dead, not because their souls are floating in spiritual realms.

But *immediate resurrection* comes with a great cost. If we are immediately raised, then we must be raised in another dimension—the dimension known as heaven. That means that we all do not rise from the dead at the same time. John Paul II recently rose, but Luther rose in the 1500s AD, and Paul in the 60s AD. I rise when I die and you rise when you die. Thus, we cannot rise together. Immediate resurrectionists could reply that heavenly time is different such that we all arrive in heaven at the same time even though we die at different times on earth. But they would still have to give up the idea that our resurrection is connected with the renewal of creation. God may renew creation as the Scriptures say, but our renewal has nothing to do with it. They would also have to give up the idea that our resurrection occurs at the end of this world's history. The resurrection would have to be an event in an altogether different history.

Some claim that we will be *immediately* raised at the Last Judgment and not in heaven. By this, they mean that we experience the resurrection as immediate even though it really isn't. We die, we are raised, and nothing happens to us in the interim. This view combines the strengths of *immediate resurrection* with the traditional belief in the *general resurrection* and its implications for community and creation. History, however, marches on in the interim and one may wonder if the same person can come into existence again after not existing for millennia. One may also wonder how Lazarus and the rich man are already raised from the dead while the rich man's brothers have not yet died. We will return to this view in chapter 9. Because this view does not hold that we are *immediately* raised after we die, I will reserve the term *immediate resurrection* for those views which hold that we are.

Death as Enemy

We sometimes think that death is a natural passage from one phase of our existence to another. The Bible both accepts and rejects that idea. It accepts that death is a *passage*. After all, we do live again after we die. But it rejects the idea that death is *natural* if that means that death is a right and good part of our journey. The Bible is clear that death is not right and not good. It is an enemy that must be vanquished: "The last enemy to be destroyed is death" (1 Cor 15:26). It has a sting: "The sting of death is sin . . . But thanks be to God, who gives us the victory through our Lord Jesus Christ" (1 Cor 15:56–7). When we are raised again, then death will lose the battle. Then the "saying that is written will be fulfilled: 'Death has been swallowed up in victory. Where, O death, is your victory? Where, O death, is your sting?'" (1 Cor 15:54–55).

Something bad happens to us when we die—something so serious that it is an enemy and that only our future resurrection will finally conquer it. The Bible does not give us a smooth transition to paradise. The *interim state* is not itself good enough to conquer death. But it is hard to see why death is so bad if we do not really die—if we live on as spirits, or whatever we will be, in paradise. Sure, it would be nice to have our bodies back. Sure, our ultimate hope is in the resurrection. But why all the fuss about death if we are still conscious, aware, and happy in the meantime? At worst, death strips us of our bodies. But it does not strip us of ourselves or our happiness.

For these reasons, many believe that the Bible teaches that we really do die when we die. Death is real. The last breath, the last heartbeat, or the last firing of the neurons in our brains mark the last moment of not just our lives, but also our existence. The resurrection of the body is the only way to overcome death and bring one back into existence. That is why Paul says that if Christ has not been raised then we would perish when we die (1 Cor 15:19).

But if we die when we die, then how can we be in paradise awaiting our future resurrections? The biblical data pulls us in different directions. Thus, many argue that the Bible does not really teach the *interim state*. There is, however, another solution: we could both die and not die. We die in that we cease to exist as full persons. But we do not die in that a part of us lives on in the interim state. That part, perhaps the soul, survives death and continues in the *interim state*. It is conscious and happy. So, in a sense, we survive in the *interim state*, but as truncated selves. The part of us that survives is still us in the sense that it preserves our memories and streams of consciousness. Grandma Jones is looking down on us from heaven in the sense that the part of her that is conscious and remembers us is looking down on us. But she herself, as her full self, is not actually looking down on us. We will explore this idea further in chapter 10.

The Resurrected Body

According to the Bible, our resurrected bodies will be very different from our current bodies. Otherwise, the resurrection of the body would not be good news. We look forward to an eternity that is free from death, disease, aging, and pain. A heaven that required hospitals and hospices would not be heaven. Our new bodies will instead be incorruptible and imperishable. That means that they cannot get old and die. It also means that they cannot get sick.

Paul says that our new bodies will be *spiritual* bodies, as opposed to the *physical* bodies that we have now (1 Cor 15:44). He does not mean that we will have immaterial bodies. That would be impossible. Bodies, by definition, are made up of some kind of material that extends in space—that has length and width. He also does not mean that we will have some kind of airy bodies—like the kinds of bodies that ghosts have in movies like *Caspar* or *Harry Potter*. Instead, Paul means that we will have bodies that are adapted to and infused by the Holy Spirit.

The Bible seems to connect our future bodies with Christ's resurrected body.[7] If we want to know what our resurrected bodies will be like, then we ought to look to Christ's resurrection body. His body could move through walls and move quickly from one place to another. His body could somehow shift out of this world and into another, which is what must have happened when Christ ascended. His body was also hard to recognize at first, so there was some slight change in his physical appearance.

Christ's resurrected body was also a very human body. It looked mostly the same as his pre-resurrection body. It could be seen and touched. It could eat and breathe. It interacted with its environment in much the way our current bodies do. It, for example, took into itself parts of its surrounding environment, such as food and probably also oxygen. So, in important ways, our new bodies will look much like and function much like our current ones, but with perks.

The Bible also *seems* to say that our new bodies will be the *same* bodies as our current bodies. These same bodies that we have now will be raised again. "So it is with the resurrection of the dead. What is sown is perishable, what is raised is imperishable. It is sown in dishonor, it is raised in glory. It is sown in weakness, it is raised in power. It is sown a physical body, it is raised a spiritual body" (1 Cor 15:42–44). Our bodies, Paul says, are buried like seeds. They will also rise again like seeds. The imagery implies that it is the same body throughout.

Yet how can this be? Our bodies rot, seeds do not. Paul has some explaining to do. But he does not do it. That task is left to us. We are

---

7. See Phil 3:21 and 1 Cor 15:49.

forced into two options: 1) Go against the most straightforward reading of Paul and argue that Paul did not really mean that our very *same* bodies will be raised; or 2) Find a consistent and cogent account of how our very *same* bodies can rise again. Most early and medieval Christians chose the second option.[8] We will explore some of the problems they ran into in chapter 8 and some creative solutions to these problems in chapter 10. But more and more Christian thinkers today choose the first option.

Not Immortal

The Bible also teaches that we do not naturally survive our deaths. Philosophers like Plato and Descartes disagree. They believed that the soul's surviving is as natural and predictable as a snake that survives the shedding of its skin. When philosophers speak of the "immortality of the soul," they are usually referring to the idea that the soul is the sort of thing that naturally lives forever. If true, then we would survive our deaths without any help from God. God sits back and watches our souls naturally leave our dying bodies in much the way that we might watch snakes shed their skins—an appealing idea because it makes eternal life certain. We would have grounds to believe that we will live on without having to place our faith in anything. Faith, in fact, would have nothing to do with it.

But such a view is not the biblical view. According to Scripture, our hope for eternal life is in God. Without God, we are gone for good. So those who wish to hold the Bible in one hand and Plato in the other will have to give up the idea that the soul naturally survives the body's death. Instead, they might say that the soul lives on, but only because God keeps it ticking.

As we have seen, the Bible says that our hope lies in the resurrection of our bodies. It might seem that resurrection depends completely on God, since it cannot happen on its own. There is nothing natural about the dead rising again. At least, that is what everybody thought until we discovered the bizarre world of quantum mechanics.

Clifford Pickover suggests that given enough time—and enough time there will be since time will keep ticking for infinity—anything that has ever existed will eventually spontaneously reappear.[9] He concludes that we need not worry about immortality because, naturally, our bodies

---

8. See Bynum, *Resurrection of the Body*, for a history of their attempts.
9. Pickover, *Beginner's Guide to Immortality*, 120.

will live again. He calls this process *quantum resurrection*—an intriguing but dubious proposition. Even if an exact quark by quark replica of my body appeared, then that does not in the least entail that it would be my body or that it would be me. In any case, such a resurrection would do nothing for me if it did not also involve a surrounding world capable of sustaining my body. Resurrection into empty space would result in a ghastly mess, or so I am told by physicists. But I suppose that, given infinity, an exact replica of myself and this world would eventually resurrect at the same time—thus avoiding the mess.

But even if quantum resurrection were a viable theory, it would not be biblical. Whatever resurrection is, whenever resurrection is, it is brought about by God and nothing other.

The Bible thus gives us some criteria for assessing the different options for how we survive our deaths. The biblical option will:

1. Accommodate the Bible's tendency to view the person as an integrated whole.
2. Either hold to an *interim state* between death and resurrection or find other viable interpretations of the relevant passages.
3. Place our hope for life after death in the resurrection of the body.
4. Either hold to the *general resurrection* in the future of this world or find other viable interpretations of the relevant passages.
5. View death as, in some sense, an enemy.
6. Explain how our resurrected bodies will be both similar and different to our current bodies in a way consistent with 1 Corinthians 15 and Jesus's own resurrected body.
7. Place our hope for life after death in God and not some natural process.

Now we will look at the pieces of the puzzle that lie just inside this frame.

4

The Middle Frame: What Does Science Say?

MANY, IF NOT MOST, Christians consider Scripture to be the highest authority for belief and practice. But that should not mean that there are no other authorities. We have gained knowledge about the world through our experience of it and through applying reason to that experience. We know some things about the way the world works and our beliefs ought to conform to that knowledge.

We know some things about the world that complicate belief in life after death. Everybody knows that our corpses decompose. Some bodies are burned to ashes. Some are instantly vaporized, as are those in a nuclear blast. How then can our bodies rise from the dead when there is nothing left of them? Any view of the resurrection of the body will have to address this problem.

But we also need to take into account what science has to say about the world. Science is our best tool for learning what the world is really like. It has proven itself repeatedly by making accurate predictions and by developing technologies that work. Science is generally careful about reaching conclusions. Findings are tested and triple tested. So we ought to take its findings as authoritative and adjust our beliefs accordingly—especially when a consensus or near consensus of scientists adopt a particular scientific theory. We ought to, for example, believe that we humans evolved from apes because evolution is a well-established scientific theory.

Scientists sometimes make claims that go beyond the scientific evidence. So we need to be careful about when and when not to believe what scientists say. Science has its limits. It cannot tell us much about the afterlife, because the afterlife could abide by very different scientific laws. Scientists who criticize ideas of the afterlife for breaking scientific laws are like fish who insist that tortoises must swim when on land. These fish are wrong to think that the way the underwater world works is also the way the out-of-water world works.

Science and the Soul

But science rightly has things to say about who we are as human persons—about our bodies, brains, and souls. As it turns out, contemporary science is, for the most part, unhappy with the idea that we have souls.

If the soul exists then it either preexists the body or is somehow created at the same time as the body. Not all Christians believe in the soul, although most do. Those who do argue that the soul's preexistence is unbiblical and goes against traditional Christian teaching. So they take the second option. The soul cannot by itself pop into being out of nothing. But God can pop it out of nothing as he had popped the world out of nothing in the beginning. God creates the soul and immediately joins it with its body.

But the theory of evolution challenges the idea that God creates the soul. According to evolutionary theory, there is a great deal of continuity between humans and other animals. We evolved gradually from other primates who evolved gradually from other mammals. But if we evolved gradually from other animals, then did God create individual souls for each animal that evolved? Or did God create souls just for our species, *homo sapiens sapiens*? But what about our predecessor, *homo sapiens*? Or other predecessors, like *Australopithecus* or *homo erectus*? Or what about the Neanderthals who lived at the same time as we did, but on a separate evolutionary track that dead-ended? The Neanderthals were surely conscious. If consciousness requires the soul, then Neanderthals should have souls just as much as *homo sapiens sapiens*. Our species also evolved gradually. There is no clear line that separates *homo sapiens sapiens* from *homo sapiens*—no clear line after which it makes sense to say that this slightly newer high-level primate has a soul whereas its parents do not.

Maybe we could grant that all conscious primates capable of thought have divinely created souls. But what about those primates who are conscious and capable of rudimentary thought? What about dolphins, pigs, crows, and other intelligent creatures? Each of these species gradually evolved from prior species. Again, there does not seem to be any non-arbitrary line that divides those animals with souls from those animals without souls.

Embryology also challenges the idea that God creates the soul. Each person developed gradually from fertilized ova in the womb. But at what point was the soul created? We might think it was created at conception. But fertilized ova can split, fuse, or die.[1] If an ovum splits to form twins, then did the soul split too? But souls cannot split. If they did, then they could not be the source of our unique personal identities. If two ova fuse together, then did two souls fuse together? Again, if they did, then they could not be the source of our unique personal identities. One-third of ova naturally die in the womb. But would a good God create souls for ova that he knew were about to die?

Suppose instead that God creates the soul later in the embryo's development—perhaps when the nervous system and brain reach a sufficient level of development. But then, would a good God create souls for fetuses of whatever phase of development that he knew were going to be aborted, naturally or not? Yet surely fetuses with brains and nervous systems have souls since their brains and nervous system are the same as other fetuses who are not about to die. We would think they ought to have the same level of consciousness as other fetuses regardless of whether they are about to die or not.

Science also has much to say about whether and how our mental features might be able to survive the deaths of our brains. Mental features are all those features that many normally think of as belonging to our minds or souls. They include thoughts, feelings, desires, memories, personality traits, and character traits. Neuroscientists study the connection between these features and what is going on inside of our brains. They are finding that our mental features are tightly linked to them, so much so that it seems that they cannot exist without the brain. It would seem that they die when the brain dies.

Neuroscience and the Mind

We all know that there is an important connection between the brain and the mind. We all know about how changes in the brain affect our mental features. Two cups of wine inebriate the mind. Two cups of coffee make us think faster. Cocaine causes hallucinations. Pharmaceuticals can profoundly affect our personalities. Too much Concerta and we become irritable and impatient. Vicodin makes us happy and hopeful.

---

1. See Nichols, *Death and Afterlife*, 207n58.

Anti-depressants reduce depression. We also know that damaging the brain damages the mind. Strokes and tumors can affect our reasoning and our memories. Alzheimer's disease causes dementia.

Brain damage can also cause radical personality changes. In 1848, a twenty-five-year-old man named Phineas Gage accidently caused an explosion while working for a railroad company in Vermont. The explosion hurled a three-foot-seven-inch iron rod through his left cheek. It went through the front of his brain and out the top of his head. He survived but as a very different person. Before the accident, he was responsible and conscientious. According to his doctor, the accident caused him to become

> fitful, irreverent, indulging at times in the grossest profanity which was not previously his custom, manifesting little deference to his fellows, impatient of restraint or advice when it conflicts with his desires, at times perniciously obstinate, yet capricious and vacillating, devising many plans of future operation, which are no sooner arranged than they are abandoned.[2]

In many respects, he became a completely different person with a weakened sense of morality.

We are right to wonder whether the doctor exaggerated the changes in Gage's behavior. But more recent cases also show that brain damage in other patients, to the same regions damaged in Gage, causes the same behavioral changes observed in Gage. We also know that tumors can cause paranoia, aggression, and impulsivity. Gage's case and others like it suggest that our personalities and moral traits are tightly linked to our brains such that they cannot exist apart from them. How then can there be a soul that bears the core of a person's personality?

Without neuroscience, we have good reasons to believe that our minds are necessarily lodged in our brains. With neuroscience, it becomes extremely difficult to argue otherwise.

Neuroscientists are moving closer to the goal of being able to tell what we are thinking by scanning our brains. In an MRI, the patient lays down on a table that slides into a cylindrical tube. Then, the machine sends radio waves into her brain. These waves send signals back to the machine that indicate which areas of the brain have the greatest blood flow. Those areas with the greatest blood flow represent the areas of the brain that are the most active. If particular thoughts are found in

---

2. Damasio, *Descartes' Error*, 8.

particular places, then theoretically we should be able to eventually read minds by reading brains.

So far neuroscientists have been able to identify which regions of the brain are typically activated when certain particular concrete nouns like "celery" are thought.[3] Usually, the thinking of a particular word will activate multiple regions of the brain, creating a brain pattern that represents the particular thought. More research should expand the repertoire of thoughts whose patterns we can identify. We may possibly someday identify the brain patterns for whole sentences, thus leading us to also read complex thoughts from scanning the brain.

We like to think our thoughts are private, especially our thoughts of other persons. But neuroscientists are discovering that our thoughts of particular persons are linked to unique brain patterns in the medial prefrontal cortex. Cornell scientists conducting a study in 2013 were surprised how well they could predict who the test subjects were thinking about by looking at their brain scans.[4]

Neuroscientists at UC Berkeley have found a way to scan the brains of persons watching YouTube videos and then reconstruct from them blurry images of the videos the persons were watching.[5] The study shows that our visual processing of the images we see takes place in the visual cortex of the brain such that particular visual patterns are linked to particular types of activity in the visual cortex. The reconstructed images are only blurry because the MRIs can only measure the levels of blood flow to different regions of the brain. But our neurons move faster than our blood levels change. The MRI can't keep up with the brain's speed. If it could, then we should be able to get clear pictures of what someone is seeing. Scientists have already used brain measuring techniques to get accurate pictures of the black and white static images that test subjects are seeing. Thus, the images in our "minds" are linked so tightly to our brains that, with the right tools, we can theoretically tell which images others are seeing with perfect accuracy even as the images are changing. It seems likely that the same is true for all other images in our minds, whether from our dreams, memories, or imaginations. The limitation is in the technology, not the tight linkage between images and neurons.

---

3. Mitchell et al., "Predicting Human Brain Activity," 1191.
4. Hassabis et al., "Imagine All the People," para. 1.
5. Nishimoto et al., "Reconstructing Visual Experiences," 1641.

Scientists have identified regions of the brain that are associated with certain types of memories. Recall when you accidentally hit a cat with your car in the night, as I once did. That sad memory and all other emotional memories are linked with a small part of the brain called the amygdala. Recall that William conquered England at the Battle of Hastings in 1066. That memory and all other memories of facts and figures are linked to a neighboring region called the hippocampus. Recall how to tie your shoe. That memory and all other how-to memories are linked to the cerebellum, located in the lower back of your brain. Recall the last two sentences you just read. That memory and other such short term memories are linked with your prefrontal cortex, which is at the front and center of your brain. Scientists can also cause us to remember certain events from our lives by stimulating certain regions of our brains with electrical currents.

And so we wonder. Will we be able to someday implant false memories? If memories are just a neuron dance, theoretically transferable from brain to brain, then how are my memories uniquely mine? My memory of the walk with my wife on the moonlit beach could just as well be yours. If it is possible to implant false memories then memory cannot be the key to our personal identities.

Neuroscientists are also getting better at reading our emotions by reading our brains. Certain emotions tend to activate certain parts of the brain. Scientists can determine a person's emotions by noting which regions of her brain are active.[6] Perhaps someday scientists will be able to make someone happy or sad by zapping certain parts of the brain. In *Star Trek: The Next Generation*, the android Data receives an emotion chip that allows him to have emotions. Emotion chips might also be in our future.

Neuroscientists are also discovering that our religious experiences are linked to our brains. Some studies show that particular regions of the brain are activated when Buddhist monks meditate and Franciscan nuns pray.[7] Radioactive tracers injected into the bloodstream during a religious high show that blood flow to the brain's temporal lobe increases while blood flow to the parietal lobe decreases. Neither result is a surprise since we already know that temporal lobe epilepsy increases one's interest in religion. The temporal lobe is a religious goldfield. The parietal lobe is a religious desert. It is the part of the brain that orients one's self

---

6. Kassam et al., "Identifying Emotions," 1.
7. Murphy, *Bodies and Souls*, 67–68.

in space and time. It helps us know where things are and when events occur. Intense religious experiences often involve a feeling that one has transcended time and space—exactly what should happen when one's parietal lobe is inactive.

Dr. Michael Persinger, a Canadian neuropsychologist, claims to have created a helmet that can induce experiences of God.[8] The helmet, dubbed the "God helmet," looks like a motorcycle helmet with wires hooking up to the wearer's head. It zaps the temporal lobe via magnetic stimulation and apparently causes some people to have the perception that a transcendent god-like being is present. We should approach these claims with caution since they rely on the subjective reports of the helmet's wearers and since his experiments need further replication to be truly scientific. Yet the result is in line with what neuroscience is increasingly learning about our temporal lobes. We might wish to remember this the next time we feel God's presence, for that presence may be felt in our neurons.

The real threat in these findings is not against the existence of God or our experiences of God. The fact that particular neurons are active when we feel God does not mean that we are not feeling God. God can activate our neurons as well as any scientist. After all, particular neurons are active when we see a sunset. It is wrong to conclude that we are not actually seeing a sunset or that the sunset does not exist. The real threat is to the existence of an immaterial soul or mind, and to the idea that our spirituality is something separate and separable from our brains. The real threat is to the possibility of life after death.

Further studies suggest that splitting one's brain can split one's consciousness. The two halves of our brains are connected by fibers called the corpus callosum. Cut those fibers in a procedure called commissurotomy and the left half of the brain doesn't always know what the right half is doing. Neither does the right half always know what the left half is doing. That a change in the brain has such an enormous implication for consciousness suggests a deep connection between consciousness and the brain—a connection so deep that one wonders whether consciousness can ever exist apart from the brain.

Commissurotomy also raises questions about the existence of the soul. Do two different souls result when the fibers are cut? If so, which is the original soul? How was the new one created? Did God suddenly create it? If there remains just one soul, then how can one soul have two centers of consciousness?

---

8. See Murphy and Persinger, "Debate Concerning the God Helmet."

Given all this evidence, most neuroscientists believe that our mental features depend on our brains. We'd better listen to them.

But evidence is different from interpretation of that evidence. Neuroscience shows that mental features are tightly linked to brain processes and regions. But it cannot tell us the nature of that link. It cannot, for example, prove that mental features depend on the brain for their continued existence. One can consistently interpret the evidence to mean that what goes on in the mind is normally correlated with what goes on in the brain. Every time I think about a dark chocolate bar with hazelnuts, the same particular region of my brain activates. But that does not mean that the thinking depends on the brain. The mind could be one thing and the brain another, like dance partners who follow the same steps at the same time. When the dance is done, the mind walks away from the brain as a dancer walks away from her partner. The mind may necessarily depend on the brain while attached to it and yet keep going when no longer attached to it. It might be able to do its thinking in some other way. Science cannot disprove the continuation of the mind after death.

Still, neuroscience makes it harder to defend the mind's survival of the brain's death. We can explain so much of our mental features in terms of brain processes. Therefore, it seems, we no longer need to posit the existence of a soul or a mind to explain those processes. The simplest explanation is often the best explanation and the simplest explanation confines our thoughts to our brains.

Our knowledge of the world works against our belief in the afterlife. If we are our bodies or brains, then all that we are becomes compost. If we are our minds, then we likely die when all our brain activities cease. No wonder that many today deny the existence of life after death. The skeptics are increasing and will likely continue to increase as neuroscience explains more of our minds. That is reason enough to do what this book does—to lay out the Christian options for death and resurrection and see how well they accommodate the findings of science.

Each Christian view on death and resurrection will need to be consistent with what we know about our corpses and what we know about our brains. They will need to be consistent with the scattering of our atoms after we die and with the tight linkage between our thoughts and our neurons. Each of the views we will consider are consistent with contemporary science, although some better fit science than others. Scripture and science both constrain our options for death and resurrection, but there is one more crucial authority that is too often overlooked.

5

The Inner Frame: What Does Philosophy Say?

Philosophy at the Baggage Claim

MY ELDEST SON ONCE loved to go to airports. Unlike other boys, he wasn't much interested in watching the airplanes take off. Instead, he wanted to watch the suitcases. So whenever we visited an airport, we always went to the baggage claim area even if we didn't need to. Most of us never stop to think about how mysterious this area really is. The luggage suddenly appears from behind some flaps as a conveyer belt carries it around a track. Sometimes someone claims the luggage as their own. But if no one claims a suitcase, it disappears behind another set of flaps. In a few minutes, it reappears again from behind the set of flaps from which it had originally appeared.

How do we know that the suitcase that just came through the entrance flap is the same as the one that had recently disappeared behind the exit flap? The suitcase that reappears looks like the suitcase that had disappeared. It is as yellow as a sunflower. It has wheels on one end and a handle so that it can be pulled. It is a medium-sized Samsonite. So we think it is the same suitcase. But we could be wrong. That is why we put nametags on our suitcases. If the suitcase has the right name written on the nametag, then we know it is the same suitcase. But even then we could be wrong. Nametags can be switched, even in the short time when luggage moves from the exit flap back to the entrance flap.

The problem is much greater when we wonder whether the suitcase we now see on the conveyor belt is the same suitcase that we checked in at Gatwick. We think that the only way we could know for sure would be to open the suitcase and see what's inside. But even then we could be wrong. Contents can be switched too. Once an item disappears from our view, it is difficult, if not impossible, to know for sure if a similar item that reappears is the same item as the one that has disappeared.

We do philosophy when we try to identify our suitcases. It is a philosophical question whether the suitcase rolling down the track is the *same* suitcase as the one we last saw at the check-in counter at Gatwick. When we make such a judgment about the suitcase, we are making a judgment about its *identity*. Philosophers call this the *problem of identity over time*. How is it that the yellow suitcase that we now see on the conveyor belt is the same as the yellow suitcase that we saw in Gatwick twelve hours ago? But we need to be clear about what exactly we mean when we puzzle over whether this suitcase is the same one that we lugged through London.

Sometimes when we say that one suitcase is the same as another, we mean that it *looks* like the other. It has the same color, shape, size and brand. It is made of the same material. This suitcase is the same as mine because it is also yellow, medium-sized, rectangular, and a Samsonite. They are the same because they *resemble* each other, because they are the same *kind* of suitcase.

But we want to know whether the suitcase rolling down the track is the *exact* same suitcase as the one we checked in—that it is that suitcase and none other. We want to know whether the Gatwick suitcase and the suitcase now before us are one object in the universe and not two—that they are one in number. Philosophers call this *numerical identity*. The suitcase at the baggage claim is the exact same suitcase as the one in Gatwick if it is *numerically identical* to it.

The exact same suitcase may not even look like the one we checked in. It may have gotten some holes during transport. An artistically inclined airline employee may have painted it with pink polka dots and silver stripes. Other suitcases on the belt may look more like the one we checked in. So being the exact same suitcase does not necessarily mean looking exactly like the exact same suitcase. Objects change over time. But they still remain the same objects.

It is also important to distinguish two different but related issues. When we are trying to find our suitcase among the luggage, we are looking for clues that will help us identify the right suitcase. Those clues are answers to the question: "How do we *know* that it is the same suitcase?" Sometimes philosophers are interested in this question. We are being philosophers when we think of the kinds of clues that will help us identify the suitcase.

But philosophers also want to know what it is that makes this suitcase the exact same suitcase. What does its identity over time consist in? What is the connection between the postflight suitcase and the preflight suitcase that makes them the same suitcase? This is a different question, because its answer may be different than the answer to the other question. I might know that this suitcase is the same as the one in London because it has my name etched on its side. But the etched name does not make it the exact same suitcase.

What could make it the exact same suitcase? The obvious answer is that its matter does. It has got the same atoms and that is why it is the same suitcase. Thus, you may wonder why philosophers fuss about such things. Consider a river. Its matter is constantly changing as the old water flows on and the new water flows in. Yet it is the same river. Or consider a Chihuahua. The atoms in her body are constantly changing as she eats and excretes. By the end of her life, she will consist of an entirely different set of atoms. But she is still the same Chihuahua we always loved. So not all material objects can so easily get their identities from their atoms.

Not everyone may agree. The ancient Greek philosopher Heraclitus famously said that you can't step into the same river twice. By the time you step in it again, even if it is only a second later, it will already consist of different water molecules and thus be a different river. If we follow the same logic, then our ten-year-old Chihuahua is no longer *numerically the same* Chihuahua as the pup we rescued from the shelter. We might agree with Heraclitus about rivers, but still think that dogs are different. But why? What is it about dogs that makes them different—that preserves their identities over time even though their atoms are always changing?

We are more like Chihuahuas than suitcases. Our atoms come and go faster than we think. Apparently, 98 percent of our atoms are replaced every year. So philosophers want to know what makes a person at a later time numerically identical to a person at an earlier time. What makes the ninety-year-old man *numerically the same* person as the nine-year-old boy? What is the *connection* between them that makes them one person and not two different persons? Philosophers call this the *problem of personal identity over time*.

We sometimes speak of someone as no longer being the *same* person as the one before. We meet Donny, the neighborhood bully of our childhood. Only now he is nice. He says that he is no longer the *same* person as that boy we once knew. But we all know that Donny does not mean that he has literally become a different person altogether—that he is no longer Donny even if he now goes by Donald. We know that he means that his personality has radically changed. He was mean then, now he's nice. Sometimes when we say that we have become different persons, we also mean that we have adopted completely new beliefs and values. We might mean, for example, that we have converted to a new religion or become an atheist. But we do not mean that we are an altogether new person so that if we were to count us now and us then that we would count two persons instead of one. The philosophical *problem of personal identity over time* is not concerned with that kind of change in identity. Such changes are not cases of becoming *numerically different* persons.

Not too much hangs on what makes the preflight suitcase the same as the postflight suitcase. But a lot hangs on whether the forty-year-old Professor Silas Langley is the same person as the whiny four-year-old named Silas. We might think it obvious, but it is a little less obvious when we realize that Professor Langley remembers nothing of being that four-year-old. So how can he be the same person? Or what about the baby who was Silas. Or the being in the womb who will be named Silas once he is born? How we answer the question of what makes later Silas's *numerically identical* to earlier Silas's may also tell us when Silas began. That may influence our beliefs about, for example, the morality of abortion. We can also ask about whether the ninety-year-old Silas living only in a vegetative state is really Silas anymore. That may influence our beliefs about, for example, the morality of pulling the plug.

The same person who lives today will one day live in heaven. At least, that is the Christian's hope. But whether and how this can be also depends on *the problem of personal identity over time*. How is the person in heaven *numerically the same* person as the person who stands before me? What makes that person the *same* person? What connects that person to this person so that they are one and the *same*? That is the most important philosophical question for each of the five options for how we might survive our deaths. It does not have an obvious answer. This is the very problem that first got people thinking about *personal identity over time*. Here is one case where philosophy owes a debt to Christianity.[1]

Heaven further complicates *the problem of personal identity over time*. Christianity traditionally holds that we will have bodies in heaven.

---

1. Martin and Barresi, *Rise and Fall*, 56.

But our new bodies will be different and better. If we died old, we will not reappear old. If we died bald, we may not reappear bald. If we died without our right finger, we will reappear with one. We may even have wings and no fingerprints. Our bodies may not even be human. Our resurrected bodies are more like battered suitcases that are repaired and enhanced as they reappear from the flap. The suitcase goes out one flap with holes. It comes back through another as a work of art, newly painted and designed. It went out dull green, it comes back spring green. It goes out with plastic wheels, it comes back with metal wheels and wings. It went out heavy and sluggish. It comes back light and flexible. How can the new suitcase be *numerically the same* suitcase if it has changed so much? Likewise, how can we be *numerically the same* persons if we have changed so much? So we will need to find something about us that makes us *numerically the same* persons in heaven as we are on earth despite all these changes.

What Are You?

The *problem of personal identity over time* gets to the heart of the question of who you are. What has to be there for you to be there? What is the core of who you are, such that without it you are no more? What is it about you that, if present, makes it so that *you* are present?

In the past, the most common answer was that you are your soul—an invisible spiritual something that is the seat of your consciousness, personality, thoughts, desires, memories, and emotions. Or maybe you, like most thinkers today, don't believe in souls. But then what are you? Are you your memories, so that you continue to exist as long as your memories continue to exist? Or are you your core personality, whatever that may be—perhaps the shy inquisitive nerdy person that you really are? Or the outgoing adventurous athletic person that you really are? Or are you your self-awareness? Are you just that sense you have of being you, so that you continue to exist as long as you continue to have this sense of being you?

It is becoming more common to believe that you are your body. You continue to exist as long as your same body continues to exist. That sounds simple enough, that is, until you remember that your body is more like a river than a suitcase.

the inner frame: what does philosophy say?   43

Your atoms can't be what make your body remain *numerically the same* body over time. Yet newer atoms always overlap with some of the older atoms. The atoms of your body are never instantly replaced by the atoms of the pizza you just ate or the atoms of oxygen you just breathed in. A continual chain of overlapping atoms connects your sixty-year-old body to your six-year-old body. Perhaps that chain makes the aging body *numerically the same* body as the boyish body. Consider a rope made of many fibers in which no single fiber runs through the whole length of the rope. It is one rope and not two because the fibers overlap. New fibers always overlap with older fibers, which in turn overlap with even older fibers and so on all the way back to the beginning of the rope. The atoms of your body are like the fibers of that rope. None of those atoms remain throughout the lifespan of your body, but their overlapping makes them all part of *numerically the same* body.

Or maybe your body remains *numerically the same* over time because it has the same ongoing life—the continuation of the same heartbeat, the same breathing, the same flowing of blood. You continue to exist as you as long as your breathing and beating continue. Or maybe it is not so much the breathing and the beating as it is the organs themselves. You continue to exist as long as your heart and lungs continue. But why should they matter as much as your brain? Perhaps you are really just your brain. As long as your brain lives on, then you live on.

There are four main types of theories about what constitutes *personal identity over time*:

1. You are something other than your body (like your soul).
2. You are something other than your body but which still needs some body or other in order to exist (such as your memories, which might be able to exist in a different body).
3. You are your body or some part of your body (like your brain).
4. You are both your body and something other than your body (like your soul).

Philosophers have adopted each of these answers to the *problem of personal identity over time*. They have also found ways for each of these answers to support the possibility of life after death. That should sound surprising. If we are our bodies and our bodies are destined for compost, then we too should be destined for compost. Yet Christian philosophers are creative folk. They find ways. We will encounter some of them in the following chapters.

Brain Surgery, Transporter Errors, and the Problem of Duplication

Philosophers tend to use thought experiments to test theories of *personal identity over time*. Thought experiments involve imagining unusual situations that are intended to help us develop better theories about reality. Here is one.

Imagine that your body is dying. Some clever neurosurgeons have found a way to remove your brain and place it into a cloned body that has no brain. But these neurosurgeons decide that two of you are better than one. So they put your left brain in one cloned body and your right brain in another. The operation is successful, but both the left-brain person and the right-brain person claim to be you. Each one also shares all your mental features—your memories, beliefs, personality traits, desires, and such. But the neurosurgeons do not realize that the two resulting persons can't both be *numerically the same* person as you.

One of the laws of logic states that if $X = Y$ and $X = Z$, then $Y = Z$. Suppose that X represents me, Y represents Dr. Langley, and Z represents the husband of Rhonda. I am identical to Dr. Langley and I am identical to the husband of Rhonda. It necessarily follows that Dr. Langley must be identical to the husband of Rhonda. If Dr. Langley isn't identical to the husband of Rhonda, then there has been a mistake. Either I am not Dr. Langley or I am not the husband of Rhonda. Fortunately, I am both so there has been no mistake.

Now let's have X represent the original you—the you who existed before the surgery. Y represents the clone who got your left brain. Z represents the clone who got your right brain.

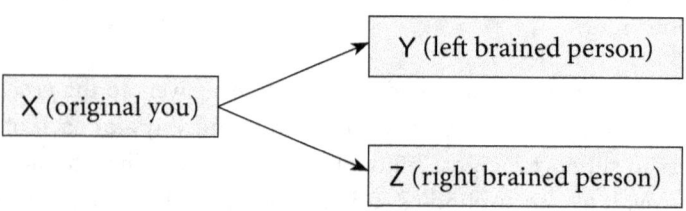

If X and Y are the same person, then X = Y. If X and Z are the same person, then X = Z. It necessarily follows that Y = Z. But in this case, Y does not equal Z. The left-brained person and the right-brained person are not the same person. How can they be? One is now watching the television in the recovery room while the other is drinking cocoa in the cafeteria. So if Y does not equal Z, then X can't be both Y and Z. One of them can be you, but not both.

Yet neither one of them has any greater claim to being you than the other. So there are no non-arbitrary reasons for choosing one over the other as being you. That leaves one alternative. You died on the operating table. You can, however, take comfort in knowing that your death led to the creation of two new persons.

Suppose, however, that one of the surgeons accidentally dropped your right brain during the surgery. It splattered. Therefore, she could not place it into a cloned body. Fortunately for you, your left brain did not drop and was safely placed in the other cloned body. That brain survived. But did you?

Most of us tend to believe that you did. But if you did, then your survival depended on whether or not the other brain happened to splatter. Makes life seem contingent, doesn't it? But here lies the rub. Your identity can't depend on what may or may not happen to something or someone else. Our survival can't depend on whether or not some other person happens to come into existence. Philosophers call this *the only X and Y principle*. Identity can't depend on whether or not there is also a Z. It challenges any theory of identity that makes one's identity depend on something that can be duplicated. Philosophers call this *the problem of duplication*. In theory at least, brains can be split and thus duplicated. So anyone who thinks that they are their brains will need to respond to this challenge. But what else about you can be duplicated? Perhaps everything.

In one episode of *Star Trek: The Next Generation*, Commander Riker is beamed up by a transporter beam from a planet to his starship.[2] But the transporter beam is somehow split in two, which results in two Rikers. One Riker successfully re-materializes on the ship. The other re-materializes on the planet. They are completely identical in mind and body at the moment of re-materialization. They both have equal claims to being the real Riker. But it is impossible for both of them to be the real

2. See Hanley, *Metaphysics of Star Trek*, 168–76, for an interesting discussion of Riker's fission case.

Riker (remember the X's, Y's, and Z's). Anyone watching the show would conclude that the two resulting Rikers are two different persons. Yet no viewer would conclude that Riker died during the transporter accident. But, as we saw with the split brain scenario, it seems we would have to conclude that Riker did die during the transporter accident.

In any case, suppose that the transporter accident never occurred and only one Riker re-materializes. We would think that Riker did survive the transport. But, according to the *only X and Y principle*, whether or not he survived can't depend on whether some other "Riker" may or may not have re-materialized. We can't conclude both that he survived the transport when no other "Riker" re-materialized and that he would have died and been replaced by two new "Rikers" if another "Riker" had re-materialized.

We are at an impasse. Both aren't Riker. At least one of them is Riker. But there is no good reason to choose one over the other. The only way out seems to be to deny that *personal identity over time* depends on having either the same minds or the same bodies. It would have to depend on some further fact of the matter, such as the existence of a soul that went with one Riker and not the other. If we are committed to either mind or body-based theories of personality identity, then we will need to explain how such theories solve the *duplication problem*. One solution might be to argue that it is theoretically impossible to split brains and bodies. It makes for good science fiction, but not for good reality.

Fission-cases and the resulting *problem of duplication* are one of the main reasons why many contemporary philosophers, such as Derek Parfit, believe that we should give up the idea of *personal identity over time*.[3] You do not die during the brain surgery, but neither do you survive. That's because there was no you to begin with. The same can be said for Riker during the transporter mishap. He neither dies nor doesn't die, because there never was a Riker to begin with.

According to Parfit, we are nothing but a stream of ever-flowing thoughts, memories desires, feelings, choices, personality traits, and bodily states. We do not worry about a stream's identity if it divides equally. We do not puzzle over which resulting stream is identical to the original stream. Both continue the stream and that is all there is to say.

---

3. See Parfit, *Reasons and Persons*. He uses many bizarre cases that are familiar to science fiction fans. There is no way around it. Science fiction is a seedbed for addressing the *problem of personal identity over time*.

Likewise, both Rikers continue the mental and bodily lives of the original Riker. There is no further fact of the matter.

Riker should be happy. Everything that he cares about lives on. His memory of boarding his first starship and his talent for playing the trumpet will live on. Even better, they live on twice over. So if something happened to one of them, the other would keep flowing on. The split has increased the odds of the survival of what he cares about. The more splits the merrier. It is like having more grandkids to carry on the family name.

Some scientists speculate that our lives split with every choice we make. One stream continues in one dimensional timeline and the other continues in another. There are potentially thousands of streams that carry forward all that you care about—your memories, desires, talents, etc. One episode of *Star Trek: The Next Generation* (no surprises here) suggests as much. A dimensional fracturing causes multiple Enterprises to appear at once. But they are all from different dimensional timelines. Riker gets to see one of his dimensional duplicates captaining one of the duplicate Enterprises. That duplicate Riker sacrifices his ship and thus his life to save all the others. But the sacrifice isn't nearly as sad knowing that most of that Riker's mental life continues in the Rikers of the other dimensional timelines. If the universe is a dividing stream, then death it seems has less a sting.

But Christians, for the most part, are committed to the view that persons do exist. Many Christians believe it is essential to the biblical understanding of salvation, judgment, and the afterlife. You can't be saved if there is no You to save. You can't be judged at the Last Judgment, if there is no You to be judged. You can't be in heaven if there is no You to begin with. The continuation of our memories, desires, and such is not enough. Christians generally hope for the continuation of our very selves and that, if not for Christ's resurrection, death's sting strikes deep. The question for us is how it is possible for *numerically the same* self to cross the chasm between death and resurrection. There are five main ways to cross it. The next chapter explores the first one.

Filling In the Puzzle: Five Ways to Die and Live Again

6

Soul-Flight, Part 1

You push the first button. You see your body crumple to the floor and are surprised that you don't crumple with it. At first, the sensation is unnerving. But then it is liberating, for you no longer feel burdened by the weight of your body. The ship explodes but it does not affect you. You are immaterial. The explosion can no more harm you than an ant can harm a giant. You drift across space. You feel as if you are observing the universe as an outsider, as if you were a scientist observing protozoa through a microscope. For an instant, you worry that maybe you lost all your memories—as if they belonged to your brain and not to you. You try to recall your most important memories. They are all there, even your memory of visiting the bridge of the spaceship when you were just five years old. You remember what it was like to eat chocolate, to hold hands, to dance. Nothing about you is missing except your body. You float down to the planet. There lying on the ground is a body that has been ready made for you. It is very different from your previous body. It is taller and stronger. The face is handsomer. The eyes are blue rather than the brown you are used to. Pleased, you float into the body and bring it to life.

You see a computer nearby. Its printer spits out a piece of paper that reads:

> Congratulations! You chose the correct button. The spaceship computer enabled your soul to separate from your body. We have constructed a new body for you that we think you will like much better. But wasn't it fun to travel to the planet without your body? If you ever wish to leave your new body, just push the red button on this computer.
>
> Made possible by the
> Uralive Teletransportation Company.

Self-as-Soul

This scenario corresponds with the most common Christian understanding of what happens after we die. When we die, we separate from our bodies. Perhaps we see our dead bodies just after we leave them. Then we float into heaven. We still see everything that is happening on earth. We see our loved ones cry at our funeral. We see them eat their dinners and go to sleep. We know that the living are comforted by the thought that we are aware of them. We lose none of our memories. We remember our first days of school, our high school graduations, our weddings, the births of our kids, and the moments before our deaths. Most importantly, we are now directly in the presence of God. We commune with him in a way that we could never do on earth. Eventually we will be reunited with our loved ones when they die and join us in heaven. Someday, God will give us new bodies, but they may not be anything like the bodies we have now.

This scenario is also based on the most common Christian understanding of who we are. According to it, we each have a soul. But we don't just *have* souls. We *are* our souls. We are not our bodies. We *have* our bodies. We use them as tools to interact with this physical world.

> Self-as-Soul: I am my soul. Any future person is the same person as me as long as she is the same soul as I am.

Our souls survive the deaths of our bodies. They are not physical beings like bodies, so there is no reason why they should perish along with the body. Since our souls survive, we too survive. We are like hermit crabs who have temporarily taken up house in our shells. But when our shells crack, we can leave them and find other shells. Self-as-Soul is a form of what philosophers call *dualism*, which was introduced in chapter 3. Today's dualists usually refer to minds instead of souls, but souls and minds mean much the same thing. I will use these words interchangeably.

Dualism frequents popular culture. In the Star Wars saga, Jedi Master Yoda teaches Luke Skywalker that we are "not this crude matter."[1] In the movie *What Dreams May Come*, heavenly guide Albert Lewis, played by Cuba Gooding Jr., tells the newly dead Chris Nielsen, played by Robin Williams, that: "Your brain is meat, and rots and disappears. Do you really think that's all there was to you? Like you're in your house right now. You're *in* your house. That doesn't mean you *are* your house. House falls down, you get up and walk away."[2]

Being John Malkovich explores the possibility that our minds can roam into another person's bodies and perceive what that other person perceives. Watching the movie is itself unnerving, because it makes the viewer feel like she too is in someone else's body. The film uses the metaphor of the puppet master pulling the strings on his puppet. The master is like the mind. The puppet is like the body. Our minds control our bodies. But our minds are no more connected to our bodies than the puppet master is to his puppet. Cut the strings, the puppet falls, and the puppet master walks away whole and unharmed.

Self-as-Soul has much in its favor. It has a long and distinguished history, embraced by saints, mystics, philosophers, and most of the commoners on the street. It is also simple. Obviously our bodies do not go anywhere when we die. They become lifeless and eventually decay until only the skeleton is left. Even the skeleton will not last forever. Self-as-Soul is the simplest way to understand how we can survive our deaths given that our corpses rot. We do not have to invent strange scenarios that could explain how our bodies survive our deaths. Neither do we have to figure out how we can be *numerically the same* persons if we have completely new bodies in heaven. According to Self-as-Soul, that person who will be in heaven is *numerically the same* person as me now because that person will have the same soul as I have now. After all, he and I are just that single soul that we share.

---

1. "The Best Yoda Quote," *YouTube* video, 0:16, posted May 27, 2012, from *Star Wars: The Empire Strikes Back*, http://www.youtube.com/watch?v=XMdR9iAflKo.

2. "What Dreams May Come—Heaven & Reality," *YouTube* video, 3:18, posted August 5, 2013, from *What Dreams May Come*, http://www.youtube.com/watch?v=OdgGxgg91Tc.

Self-as-Soul also explains those scriptural passages that suggest that something of us can exist apart from our bodies. Paul says "absent from the body . . . present with the Lord" (2 Cor 5:8 KJV). We do not have to find scriptural interpretations that try to show how such passages do not mean what they seem to say. This view can also explain *Sheol*. The ancient Hebrews could go to *Sheol* after they die because their souls can go to *Sheol* after they die.

This view also makes possible a belief important to most Christians throughout history—the belief that our deceased loved ones exist right now even though the resurrection has not happened yet. It is possible because their souls can exist right now in heaven. Many a eulogy comforts us by suggesting that the deceased is now with God and looking down on us. With Self-as-Soul, such a belief is not a charade to make us feel better. It is based in a truth.

Biblical Challenges

There are, however, some important biblical challenges to Self-as-Soul. The last chapter suggested that the Bible, especially the Old Testament, tends to view persons as living *bodies*, rather than as *souls* inhabiting bodies. We have also seen how the Bible views death as an enemy and teaches that we can't survive our deaths without God's help. But, according to Self-as-Soul, our souls naturally survive the deaths of our bodies. That makes death more a blessing than a burden. Death is more like a friend who guides us into heaven than a Grim Reaper who is out to get us. If Self-as-Soul is true, then we do not need Christ to conquer death.

The Bible also places our hope for an afterlife in the resurrections of our bodies. But according to Self-as-Soul, getting a better body back is an extra add-on, a welcome accoutrement. It is like swapping a tattered coat for an Armani suit—nice but unnecessary. If we are just our souls and if they survive our deaths, then the Bible's emphasis on the resurrection seems misplaced. Resurrection should then be tangential to biblical teaching. But instead Paul makes it the cornerstone of his theology of the afterlife.

Some defenders of Self-as-Soul modify it to make it more biblical. They concede, for example, that the soul can't survive death without God's help. God must zap it so that it can survive death. This modified view will, however, need to explain why souls naturally perish with their bodies. Dualists typically believe that soul and body are two radically different sorts of things that are hooked together no more tightly than a train engine is hooked to the car it tows. The soul should survive its unhooking with the body as easily as the engine survives its unhooking from the car. The modified view may therefore need to integrate soul and body more deeply than dualists desire.

Others rethink the standard biblical interpretations. As we have seen, many New Testament verses seem to support *dualism*. Perhaps then the New Testament offers a more dualist view that corrects more primitive Old Testament *holistic* tendencies. Perhaps the Hebrew view evolved into a more *dualist* view as the Hebrews increasingly understood that God intended for each individual person to live on after death so that the good could be rewarded and the evil could be punished. Many wicked people prosper their whole lives and never get their comeuppance. Many good people suffer their whole lives at the hands of the wicked and never get rewarded. If this life is it, then God is not just. The soul's survival after death is the easiest way to explain how we can live after we die and get our just desserts.

Some also suggest that the resurrection of the body is a metaphor for the survival of the soul after death. Parents use metaphors all the time to help their kids understand something of what they can't yet fully grasp. For example, mothers tell their kids that little bugs are making them sick. She can't tell them the literal truth, because their minds have not developed enough to understand what germs are. Likewise, Paul's uneducated first-century Roman readers are unable to understand immaterial invisible somethings surviving their deaths. But they understand bodies, because they see them all the time. It is easier for them to understand some kind of spiritual body leaving their physical bodies at death, even though Paul knows that it is really their immaterial souls that leave their bodies.

Very few Christian *dualists* accept this interpretation. Most concede that the resurrection is physical and a good thing. We are fully aware and happy without our bodies, but we can't really interact with a physical environment without them. We look forward to having them back so that we can again smell roses, taste coffee, feel the grass beneath our feet, and see each other's smiles. It is like traveling in Rome. We enjoy touring the Vatican, marching up the Spanish Steps, and tossing coins in the Trevi fountain. But we still miss the comforts and familiarity of being at home. We look forward to going home even though we are perfectly happy in Rome. A body is like a home. We can live life fully without it. But we still like to come back to it. So we hope for the resurrection like we hope for a homecoming.

The Problem of Soul-Body Interaction

Many philosophers criticize Self-as-Soul because it has a hard time explaining how souls can interact with bodies. Souls are immaterial. They do not have sizes, shapes, or surfaces. Bodies do. They move each other by pushing or pulling each other, which requires making contact with each other. The white ball pushes the eight ball into the corner pocket because part of its surface touches part of the surface of the eight ball. The engine pulls the coal car because the two are connected by a hook. But if the pusher has no surface then it can't make contact with anything and thus can't push or pull anything. Souls have no surface. Therefore, they can neither push nor pull. Neither can they be pushed or pulled. The soul can't *push* a neuron to fire in a particular way to cause the brain to remember the white cliffs of Dover. Neither can the soul *push* our brain to cause the body's hand to raise. Neither can the ear's hearing of a Bach cantata *push* the soul to thinking about the beauty of Bach's music.

Descartes, a sixteenth-century French philosopher, is well known for his defense of *dualism*, but he never successfully explained how mind and body could interact. He suggested that soul and body make direct contact in the pineal gland, which is a small gland at the base of the brain.[3] Today we might choose some other more promising region of the brain. But choosing a particular part of the body as a contact point does not solve the problem, because it raises the question of how the soul can make contact with that part of the body.

Even without belief in souls, most Christians still need to resolve the problem of how immaterial beings can interact with material beings. That is because we generally believe in miracles. God could not raise Jesus from the dead, for example, if God could not act on Jesus's dead body. God could not even have created the world in the first place. How can an immaterial being such as God *touch* a material universe?

Dualists often reply that we do not have to know exactly how mind and body interact. We do not yet know all the possible ways in which entities can interact with each other. It is not logically impossible for spiritual and material beings to interact, so keep an open mind and maybe we

---

3. Descartes, "Passions of the Soul," 340.

will figure it out someday. Scientists do not yet fully understand how light is both a wave and a particle. But they would be wrong to deny it is both just because they do not yet understand how.

Dualists also point out that *physicalists* have a mystery of their own. *Physicalists* believe that only material things exist and thus that souls do not exist. But they have trouble explaining how matter can give rise to consciousness. How can something as profound as our own mental lives arise simply from the natural development of better brains? We each have an inner life that is uniquely our own. There is something that it is like to be you and something that it is like to be me. I can't know what it is like to be you by examining your brain. Even if I knew everything about your brain, I still could not know what it is like to be you. I also could not know what it is like for you to taste chocolate. I might be able to examine your brain and discover that you are having the experience of eating chocolate. I might be able to discover that you think it tastes good and that you want more. But I can't discover how it tastes to you or how you experience the pleasure of tasting it or how your addiction to chocolate feels to you. Licking your brain will not help, because the way you experience the taste of chocolate isn't there.[4] Your unique experience of chocolate is a different kind of thing altogether than the neurons that are firing when you taste the chocolate. Your experience is subjective. Your neurons are objective. So it is hard to explain how the experience could emerge from the neurons. Thus, it is difficult to explain how your unique experience of chocolate emerged from your brain.

Physicalists have two options. They can agree with the dualist that consciousness is real, but that consciousness does not exist in an immaterial entity like a soul. Instead it exists in the brain, but it is much more than the brain. Think of it as the second story of a building. It requires the first story to exist. But it is something in addition to the first story. You would not be able to explain everything about the building by examining

---

4. Contemporary philosopher Thomas Nagel provides a charming account of licking brains in his book *What Does It All Mean?*, 30. He is also well-known for an article he wrote titled "What Is It Like to Be a Bat?" Nagel suggests that we can't understand what it is like to experience the world as a bat does. Knowing all the physical facts about the mechanism that the bat uses to navigate the world through sonar isn't enough to know what it is actually like to experience the world through sonar rather than through sight. So there is more to a bat than just its physical make-up. So too with humans. Nagel does not endorse *dualism* though. He believes that our minds are more deeply integrated with our bodies. We are unified beings with mental and physical aspects, such that neither can be reduced to the other.

all the contents of the first story—its walls, furniture, floors, ceilings, and the persons who inhabit it. Likewise, you can't know everything about the mind by only examining its first story, the physical brain. You would have to look at its second story, its consciousness. Your unique experience of chocolate is on the second story and nobody but you can climb the stairs to get there. But this solution still does not resolve the mystery of how consciousness arises from matter—of how the second story got built.

Or *physicalists* can deny our consciousness altogether, in the sense that there is anything that it is like to be you.[5] Your unique experience of tasting chocolate is an illusion—a trick of the brain. If I were to examine everything in your brain, I would know everything there is to know about your mental life and experiences. This option removes the mystery but it also removes your unique experience of tasting chocolate—which goes against some of our strongest intuitions about ourselves.

Either way, *physicalism* is not perfect either. Depending on one's intuitions, the *physicalist*'s problems may be greater than the *dualist*'s problem of explaining how soul and body interact. Holding on to our deep-seated intuition that consciousness is real may override our lack of understanding of how soul and body interact. Such understanding may yet be forthcoming.

Souls, Bodies, and the Conservation of Energy

Dualism may not have to explain exactly how the soul and body interact. But it does need to explain how that interaction squares with science. The law of the conservation of energy is one of the fundamental laws of physics. According to it, the total level of energy in the universe must always remain the same. Thus, no energy can enter or leave the universe. But if our souls tell our bodies what to do or our brains what to think then they are inputting new energy into the universe. If your soul tells your arm to raise and it raises, then the soul adds energy to the physical universe by putting new energy into your arm so that it can raise. You increase the total amount of energy in the universe every time you decide to eat Corn Flakes or throw a frisbee. Furthermore, suppose that you stub your toe. The toe sends a signal (energy) to your brain which then sends a signal (energy) to your soul, and you feel pain. But that would mean that energy is sent out of the universe and into your mind. The universe loses energy

---

5. See Daniel Dennett's book *Sweet Dreams* for such an account.

every time your body sends a signal to your mind—whenever you see a rainbow, hear a horn honk, or feel a pin prick. The same applies to God. If God raises Jesus's dead body then God inputs new energy into the universe. If God *sees* Francis feed the birds, then energy leaves the universe. According to this law, neither God nor souls should be able to interact with the physical universe because any such interaction requires a transfer of energy into or out of the universe.

Fortunately, the world of subatomic particles may open a crack in the universe that allows God and the soul to step in. Seeing how requires a detour to the world of Napoleonic France. Pierre Simon de Laplace, whose brain was apparently smaller than average, was one of the greatest scientists and mathematicians of his time. He is most known for telling Napoleon that he had no need for the hypothesis that God existed. But he is also known for claiming that we could know the entire future of the universe if we knew the location, speed, and direction of every particle in it. We could know who will be president in 2016, whether the Red Sox will ever again win a World Series, and whether we will ever get to Mars. Think of the universe as a vast billiards table without any pockets and each particle as a billiard ball. The balls are continually in motion bouncing off each other and the walls. If we knew the location, speed, and direction of every ball at any moment then we could know the exact future trajectories of each ball. This picture of the universe leaves out the possibility that God or souls might sometimes push the particles off course, thus creating an unpredictable future. But Laplace's point is that this is not possible. Particles can explain everything there is to know about what causes what to move when and where.

Quantum mechanics dashed Laplace's dream. It showed that the direction that a subatomic particle takes is not completely determined by the particles that push it. In some cases, knowledge of the location, speed, and direction of all the particles that are pushing a given particle still would not give us knowledge of which direction that particle will move. It could conceivably go either way. Think of a raindrop that falls on the exact center of the peak of a roof. Imagine that there are no other factors, such as wind or the earth's spinning, that can cause it to go down one side of the roof rather than the other. It could equally fall in either direction. So too subatomic particles can sometimes equally go in two or more directions.

Such indeterminacy implies that the future is not written in stone. If a particle can sometimes just as easily go one way than other, then we can't always predict which way it will go. A hurricane might sometimes as likely head north to New York as head south to Miami, because all the particles that effect its movement might just as likely push it one way rather than another. We could not predict the hurricane's movement even if we had instruments that give us perfect observations of all the factors that affect its movement.

If this is correct, then sometimes only pure chance determines whether a particle will go one way rather than another. Here lies the crack. God could sometimes give particles the *information* that they need that will lead them to go one way rather than another. So could souls. Imagine a train that is zooming toward a fork in the tracks. Various forces such as the slope of the ground, the nature of the tracks, how much coal is in the train's engine, and such, determine how fast the train will keep zooming past the fork. Next to the fork is a track switcher. That switcher, and none of these other factors, will determine whether the train takes the left or the right fork. In a sense, the switcher gives it *information* about whether to go left or right that the other factors can't give it. The physical universe is like the tracks and God is like a switcher. The particles get their *energy* from the rest of the material world, but they sometimes get their *directions* from God. By influencing particles in this way, God can influence anything in the universe. He can send a hurricane south instead of North. God can raise Jesus's body from the dead by giving *information* to the particles of his body so that they go in the direction of restoring life rather than in the direction of decomposing his body.

Souls are also like track switchers. They give the particles of the brain external *information* that direct them one way rather than another. In that way, they can cause neurons to fire one way rather than another. Thus, souls can cause the brain to remember the taste of chocolate and to cause the body to walk into the chocolate store. The energy that causes the neurons to fire comes entirely from the material world, but the soul may sometimes determine which way a neuron fires, or which way that energy is directed. Souls influence the material world through giving it *information* rather than through pushing, pulling, or energizing it. The giving of information no more involves an injection of energy than a GPS giving directions. Thus the soul can influence the body without adding new energy into the universe. Conversely, our brains influence our souls by sending them *information* rather than energy. You do not have to worry about draining the universe of its energy every time you smell coffee.

Neuroscience and the Soul

As we saw in chapter 4, contemporary neuroscience also challenges Self-as-Soul. Many well-known contemporary thinkers believe that science has killed the soul, or at least the version of the soul espoused by Self-as-Soul. Among them are the biologist Richard Dawkins, the psychologist Steven Pinker, and the philosopher Daniel Dennett.[6] As we have seen, neuroscience shows that there is a close connection between our mental states—thoughts, memories, personality traits, desires, experiences—and our brain states. Some interpret this connection to mean that our mental states are just brain states. Love is nothing but a movement of neurotransmitters in a network of neurons. Others interpret this close connection to mean that our mental states are different from our brain states but can't exist without them—like a second story resting atop a first story. Remove the first story and the second story collapses. Many thinkers also conclude that there is a close connection between brain states and consciousness and free will. Some even claim that we do not really have consciousness or free will. We have been duped by our brains into believing that we do.

But we do not even have to go as far as denying consciousness to kill the soul. So long as we acknowledge that all of our mental features depend on the brain, then there is no longer any reason to believe that the soul exists. We can explain everything about us without it. Many contemporary Christian thinkers have been so impressed with the correlation between such findings of neuroscience and the biblical emphasis on our bodily natures that they have put together a book called *Whatever Happened to the Soul?*[7] Some of these thinkers are evangelicals. It is not just "crazy" liberals who have given up on the soul.

But the data from neuroscience does not conclusively show that we do not have souls. It shows that neurons fire in particular regions of our brains when we think about the purple of a pansy, remember the smell of lavender in the spring, or choose to stop and smell the roses. It does not prove, although it might imply, that the thoughts, memories, and choices

---

6. See Dawkins and Pinker, "Is Science Killing the Soul?," and Dennett, "Non-Believer."

7. See Brown et al., *Whatever Happened to the Soul?* The book includes a number of essays by psychologists, philosophers, scientists, and theologians who are all impressed by the convergence of neuroscience with the Bible's tendency toward a *holistic* understanding of human beings.

occur in the brain or that the brain causes them. It only shows that there is a *correlation* between our mental activities and our neural activities in our brains. For this reason, science cannot ever conclusively prove that the soul does not exist.

Dualists often think of the brain as the soul's tool to interact with the physical universe. Descartes used the analogy of a violinist and her violin. The violinist has the ability to play the violin. The violin allows her to manifest her ability to the rest of the world. When we see the violinist play the violin, then we can see that she knows how to play the violin. Suppose that a metal beam punctures the violin. She tries to play it and it comes out wrong. Sometimes it does not play at all. But that does not mean that she no longer has the ability to play violin. It means that she will now have to keep that ability to herself, unable to show to others that she has it.

The soul is like the violinist and the brain is like the violin. The soul needs the brain to show to the physical world its ability to think, remember, and make choices. But she can't display those abilities to the world as well if the brain is damaged. She still has the ability to think about the purple of a pansy, remember the smell of lavender in the spring, or desire to stop and smell the roses, but nobody in the physical universe will know. That is how brain damage causes dementia. It blocks the soul's connection to the brain so that the soul's ability to think can't manifest itself in the brain. A person with dementia *appears* mindless to us, but her abilities to think and remember are still present deep down in her soul. Perhaps she can't think at all. But the *potentiality* for thinking is still there, lodged in her soul, ready to be actualized the moment her brain will let it.

Still, the best explanation is usually the simplest explanation. According to the rule of thinking known as Ockham's Razor, we should not think that more things exist in the universe than are necessary to explain any given data. The brain can explain the mind. We do not need the soul to explain it. We therefore have no good reason to believe that the soul exists.

But we have seen how *physicalists* have a difficult time explaining how matter can give rise to consciousness and free will. *Dualists* argue that the soul is the only thing that can explain why there is something that it is like to be you—why you experience the taste of chocolate in your own unique way. They also argue that the soul is the only thing that can explain your ability to freely choose to eat chocolate instead of cherries.

If you do not have a soul, then your neurons made you choose the chocolate and duped you into believing that *you* freely chose it.

Dualists also argue that we need the soul to explain why your experience of the world, such as experiencing a bar of chocolate, is a unified experience. Some neurons register the sweet smell of the chocolate. Other neurons register the chocolate's brown color and rectangular shape. Others register its hard but softening surface. Others register the snapping sound it makes when it breaks. Still others register its earthy, fruity, nutty taste. But we do not experience its smells, colors, textures, shapes, sounds, and flavors as disconnected experiences. We experience them all together at once and as one single experience. We cannot do that unless there is something other than the disconnected neurons themselves that can unify them. That something is the soul. So the soul may well be the best explanation of all the data.

But then there is Phineas Gage. In chapter 4, we saw that damage to his brain caused his personality to completely change. If Phineas had a soul that is the center of his personality, then that soul should continue after his accident and exhibit, for the most part, the same personality. Phineas should still be Phineas. Yet that is not what happened. His personality changed drastically and for the worse. How then could he have had a soul?

The *dualist* can appeal to the analogy of the violinist and the violin. The true Phineas Gage remains, but he can no longer express his true personality in his body, just as the violinist's ability to play the violin remains even though she can no longer express it. His true personality can no longer cause him to wear his emotions on his sleeve or respond to stress with the coolness of a Vulcan. The true Phineas lived out the rest of his bodily life unable to express his true self.

The *dualist* can also say that Phineas's accident blocked one part of his personality but released another. Both the pre and post-accident personalities represent his core personality. We know that everyone's personality changes over time. A person's eighty-year-old personality can be as different from her eight-year-old personality as the Phineas's post-accident personality was from his pre-accident personality. We tend to accept that the eighty-year-old personality is an expression of the same core personality as the eight-year-old personality. We should accept the same for Phineas.

Still, the simpler conclusion is that there is no such thing as a core personality. You may think that your shyness, intelligence, and love of classical music are essential to who you are. But perhaps you are wrong. You could just as easily be an outgoing hard rock fan. You may think that your easygoing, fun-loving, life-is-to-be-lived nature is essential to your identity. But you are wrong. You could just as easily be the hermit type. The good news would then be that we can endlessly reinvent ourselves. You may not like being boring and humorless, well, some day you might be the life of the party.

Self-as-Soul can concede that we do not have core personalities. But it can do so only by giving up the popular idea that the soul is the seat of our true personalities.

Our Bodies, Our Selves?

Self-as-Soul believes that we are souls loosely connected to our bodies. But do we really experience ourselves that way? Perhaps sometimes we do when we close our eyes and think about mathematics or philosophy as Descartes often did. The characters in the movie *Being John Malkovich* get a chance to be in John Malkovich's body. They experience the world through his body as if his body were their own. But they experience it as something apart from themselves—as an object that they are inhabiting. If *dualism* is true and we can hop from body to body like a hermit crab changing shells, then that is how we ought to experience our bodies. But do we? Many would say that we experience our bodies as ourselves, or at least as intimately linked to ourselves.

Some *dualists* suggest that our souls are intimately connected to our bodies while joined to them. Bodies are more like spouses than coats. Two persons become like one person when they wed and experience life together in a profound and intimate way. Yet if they were to divorce, they would each leave the marriage with their full selves intact. Likewise, the soul temporarily experiences a profound unity with the body, but survives its parting from the body whole and complete.

Yet souls and bodies are not like persons. They do not make vows to each other. Nor do they share links of empathy and sympathy in the way that husbands and wives do. There is no communing of thought and emotion. If anything, the soul has all the thoughts and the body has all the emotions. What then so intimately binds the two together? What is the source of their special connection? Functioning together is not enough. Train cars do that.

Despite what the disciples of Dawkins and Dennett might say, science has not disproved the existence of the soul. Despite its drawbacks, Self-as-Soul will continue to provide a viable option for how we survive our deaths. Yet it faces enormous challenges. Things are likely to get worse for it as neuroscience progresses. The next chapter explores two versions of Self-as-Soul that try to successfully meet those challenges by more closely knitting soul and body together.

7

Soul-Flight, Part 2

Soul Sleep

You press the first button. But it does not work out as you had thought. You instantly go unconscious. But then you wake up on the planet below with a brand new body. It is better than the one you had before. It is taller. Its eyes are a brighter blue. It has a shorter and perfect nose. The face is very different. Nobody would be able to recognize you. The fingerprints are different. In fact, there are not any fingerprints at all. Upon waking up you are told that your soul drifted down to the planet. But you were unconscious the whole time. In fact, the whole process was much like falling asleep at night and waking up again in the morning. But this time you wake up without the grogginess that usually greets you in the morning. Your new body never gets groggy. You are sad that you did not get to enjoy the ride down to the planet, but you are happy nonetheless. You will never be groggy again.

This scenario corresponds to a view called Soul Sleep. According to it, you survive your death as your soul leaves your body. But you become unconscious when separate from your body. Then you become conscious again once your soul joins with a new body at the future resurrection. It is as if your soul was asleep. Many of us may have never heard of this idea before. When was the last time that you heard the term "soul sleep" in a sermon? Yet it has a respectable theological history. The Bible sometimes refers to death as "falling asleep." This view interprets that literally. Martin Luther, who began the Protestant Reformation, held this view. So did some of the early Anabaptists—those Protestant Reformers whose main descendants are the Mennonites of today.

Soul Sleep has two major advantages over the traditional dualist view. First, it can better accommodate the findings of neuroscience. As we have seen, neuroscience strongly suggests that our mental activities take place in our brain. It also strongly suggests that they must take place in some brain or other. We also know that brain damage also damages our minds, especially our abilities to think and remember. *Traditional dualism* has a difficult time explaining how this can be. Soul Sleep grants these conclusions. Thoughts and memories do require brains. That is why we are unable to think and remember while our souls are separate from our bodies. That is why we are unconscious. We only regain the ability to think and remember when we get the new brains that our new bodies will have. The soul is like a light bulb that needs a light socket to function but that can still exist without one. Insert the soul into another brain and it will light up again.[1]

Second, Soul Sleep makes better sense of why the Bible considers death to be an enemy. While we do not cease to exist when our bodies die, we do lose our consciousness. But that is not good news. Who wants to be in an eternal coma? If death does that too us, then no wonder it is an enemy. The Grim Reaper is in fact grim.

The resurrection of the body is good news because it restores our consciousness. We get to think again. We get to remember again all those fond camping trips we went on as kids. We get to see stars again and hear music again. We place our hope in the resurrection not because it is necessary for our survival after death, but because it is necessary for our *conscious* survival. It makes the afterlife worth looking forward to.

Even so, Soul Sleep has some problems of its own. For one thing, it sacrifices a traditional Christian belief. If we are asleep between death and resurrection, then our loved ones are not currently watching over us. Nor are they currently enjoying God's presence.

This theory faces a more serious problem. If our souls are doing nothing when they are separate from our bodies, then in what sense do they exist at all? If something exists, then it seems it must be doing something. The only thing the soul, when separate from the body, seems to be doing is preserving our personal identities—keeping us in existence. But

---

1. The analogy comes from Swinburne, *Evolution of the Soul*, 310–11.

that really is not doing anything at all. That is like saying that we exist because we are existing. We need something more to go on.

So perhaps we can slightly modify Soul Sleep to accommodate these problems. Suppose that the soul has a minimal awareness. Perhaps it is just an awareness of God. Perhaps the soul can also be aware of itself through its awareness of God's awareness of it. This restores something of an *interim state* and gives the soul a modicum of blessedness before the resurrection. It also gives it some activity and thus some basis for its continued existence. Yet, as we saw in chapter 4, some evidence suggests that our experience of God takes place in particular regions of the brain. Even so, there could still be something of our awareness of God that transcends our neurons. These objections are not enough to lay this view to rest.

Emergent Dualism

You push the first button. You feel yourself separating from your body. You watch the spaceship explode, the stars pass by, and the green fields of the planet getting larger and larger as you approach it. You also think back on those great camping trips. You see a body waiting for you. You enter it and once again have a body.

This scenario sounds exactly like the one in the last chapter. Your experience in getting to the planet is exactly the same. Likewise, it represents the same understanding of death and resurrection—the same story of how you get from your corpse to your new body. You are your soul. Your soul separates from your body at death and remains conscious in its disembodied state. Then it joins a new body at the resurrection. But there is another way of understanding this story that, in some ways, makes it less objectionable to Scripture, science, and philosophy.

This new understanding is based on the concept of *emergence*. When we think of the word "emerge," we usually think of bunnies emerging from bushes or flowers emerging from buds. But we may also think of a stereoscope—the iPad and smartphone of yesteryear. It looks like bulky plastic glasses. Within it are two juxtaposed two-dimensional images. But when you look through it, a single three-dimensional image "magically" *emerges* from the two flat images.

That is how our souls, according to this second modification of Self-as-Soul, come to be. They *emerge* from our brains. That is different from the original Self-as-Soul view, in which our souls come into existence seemingly out of nothing. But our souls are more like the 3-D image of a stereoscope than a bunny from a bush. According to this view, *emergence* also means that the emergent thing comes into existence *out of* what it emerges from. More exactly, the emergent thing comes into existence when the things it comes out of are arranged in just the right kind of way. The 3-D image appears only when the two 2-D images are side by side such that the left eye can only see the left image and the right eye can only see the right image. So the soul, or the mind—and remember they are much the same thing for Self-as-Soul—only *emerges* when neurons and other such brain-y stuff are arranged, or organized, in just the right way.

There are some crucial differences between the emergence of souls and stereoscopic images. According to *emergent dualism*, *emergence* also means the arrival of something unexpected—something that can't be foreseen. Suppose that you know everything about the physics of stereoscopes and human vision. You would probably be able to guess what is going to happen when you look through the stereoscope. But suppose you knew everything about the physics of cells and neurons. You would not be able to foresee, based on that knowledge alone, that the soul is going to emerge from it.

Another difference is that images cannot really do much of anything on their own. They have got no powers. But emergent souls have powers. They can do things that neurons and such cannot do on their own. They can have the experience of smelling chocolate. They can think about life, death, and the hereafter. The soul may normally depend on the brain to do these things, but the soul is the entity doing them. Brains without souls cannot think or smell. The emergent soul also has powers to change what is happening in the brain. It can, for example, alter the firing of the brain's neurons in order to cause the hand to reach into the cookie jar. Thus, emergent dualism can explain how we have free will—how we can sometimes make free choices. It can explain why we cannot always blame our neurons for making us steal the cookies. Stereoscopic images, on the other hand, cannot alter the flat images from which they emerged.

Finally, we do not normally think of images as "things" with "substance." But *emergent* souls are "things" with "substance." They are real entities in the universe. If you are counting up the number of "things" in the room, you would count the soul and the brain as two different things.

But you would not usually count the 3-D stereoscopic image as another thing that is added to the two flat images and the stereoscope.

Emergent souls are more like mobs than stereoscopic images. Mobs form when individual persons begin to interact with each other in a particular way, as they come together around some common cause, feeling, or idea. Those individual persons get so caught up in it that they do things as a part of the mob that they would not have otherwise done. The mob alters their behavior. If you count up the number of "things" on the scene, you might then want to count the mob as another "thing" in the sense that it is a real entity with causal abilities.

No one can predict when a mob will arise and what it is going to cause its participants to do. Mobs can inspire people to great good. But they can also result in tragedy. Recently, a referee in a soccer game in Santa Ines, Brazil, stabbed a player to death. A mob formed as spectators swarmed onto the field and stoned the referee to death. Then they tore his body apart. Some report that they then placed his head on a pike as if they were ancient "barbaric" Assyrians putting the head of the enemy king on display. The members of the mob were likely ordinary people—nice but into sports. They would not do such things on their own. But they were swept up in the spirit of the mob.

Some *emergent dualists* believe that life also emerged in this way. Proteins come together in just the right kind of way and then a living cell emerges. The cell takes on a spirit of its own, a life of its own, and begins to act back on the proteins that make it up. It causes them to behave in ways they would otherwise not behave in. It causes them, for example, to self-regulate and perpetuate. The cell is therefore more than its molecules and cannot be fully explained in terms of them.

Emergent dualism takes sides in a big debate that is happening in many different fields, such as philosophy, history, psychology, biology, and physics. That debate has to do with whether or not everything can be fully explained in terms of the interactions of elementary particles according to the laws of physics. Can physics explain everything? Are we nothing but collections of atoms? If you think the answer is yes, then you are a *reductionist*. This view is also called nothing-buttery and it is more common than we might think. Many contemporary scientists and philosophers are *reductionists*. But there are also many who oppose it. They are called *non-reductionists*. But *non-reductionism* comes in two varieties. According to the first variety, the *emergent* entity has powers, but is not a thing in itself. According to the second, it is a thing in itself. Perhaps mobs exemplify the first variety. But *emergent dualists* believe that souls or minds exemplify the second.

Emergent dualists also use the analogy of a magnetic field to explain the *emergent* soul. Electricity pumped through a coiled wire causes the electrons of the atoms to align in just the right way for a magnetic field to emerge. The magnetic field is a real entity that did not exist before but somehow came out of the coiled wire when the conditions were just right. The field can do things on its own, such as line up iron filings. Our conscious minds are like *emergent* fields that envelop our brains when our neurons are arranged in just the right way. Only they tend to line up balance sheets instead of iron filings.

The problem though is that the magnetic field will cease to exist when the magnet is destroyed. If the soul is generated by the brain and needs the brain to function, then it should similarly cease to exist when the brain dies. But even though the brain generates the soul and the soul *normally* needs the brain to function, it is possible for an omnipotent God to maintain the soul's existence after the brain dies. The soul is, after all, a substance in its own right. It may have emerged from the brain, but it is its own entity. It is neither the brain nor a part of the brain nor an aspect of the brain. It normally depends on the brain to do what it does, but it is possible that God could zap it with an ability to continue to function apart from the brain. Thus at death, the soul persists, possibly maintaining consciousness. Since we are our minds, we continue to exist apart from our bodies.

Some theories in physics suggest that gravity can theoretically maintain a strong magnetic field in existence after the supporting magnet is destroyed. On some theories, black holes are gravitational fields that sustain themselves after the body that generated them is destroyed.[2] If our minds are like fields generated from our brains, then it is conceivable that they could exist without them. Some might say, however, that fields are not real entities in themselves. The magnetic field appears to survive the magnet's death because the effects of the magnet are lingering longer. Similarly with the black hole and its gravitational field. So whether such analogies help depend on whether fields turn out to be real entities in themselves.

In any case, it is no more natural for the mind to exist disembodied than for a magnetic field to exist without its magnet. The mind's existence

---

2. See Hasker, *Emergent Self*, 232. Hasker is the foremost contemporary Christian philosopher who defends *emergent dualism*.

is sub-par. It cannot function as well without a brain. The resurrection of the body is therefore important because it restores the mind to its proper and optimal state of being. But not just any body and brain will do. It will need a new body and new brain that are sufficiently similar to its original body and brain. It is specially linked to the particular type of body and brain from which it emerged and through which it normally functions. Not just a human body in general, but a human body much like the original in specifics as well—with similar neuronal patterns in the body, similar DNA, and such.

If the original body is tall, thin, with straight black hair and pointed ears, then the resurrected body will need to be *relatively* tall, *relatively* thin, with *relatively* straight black hair, and with pointed ears. If the neurons in the brain are arranged in such a way to promote pervasive logical thinking and strict control of emotions, the neurons of the resurrected brain will need to be *relatively* arranged in such a way to promote pervasive logical thinking and strict control of emotions. But you may not like all the features of your body and your brain. You may hope for a taller body or a more quick-witted brain. *Emergent dualism* allows for this in that the resurrected body does not need to *perfectly* match the original body. The new body may be taller but in a way that fits its own unique nature—in a way that is in line with your uniqueness. The brain may be more quick-witted but in a way that fits your mind—that is in line with what makes you you.

Why Emergent Dualism?

Emergent dualism has a lot going for it. Suppose that you strongly believe that you have a soul, that that soul is you, and that it survives after your body dies. But suppose that you are unhappy with the way that Self-as-Soul typically treats our bodies. According to it, the soul wears the body like a coat. It has no special connection to the body and can just as well take it off and try on a new one. But you believe that the connection between soul and body is tighter than that. You believe that there is some special link between your soul and your body.

You are also concerned about the scientific challenges to the soul from chapter 4.

- How does God's creation of the soul square with the theory of evolution which states that we evolved gradually from other animals?

- How does God's creation of the soul square with the fact that ova in the womb can split or fuse?
- How does God's creation of the soul square with the fact that some fetuses die in the womb or are aborted?
- How does the existence of the soul square with the findings of neuroscience which suggest a tight link between our minds and our brains?
- How does the existence of the soul square with cases in which two distinct centers of consciousness emerge when the link between the two hemispheres of the brain is cut?

You are also concerned that *traditional dualism* can't explain how mind and body can interact. How can the mind tell the arm to raise when mind is so different from body? How can the body tell the mind to feel the pain of the bang on the head when body is so different from mind?

Finally, you are struck by the biblical passages that suggest that life after death does not happen naturally. *God* makes it possible. But, according to traditional dualism, the soul naturally survives the body's death just as a snake naturally survives the shredding of its skin. You are also unsatisfied with *traditional dualism*'s inability to explain why the resurrection of the body is important. If the soul is capable of a full existence without a body, then the resurrection is nice but not all that important. It is like getting a Christmas present from your distant aunt. You are thankful for the gift and may even really like it but your life would go on just fine without it. You are also struck by the Bible's tendency to see our minds and bodies as tightly woven together rather than as separate substances within us.

If you are struck by all these considerations, then you have a problem. The belief that you are your soul fits neither Scripture nor science. *Emergent dualism* offers a way out—a way to hold on to both the soul and Scripture and science. That makes it worth taking seriously.

Emergent dualists believe that soul and body are tightly connected because the soul emerges from the body and normally depends on it to function. They also therefore do not believe that God creates the soul, thus sidestepping the problem of the soul's origin faced by *traditional dualism*.

Emergent dualism also better squares with the theory of evolution and its implications for our deep connection with other animals. Minds emerge when the parts are organized in just the right kind of way. *Traditional dualists* face the problem that it is arbitrary to suddenly grant souls to hominids at a particular point in their evolution since that evolution was gradual. It also seems wrong to deny souls to other hominid species at the time who also seemed to be conscious. In any case, it also seems wrong to deny consciousness to other animals, especially the higher animals.

Emergent dualism easily allows for consciousness to arise far down the animal spectrum. It arises the first time neurons are arranged in just the right kind of way to produce consciousness. There is no arbitrary cutting off point. The mind emerges as a natural part of evolutionary history without needing special intervention from God. We are as deeply connected to other animals as the evolutionist would have us be. Animals are as conscious as our intuitions tell us. We do not have to deny the feeling we get when we look a dog in the eye and experience another conscious being. *Traditionalist dualists* have to do that. But not *emergent dualists*.

Embryology also poses no problems for *emergent dualism*. The emergent soul does not emerge until after the brain begins to develop, which is five weeks after conception. That is long after ova are able to divide or fuse. Since God does not create the soul, God is never placed in the morally objectionable position of creating a soul for a fetus that he knew would be aborted.

Emergent dualism maintains a much closer connection between mind and body than does *traditional dualism*. Because the mind emerges from the brain, it normally functions in and through the brain. Neurons both birth and berth the mind. Thus, *emergent dualism* has no problem with the neuroscientist's claim that mental activities are dependent on the brain. It comes as no surprise that a bang on the brain can black out the mind. It is no more surprising than how whacking a magnet can weaken or even destroy its magnetic field.

Emergent dualists also have less difficulty with the distinct centers of consciousness that seem to result from the splitting of the brain's hemispheres. An *emergent* field can conceivably split in two. God need create no new soul because a new soul can naturally emerge out of its brain hemisphere.

The problem of mind-body interaction also does not bother *emergent dualists* as much. If the mind emerges from and depends on the body, then mind and body are not so radically different after all. They naturally belong together like marble and a Michelangelo. If matter births mind, then surely the two can communicate with each other.

Thus, *emergent dualism* is more satisfactory scientifically and philosophically. It is also more satisfactory biblically. Our survival after death is not natural. It depends entirely on God, since we only survive if God chooses to miraculously support our soul's continuing existence. *Emergent dualism* also makes more sense of the resurrection of the body than *traditional dualism*. The soul wants a body back because it is in an unnatural and incomplete state without it. Like Scripture and unlike *traditional dualism*, *emergent dualism* closely links soul and body.

The Problems with Emergence

Yet *emergent dualism* has its problems. You might think that *emergent dualism* sounds like magic. It might remind you of stories like the *Sorcerer's Apprentice* where lifeless brooms suddenly start to move around and sweep the floor on their own. You are not alone. Some philosophers criticize this view for claiming that the mind magically emerges from the brain.

Emergent dualists try to get around this problem by claiming that matter has always had within it the ability to give rise to mind whenever the circumstances are just right. At creation, God placed within matter a latent power to produce minds. But nothing comes of it until evolution reaches just the right stage when the matter of the brain of some species is rightly arranged. Then, the power is activated and the first mind emerges. Similarly, the matter of the embryo has within it the power to generate a mind that is activated once the cells of the embryo are arranged in just the right sort of way for a mind to emerge. So our souls did not magically pop into existence out of nothing. They were part of God's original plan when he created matter in the first place. Some atheist philosophers now court the idea that the possibility of consciousness was somehow "inherent in the universe long before there was life."[3] How else, they argue, could something as immaterial as mind arise? They, of course, deny that God put such potentialities in the universe.

Others object to the *emergent dualist*'s account of bodily resurrection. God has two choices. He can first create a dead body—a shell, a husk, a coat—and then join the soul with it. Or he can create an already functioning body and join the soul with it. The former will not work because the soul can only join with a body in which its matter is arranged in

---

3. Nagel, *Mind and Cosmos*, 32.

just the right kind of way—but that can only happen if the body is already functioning. A corpse has a structure, but not a functioning one. The latter will not work because a functioning body with a functioning brain should naturally generate its own soul. It would be too late for the soul to join with it. Neither option works. Therefore, if *emergent dualism* is true, then our souls are doomed to a disembodied eternity—unless there is a way for God to create the body at the very same moment that he joins the soul to it. It seems there is no reason why he could not.

Emergent dualism may also not satisfy the neuroscientists. If they are right that consciousness always requires a physical brain or something like it, then *emergent dualism* fails to explain how a soul can continue to function after the death of the body. Perhaps not even an omnipotent God can work this miracle.

Memories, in particular, seem connected to particular regions and processes of the brain. Can they survive that brain's death and continue to exist disembodied? It is becoming more difficult to believe that. Perhaps God could restore them to us when we are resurrected. Perhaps he could implant our memories in our resurrected brains by arranging the neurons in just the right kind of way. Perhaps. But they would no longer be the same memories. They would be copies or replicas of them. My memory of the moonlit beach remains the same memory insofar as it was caused by my being at that moonlit beach. An implanted memory is a false memory even if it perfectly resembles a memory I once had.

Emergent dualism also fails to link body and soul as tightly as the dominant interpretation of Scripture suggests. According to that interpretation, body and soul are two aspects of the single unified person and not two separate substances. They are one thing not two. But *emergent dualism* makes them into two. Scripture also places our hope for life after death primarily in the resurrection of the body. *Emergent dualism* can explain why the resurrection is necessary for a full existence, but it does not place our primary hope in it. That hope is shifted to the moment when we die—to God's making sure we continue to exist after our bodies die.

Emergent dualism is an improvement over *traditional dualism*. But even it seems to fall short both biblically and scientifically. The next chapter considers a view of death and resurrection that tries to be both more biblical and more scientific. But it comes at a price. The soul will have to go.

8

Particle Beam: Resurrection as Reassembly

You push the third button. You instantly feel as if your body is about to break up. Your fingers and feet fade away. The inside of the spaceship blurs. You can no longer see or hear. You feel that the atoms in your brain are disconnecting. Then, nothing. Then, something. A sense of neurons reconnecting. A dim vision of your fingers and feet reassembling. A blue sky and a grassy meadow fade into view. You look at your body to see if all your limbs are there. They are. You feel like a computer that has been disassembled and reassembled.

Your body is the same body but it feels a bit different. You no longer have that nagging pain in your lower back. In fact, you no longer have any pain at all. Your body feels more alive than it has ever been, despite the feeling that it was recently disassembled.

You hear a hum. You turn toward it and see that it comes from a printer attached to a computer. Out of the printer comes a piece of paper. You read it.

> Congratulations! You chose the correct button. The moment you pressed it, the spaceship computer began to disassemble your body into its atoms. It started with your fingers and toes and worked its way up to your brain so that you could enjoy watching it work. It collected all your carbon, oxygen, hydrogen, iron, nitrogen, zinc, magnesium, and such and beamed them down to this planet.

> Before disassembling you, the ship's computer scanned your body and sent its scan to the computer right here next to you. That computer used that information to put all your atoms back together in just the right places. It worked rather well, as you can see. Every single atom of yours was put back into the exact spot in your body that it was in before disassembly. A remarkable feat, don't you think? Your memories, personality traits, desires, and such are exactly the same because the atoms that make them up are in exactly the same places. But we made a few minor insignificant changes. We did remove the atoms that made up the substance P in you that caused you pain. We thought you might like that. This note certifies that the scan was thorough and accurate. You never doubted that Captain Kirk of the Starship Enterprise survived a thousand such transporter beams. So be assured that you have survived this one.
>
> Guaranteed by the
Uralive Teletransportation Corporation

Resurrection as Reassembly

This scenario is the most easily understood of the five options for how to understand death and resurrection. Suppose that you are moving to a new state and your bookshelf does not fit in the moving van. You are fond of this bookshelf since you had it with you since you were a child. You do not want to get rid of it and buy some new bookshelf when you get to your new home. You want that exact same bookshelf—*numerically the same* bookshelf—to be in your new home. No Uralive Teletransportation Corporation yet exists to provide you with transporter beams. So you decide to disassemble your bookshelf. You remove the shelves. You unscrew the main supporting boards from each other. You slide all the boards into the open spaces in the truck and pocket the screws. Then you reassemble the bookshelf from those same boards and screws. It is the exact same bookshelf. Why? Because it is made out of the exact same boards and screws.

Similarly, suppose your computer breaks down. You take it the Geek Squad at Best Buy. They say the problem is so serious that they will need to disassemble the computer, do some repairs on the parts, and then reassemble it. Few of us would doubt that the repaired and reassembled computer is *numerically the same* computer as the one you had before. It has the same parts after all.

The same principle easily applies to death and resurrection. At death, one's body begins to break apart. Parts of it are eaten by bugs. Parts of it slowly waste away as the body rots, erodes, composts, and such. But at the resurrection, God collects all the parts, be they whole limbs, bones, tissues, dead cells, molecules, or atoms, and reassembles them to make the same body as the original living one. He puts all the parts back in the same place they occupied when the body died. God is the Geek Squad of human bodies. The resurrected body then is the exact same body, the *numerically same* body, as the original one because it consists of the same parts in the same places.

This view also preserves our mental features. Our memories, thoughts, desires, and personality traits are the same because our neurons are the same. It is no different than a reassembled computer. Everything stored in its memory is the same because its microchips are the same.

Reassembly appeals to those who believe that we are our bodies. Our bodies are ourselves. I am the same person at sixty-four as I am at six because I have the same body.

> Self-as-Body: I am my body. Any future person is the same person as me as long as he is the same body as I am.

Why Reassembly?

Reassembly has a lot going for it. It avoids all the problems with the soul that plagued the Self-as-Soul view in chapters 6 and 7. If science has killed the soul, then this view is a welcome alternative to Self-as-Soul. Science suggests that our mental features are neural networks in our brains. They ought then to perish when the body dies. But if they are just neural networks in our brains, then they should be able to be restored if those neural networks are restored. Those networks are restored when the neurons are again configured in the exact same way. The same neurons in the same places make the same mental features.

Suppose you agree with what Francis Crick calls the "Astonishing Hypothesis" that

> you, your joys and sorrows, your memories and your ambitions, your sense of personal identity and free will, are in fact no more

than the behavior of a vast assembly of nerve cells and their associated molecules ... You're nothing but a pack of neurons.[1]

This view seems to be a version of the self-as-brain view. According to it, I am my brain. Nothing more, nothing less.

> **Self-as-Brain:** I am my brain. Any future person is the same person as me as long as he is the same brain as I am.

If you hold this view, then you might think that you have no hope for an afterlife. The death of the brain would be the death of you. But Reassembly can restore *numerically the same* brain. It gives hope for an afterlife to even the most die-hard materialist.

There are also philosophical reasons for thinking that the resurrected person can't be *numerically the same* person as the original person if she hasn't got *numerically the same* body as the original body. Suppose that someone shows up claiming to be a long-lost heir. He looks like the long-lost heir and knows everything the long-lost heir would know. He even begins to convince others who knew the long-lost heir that he is in fact the long-lost heir. Meanwhile, researchers confirm that the long-lost heir's body has been found in Sydney. We would then conclude that "the claimant cannot be the long-lost heir, whose body we know lies buried in Australia, and if he honestly thinks he is then we must try to cure him of a delusion."[2] How then could a newly resurrected person be *numerically the same* person as the original person when her body is still lying in the grave at St. Vincent's?

Reassembly is also more straightforwardly biblical than Soul-Flight. In 1 Corinthians 15, Paul writes:

> So it is with the resurrection of the dead. What is sown is perishable, what is raised is imperishable. It is sown in dishonor, it is raised in glory. It is sown in weakness, it is raised in power. It is sown a physical body, it is raised a spiritual body ... For the trumpet will sound, and the dead will be raised imperishable, and we will all be changed. For this perishable body must put on imperishability, and this mortal body must put on immortality. When *this* perishable body puts on imperishability, and *this* mortal body puts on immortality, then the saying that is written will be fulfilled: "Death has been swallowed up in victory.

1. Crick, *Astonishing Hypothesis*, 3.
2. Geach, *God and the Soul*, 27.

Where, O death, is your victory? Where, O death, is your sting?"
(1 Cor 15:42–44, 52b–55; italics mine)

This passage implies that the body that is raised is *numerically the same* body that perished. Soul-Flight does not require that the two bodies are the same. Neither can it account for how the two bodies can be the same. Reassembly both requires their identity and explains its possibility.

The concept of resurrection itself suggests as much. Resurrection means the bringing back to life of a body that has died. Reincarnation means coming to exist in a different body. Resurrection means coming to exist again in the same body. Soul-Flight more closely resembles reincarnation than resurrection.

Reassembly also better handles the empty tomb. Jesus's resurrection meant the resurrection of his corpse—of the very matter that had made up his original body. Yet the resurrected Christ is the "first fruits of those who have died" (1 Cor 15:20), which implies that our resurrection will be much like his. But Soul-Flight does not involve the resuscitation of the corpse. It cannot explain the importance of the empty tomb. If Soul-Flight were true, one would have expected Jesus to rise with an altogether different body while his corpse remained in the tomb. That would have communicated to us how we would be raised and assured us that nothing that could happen to the corpse would endanger our own future resurrection. But if resurrection requires reassembly, then of course Jesus's resurrection would require the resuscitation of his corpse.

Reassembly is also in line with the traditional Christian understanding of death and resurrection. That does not necessarily make it correct. But it makes it worth taking seriously. If many, if not most, Christians through the ages have found truth and meaning in it, then we too do well to find out why. Many feel more deeply connected with Christians of the past, and their hopes, desires, and thoughts, when sharing beliefs with them. It adds to the mystic feeling of being part of something greater and grander that persists through the centuries—of being part of the historic Christian tradition.

Resurrection as reassembly was the standard Christian understanding of death and resurrection from the early Church to just before the Reformation. It is still a major Christian belief today, although not as dominant as it was before the Reformation. Even the two greatest pre-Reformation Christian thinkers held this view. St. Augustine writes:

> Far be it from us to fear that the omnipotence of the Creator cannot, for the resuscitation and reanimation of our bodies, recall all the portions which have been consumed by beasts or fire, or have been dissolved into dust or ashes, or have been decomposed into water, or evaporated into the air.[3]

St. Thomas Aquinas writes:

> And consequently if it be not the same body which the soul resumes, it will not be a resurrection, but rather the assuming of a new body . . . Thus the matter that will be brought back to restore the human body will be the same as that body's previous matter.[4]

Medieval Christian art contains many images of body parts being snatched out of the mouths of animals. It shows how powerful was the idea that God would collect the pieces of our body at the Last Judgment and then use them to reassemble our bodies.

Medieval Christians also favored Reassembly because it supported their devotion to the relics of the saints. Churches and monasteries around Europe would collect what they believed to be the bones, teeth, hair, or other body parts of Christian saints. They believed these relics were holy. Some believed these relics had healing powers. Imagine how one's devotion to such relics increases when one believes that these very body parts will one day be resurrected to again form the very bodies of these saints.

Early and medieval Christians, such as Augustine and Aquinas, also tended to believe in an immortal soul.[5] The combination of Reassembly and Soul-Flight is perhaps the most commonly held position about death and resurrection in Christian history. Many such Christians held Self-as-Soul and yet considered it important that the person get *numerically the same* body back at the resurrection, meaning that her resurrected body needed the same matter as her original body. But combining Reassembly with belief in an immortal soul removes many of the advantages that Reassembly has over Soul-Flight.

---

3. Augustine, *City of God* 22.20, 843–44.

4. Aquinas, *Summa Theologica*, suppl. 79.1, 2878. There is some debate, however, about the degree to which Aquinas believed in Reassembly. See Langley, "Aquinas, Resurrection, and Material Continuity," 141–42.

5. Aquinas, as we will see in chap. 10, has a different understanding of soul than Soul-Flight.

Reassembly Reconsidered

At first sight, Reassembly is simple, straightforward, and promising. A little reflection, however, shows that it has serious problems—problems that render it unacceptable to many. With some modifications, this view can surmount these problems. But doing so weakens its appeal.

Since you began reading this chapter, you may have noticed a strand of hair fall from your head. You also may have sipped some water or eaten some peanuts. We are always losing parts of our bodies. We are also often adding new parts as we eat and drink. Our bodies are like neither bookshelves nor computers. Our parts change and not just a little bit every now and then. Our parts constantly and continually change. The bookshelf you just moved into your new home has much the same matter as the bookshelf of your childhood. But your body does not. Your cells are continually being replaced. The only cells in your body that have not been replaced are the neurons in your brain's cerebral cortex and maybe a few others.[6] Even so, the atoms that make up those neurons are replaced. On some estimates, 98 percent of the atoms that make up our bodies are completely replaced every year.[7]

If having the same body requires having the same matter then our current bodies are *numerically different* bodies from our childhood bodies. But that seems wrong. Sameness of body must not require sameness of matter.

Furthermore, God could choose to reassemble our resurrected bodies out of the matter our bodies had at childhood instead of the matter they have now or that they will have when we die. God could even choose to make resurrected bodies out of all three sets of matter. The result would be three bodies, one consisting of our childhood matter, another of our current matter, and another of the matter we have when we die. But which one would be the real body? Which one would be me? They can't all be me. But it seems arbitrary to designate one as the real me. This is *the problem of duplication* discussed in chapter 5.

The above two problems are solved by claiming that the resurrected body requires the matter it had at death. It is *numerically the same* body as the original body if it has *numerically the same* matter as the original body had at death. A future body made from the matter of my childhood

---

6. See Nowakowski, "Stable Neuron Numbers, " 12220, and Wade, "Your Body Is Younger," lines 6–8.

7. Fowler, "Why New Atoms Aren't a Fountain of Youth," lines 3–5.

body would not be the same body. It would not be me. But why should the matter we have at death be so important?

To see why, we will need to adjust our understanding of what preserves the numerical identity of the body. Instead of requiring sameness of matter, sameness of body requires that the body be part of the same overlapping chain of matter. My body continually sheds skin, hair, and carbon dioxide. It continually breathes in oxygen and takes in food and drink. Some matter is lost. Some matter is gained. But in each change, there is always some matter that remains. The change is gradual. There is never a time when the matter of my body at 2 p.m. will be completely different from the matter of my body at 1:59 p.m., or 1:59 p.m. and 59.9999999999 seconds. There is always overlap. My body today is *numerically the same* body as my six-year-old body because it is a continuation of the same overlapping chain of matter. My sixty-four-year-old body will be *numerically the same* body as my body now because it will be a continuation of the same overlapping chain of matter as my body now. No bit of matter need remain a part of my body throughout its entire lifespan.

The resurrected body must consist of the matter the body had at death in order to continue that overlapping chain. If it had the matter of your childhood body instead, then it could not be part of the continuous history of your body. It would not be continuous with the history of your body since childhood.

Consider a ship. Philosophers call it the ship of Theseus, named after the Greek hero who slew the minotaur in Crete and then sailed back to Athens. Every now and then, a plank of wood on the ship is replaced until eventually not one of the ship's planks is the same plank that the ship originally had. It is still the same ship because there is a continual overlapping of planks, such that most planks remain the same when any planks are replaced. But suppose that the ship is finally disassembled and someone stores its planks in a warehouse. The ship is then reconstructed out of those same planks. Meanwhile someone else has been collecting all the ship's original planks. She then reconstructs the ship out of those original planks. Both ships have the same structure as the original ship. But only one is the same ship as the original ship—only the one that is rebuilt from the planks the ship had when it was disassembled. Only that one is part of the ship's continuous history. Only it continues the chain of overlapping matter.

But Reassembly faces a greater difficulty. An omnipotent God can easily identify the scattered atoms of our bodies and then reassemble our bodies from them. He can easily snatch our limbs from the mouths of the sharks that ate us as medieval art will testify. But it is not only sharks and lions that eat us. We also eat each other. Desperate situations can lead us to cannibalism, as shown by the case of the Donner Party that was stranded by snow in the Sierras in 1846. Some died and starvation drove some of the others to eat them. Yet God will resurrect every member of the Donner Party. But who gets whose atoms? Jim dies. Tom eats Jim. Tom then chokes on Jim's ribs and dies. Then Bill eats Tom and dies. The matter of Jim's body when he died is also in Tom's and Jim's body when they died. Who gets the matter of Jim's body at the resurrection?

This is a gruesome challenge. But it is a very important one if you believe in Reassembly. Many of the greatest thinkers of early and medieval Christianity took it seriously and worked out solutions to it.

God could resurrect Jim first. Then let his body naturally change until it consists of a different set of atoms. Then God could use the atoms that his body sloughed off, the ones that made up both Tom and Jim's bodies when they died, and then resurrect Tom's body from them. Then God will resurrect Bill from the atoms that Tom's body eventually sloughs off. This solves the problem but at the expense of the traditional belief that all are raised at once. Not everyone is willing to part with that belief and its communal implications, which we will further explore in chapter 15.

Christian thinkers have traditionally adopted another solution that is consistent with the idea that all are raised at once. According to this solution, the resurrection does not require all of the matter of one's body when one dies. It requires just enough. In the case of Tom, Jim, and Bill, Jim gets the matter his body had when he died. Tom gets the matter his body had when he died that he did not get from Jim's body. Bill gets the matter his body had when he died that he did not get from Tom's body. God can always add more matter to Tom's and Bill's resurrected bodies to give them enough matter to round out their resurrected bodies.

Things can get messier. Suppose that Jim dies, his body decomposes, and his atoms disperse into the soil and eventually scatter throughout the ecosystem. But Tom is a locavore. He only eats food grown in his ecosystem. As it happens, his body ends up consisting of the exact same atoms that Jim's body consisted of when he died. Then Tom dies and his atoms disperse throughout the ecosystem. But Amelia, another locavore, eventually winds up with the exact atoms that both Tom and Jim had when they died. Then she dies. And on and on with Jack, Julie, and John. Six persons now have died with bodies that were made of the exact same atoms. What is God to do when it is time to resurrect them all? Who will get which atoms?

God could resurrect them at different times, as we saw above with the reply to the cannibal objection. But what to do if all are to be raised at once? God could intervene in the ecosystem to prevent such a scenario from occurring. He could miraculously scatter Jim's atoms beyond that ecosystem. He could, for example, subtly move some of his atoms into a river that takes them out to sea. He could also miraculously move Jim's atoms to pass through Tom so that they are not absorbed into Tom's body and similarly for Amelia, Jack, Julie, and John. God could do this. It is possible. But it is difficult to support. It makes God into a major player in the ecosystem—intervening far too frequently than science would support.

The only other solution is to divide up the matter between Jim, Tom, Amelia, Jack, Julie, and John. That would mean that they each only get one-sixth of the matter they had when they died. But is one-sixth enough? Just how much is enough? If one-sixth is enough, then how about one-seventh, or one-eighth? Why should one-sixth be enough but not one-seventh or one-eighth? Any answer seems arbitrary—except perhaps the answer that the resurrected body needs 50.1 percent of its original matter. The reason has to do with *the problem of duplication* discussed. God could theoretically use half of the matter of my original body when I died to reassemble me at the resurrection. God could theoretically also use the other half of the matter of my original body when I died to reassemble another me at the resurrection. Both would have an equal claim to be me. But both cannot be me. So neither is me. Thus, whether or not God happened to reassemble two of me would determine whether or not the reassembled being is me. But whether that being is me cannot depend on whether or not something or someone else happens to exist. It seems then that even a single person reassembled from half of my atoms cannot be me. God would, of course, never reassemble two of me. But he could and that is enough to call into question the identity of the reassembled me. The only way to avoid the problem is to require that at least 50.1 percent of my original atoms be used to reassemble me at the resurrection. But that may be too high a bar to avoid the problems of cannibals and ecosystems.

Maybe instead the resurrection only requires one key bit of matter—a bit that is particularly important to the identities of our bodies. We can imagine a computer that has one key microchip. As long as we rebuild a computer using that same key microchip, then the rebuilt computer will be numerically the same computer as the original one. It does not matter whether the rest of the newly rebuilt computer consists of the same matter.

Many Jewish rabbis have chosen one special small bone in our bodies. It, unlike other parts of our bodies, survives until the resurrection. Then God gathers other matter around it to reassemble our bodies. Today, we might choose just the matter that made up the neurons of our cerebral cortex. After all, we keep them throughout our entire lives. Maybe they are especially important to our *numerical identity*. Or instead we might choose one key brain cell that is the equivalent of a computer's one key microchip. It is the only matter that matters because it is the matter that contains the core of who we are.

Or maybe God needs only one strand of our DNA. Then God can reassemble our bodies using that one strand of DNA. The resurrected body would be *numerically the same* body because it contains a strand of DNA that was in the original body. Heaven is Jurassic Park, God is its master scientist, and we the dinosaurs brought back from extinction. We should not quickly dismiss this solution because it is the most straightforward interpretation of Paul's description of the resurrection in 1 Corinthians 15. There, he compares the body's death and resurrection to the sowing of a seed. And what is a seed but the carrier of a plant's DNA? Paul knew nothing of DNA, but he knew that the seed provided material continuity between the new plant and the old. Perhaps Paul's image was more apt than he knew.

The problem is that our DNA decomposes too. We are lucky to get DNA samples from even a few extinct species. God would need to miraculously intervene in the earth's history to preserve DNA strands from every human who has ever lived. If so, then where are they now? Also, suppose that two of my DNA strands survive to the end of time. God could theoretically reassemble a body from both of them. But both can't be me. So neither can be me.

Reassembly faces yet another challenge. It depends on the resurrected body having enough of the same *matter* as the original body. But what is matter? And what type of matter is the matter that matters? Reassembly usually favors atoms. The resurrected body will need to have enough of the same *atoms* as the original body. But why *atoms*? Atoms can split into protons, neutrons, and electrons. So why not favor them instead? Yet protons and neutrons can change into each other and into other subatomic particles. They are not all going to hang around intact until the resurrection. But why stop there? Protons and neutrons consist of quarks. Yet different types of quarks can change into each other. Even they will not last until the resurrection.

It is not easy to specify which kind of matter is necessary for resurrection. It is not clear that there is any kind of matter that will necessarily continue to exist until the end of time. We are not even sure we know what matter is. Reassembly will have to address these problems if it is to succeed.

Reassembly is difficult to defend. Thus, few consider it viable today. Yet it is neither inconsistent nor incoherent. God could arrange things so that everyone gets enough of the matter from their original bodies that they need. Before too quickly dismissing Reassembly, we should remember the words of British philosopher Peter Geach:

> The traditional faith of Christianity, inherited from Judaism, is that at the end of this age Messiah will come and men rise from their graves to die no more. That faith is not going to be shaken by inquiries about bodies burned to ashes or eaten by beasts; those who might well suffer just such death in martyrdom were those who were most confident of a glorious reward in the resurrection.[8]

Those who most ardently believed in Reassembly knew well that their bodies were in danger of being fed to the lions.

Given its problems, however, surely there is a better way to assure the resurrection of *numerically the same* bodies that we have now. There is. Chapter 10 considers it. The next chapter considers a view of the resurrection that denies both the existence of the soul and that our resurrected bodies need to be *numerically the same* bodies as those we have now.

---

8. Geach, *God and the Soul*, 29.

9

Data Stream: Resurrection as Re-creation

You push the third button. You feel tingly, as if you are about to faint. Then you feel nothing and are aware of nothing. In fact, you no longer exist. Nothing of you is left except your dead corpse that is now lying on the floor of the spaceship. But you are neither aware of your corpse nor of the fact that you do not exist. But you soon regain consciousness. You feel a heart beating. You feel the cool earth beneath your body. You open your eyes. You see pleasant blue skies above you and grassy meadows around you. You look at your new body. It looks almost exactly like the one you had on the spaceship. It has the same hair color and the same height. But you no longer have the scar on your belly from when the spaceship's physician removed your appendix. You also no longer have the pain in your right knee that troubled you for years. You start to think about your life on the spaceship and you find that you still have all your memories of it. You believe, as much as you believe anything, that you are still you.

Nearby is a computer. Attached to it is a mirror. You gaze at your reflection in the kind of wonder that comes from being surprised by what is ordinary. You see the same face and the same eyes staring back at you that you had always seen when you looked into a mirror. You hear a humming sound. You turn and see that it comes from a printer that is attached to the computer. A piece of paper emerges from it. You read the paper:

> Congratulations! You chose the correct button. The spaceship computer scanned you at the moment that you pushed the button. It recorded everything about you—both your physical and psychological features. This note certifies that the scan was thorough and accurate. It successfully included every memory, desire, and personality trait. Nothing about you was lost. The data was sent directly to this computer. This computer used that data to construct a body nearly identical to the one you had on the spaceship. The constructed body includes reconstructions of all your psychological features as well. But the computer did not reconstruct any bodily defects, such as the scar on your former belly and the pinched nerve in your former right leg. You never doubted that Captain Kirk of the Starship Enterprise survived a thousand such transporter beams. So be assured that you have survived this one.
>
> Guaranteed by the
Uralive Teletransportation Corporation.

Resurrection as Replication

John Hick, one of the foremost philosophers of religion of the twentieth century, defends such an account of how we might survive our deaths:

> Suppose, first, that someone—John Smith—living in the United States were suddenly and inexplicably to disappear before the eyes of his friends, and that at the same moment an exact replica of him were inexplicably to appear in India. The person who appears in India is exactly similar in both physical and mental characteristics to the person who disappeared in America. There is continuity of memory, complete similarity of bodily features including fingerprints, hair and eye coloration, and stomach contents, and also of beliefs, habits, emotions, and mental dispositions. Further, the "John Smith" replica thinks of himself as being the John Smith who disappeared in the United States. After all possible tests have been made and have proved positive, the factors leading his friends to accept "John Smith" as John Smith would surely prevail and would cause them to overlook even his mysterious transference from one continent to another,

rather than treat "John Smith," with all of John Smith's memories and other characteristics, as someone other than John Smith.¹

Hick believes that we should think that the "John Smith" replica is the same person as the John Smith who disappeared in America. We should think this because he has all the same features as the original Smith, and even believes that he himself is the original Smith.

Smith's body disappears in one place and an exact copy of it appears in another place. Death is different. When we die, our bodies do not disappear. They remain as corpses. So Hick slightly alters the story:

Suppose, second, that our John Smith, instead of inexplicably disappearing, dies, but that at the moment of his death a "John Smith" replica, again complete with memories and all other characteristics, appears in India. Even with a corpse in our hands, we would, I think, still have to accept this "John Smith" as the John Smith who had died. We would just have to say that he had been miraculously re-created in another place.²

According to Hick, we still have every reason to believe that the replica Smith is *numerically the same* person as the original. If everything else about Smith is the same, why should a corpse in America matter? If we believe that the replica is the same as the original in the first scenario, then we should also believe it in the second. Whether or not Smith remains Smith should not depend on whether or not there happens to be a corpse in Cleveland.

Hick alters the story one more time:

> Now suppose, third, that on John Smith's death the "John Smith" replica appears, not in India, but as a resurrection replica in a different world altogether, a resurrection world inhabited only by resurrection persons. This world occupies its own space distinct from that which we are now familiar. That is to say, an object in the resurrection world is not situated at any distance or in any direction from the objects in our present world, although each object in either world is spatially related to every other object in the same world.³

If we believed that the replica is the same person as the original in the first two scenarios, then we ought to believe it in the third. The same markers for identity are present: same bodily appearance, same

---

1. Hick, *Philosophy of Religion*, 125–26.
2. Ibid., 126.
3. Ibid.

memories, same beliefs, same habits, and even the same "stomach contents." The resurrected John Smith has no doubt that he is the same person as the original John Smith.

According to this view, we die when we die. God remembers everything about us, down to the number and location of every hair follicle and neurotransmitter. But God instantaneously creates an exact replica of us in heaven. Our experience is no different than Smith's or a person who has been reconstructed from data in a computer. Resurrection is survival by data stream, only the data is streamed through the mind of God instead of a computer. If Smith can survive, so can we.

On this view, resurrection involves no direct connection between the old body and the new. The new body only needs to look like the old body. That means that we are not our bodies. Our current body is a temporary home. We do, however, need some body or other. On this view, we may be closely connected to whichever body we have—we may be interwoven with it into one integrated being—but we can survive the unweaving. It therefore bears an important similarity with the view that we are our souls. The major difference is that, unlike that view, we need a body to survive. We also need one that bears important similarities to our current bodies.

But how similar do the resurrected and original bodies need to be? The greater the similarity, the more willing we are to believe that we have survived. But that is not good news for many. Must the re-created body have a wrinkled face and severe arthritis? Must it have the scar on your belly that resulted from the removal of your appendix? For that matter, must it have an appendix? Must it have the scar that you have had on your forehead ever since your forehead smacked a sidewalk when you were eight?

What about the age of your re-created self? If you died as an octogenarian, will you need to rise as an octogenarian. If you died at birth, will you need to rise as a baby? We might not be so willing to accept Hick's scenario if the re-created body is too different from the body that died. Suppose that Smith were seventy and a replica of his twenty-year-old self appeared in Calcutta. We would be more hesitant to believe that the replica really was Smith.

God could create a replica that resembles your body at death and then quickly transform it into something like your scar-free twenty-year-old body. That would guarantee sufficient bodily similarity, give you a better body, and make Re-creation more plausible.

Re-creation also denies any direct connection between the old mind and the new. The new mind has the same memories, beliefs, emotions, and personality traits as the old mind. But that mind ceased to exist at death. Resurrection, according to Re-creation, is a complete re-creation of the person out of nothing.

Thus, Re-creation means that the person completely ceases to exist at death and then later begins to exist again. Philosophers call this "gappy existence" because there is a gap in the person's existence—a moment when the person does not exist at all. We are snuffed out like the flame of a candle. But somehow the same flame can be lit on another candle.

According to Hick's scenario, resurrection is immediate. We exist again with a new body in heaven immediately after our original bodies die. As chapter 3 showed, some scriptural verses seem to support *immediate resurrection* but even more verses seem to challenge it. But Re-creation does not necessarily entail *immediate resurrection*. God might choose to create replicas of us all at the end of history. The experience of death and resurrection is the same whether the resurrection occurs today, tomorrow or at the end of time. The dead do not experience the passing of time because they do not exist. When we awake many millennia from now, it will seem to us but a second after we died—as if we woke up from a timeless and dreamless sleep.

Re-creation has much in its favor. As chapter 4 showed, neuroscience suggests that our minds are deeply rooted in our brains such that they can neither function nor exist without brains or something like them. That implies that we too cannot exist without our brains. Re-creation finds a way for us to survive death that is fully consistent with these implications. God makes new brains that resemble the old, thus re-creating all our memories, beliefs, and personality traits. Life after death does not require that we ever have to exist without brains.

As chapter 3 showed, the Bible tends to view us as living bodies rather than embodied souls. Re-creation offers a view of the afterlife that is consistent with such a *holistic* conception of the human person. It views us as psychophysical wholes, such that we can never exist apart from our bodies.

But Re-creation has difficulty squaring with specific biblical passages. Chapter 3 also showed that many biblical passages suggest that the dead are conscious between death and resurrection. Re-creation can interpret these passages in terms of *immediate resurrection* but only by sacrificing the biblical idea that we will all be raised together in the future at the Last Judgment. This view also has trouble explaining Paul's saying that "we would rather be away from the body and at home with the Lord" (2 Cor 5:8).

This view also cannot explain the biblical idea of *Sheol*. How can anyone go to *Sheol* if they cannot exist disembodied? God would have to resurrect persons in *Sheol* with re-created bodies. But the Bible never connects resurrection and *Sheol*. In any case, a fully resurrected person would not have the shadowy existence that persons in *Sheol* have. Re-creation will need to interpret *Sheol* in some other way, perhaps as metaphorical rather than literal.

Surviving the Chasm of Nonexistence

Re-creation also faces philosophical challenges. God may be able to create a replica of you in heaven, but what is it that will make that replica you? Re-creation needs to explain what preserves your identity across the chasm of complete nonexistence. Nothing crosses that chasm, so how then is it that you cross it?

There are three main possibilities. According to the first, you are the same person when you rise again because you have a body with the same organization and structure as your original body. You are not your body, but you are the structure that your body has.

> Self-as-Structure: I am a bodily structure. Any future person is the same person as me as long as she has the same bodily structure as I have.

Your identity lies in an organizational structure or pattern that remains the same throughout your entire life. It is something like your DNA, or perhaps it is your DNA. Your current body has the same DNA and the same fingerprints as your baby body. That DNA and those prints prove that a pattern persists. That underlying pattern makes your replica you, not the replica's outward appearance.

The fourth major view on death and resurrection, which will be explored in the next chapter, is based on this idea that you have an underlying pattern that makes you you. But the fourth view identifies your pattern with your soul. It is the pattern for both your body and your memories, beliefs, desires, and personality traits.

data stream: resurrection as re-creation 95

According to the second possibility, your mind is like a sophisticated computer program. Your body is like the physical computer. Your mind needs some body or other to function, just as a computer program needs some computer or other to run. If your computer dies, the same program can run on another computer. If your body dies, your same mind can function in another body. Since you are your mind, you will survive in that body.

> **Self-as-Software**: I am a highly complex program, much like a computer software program. Any future person is the same person as me as long as she is the same program as I am.

We like to think that our minds are more than highly complex versions of this:[4]

```
function silas (mood, food){
    if (food == "chocolate"){
        do {
            if (mood == "happy"){
                eat (food);
            } else if (mood == "sad"){
                eat (food);
                mood = "happy";
            } else if (mood == "so-so") {
                reject (food);
                mood = "sad";
            }
        }
        while (mood == "sad");
    } else {
        alert ("I want chocolate!");
    }
}
```

But consider what a computer program does. Suppose that you are playing a video game on the computer. You press certain keys on the keyboard, move the mouse in certain directions, and click the mouse button

---

4. For the technologically curious, this code is an example of Javascript.

every now and then. Your key-pressing, mouse-moving, and button-clicking are input. The video game then processes that input according to its programming and then gives an output. The output consists of an image on the screen moving in certain directions and performing certain actions. Our minds are like this in a way. They receive input from the world around them—the smells and colors of a chocolate bar. They then process that input: the smell of chocolate and the appearance of chocolate means a chocolate bar is present; memories of eating chocolate means that the chocolate bar causes pleasure and is desired; knowledge that chocolate has antioxidants means the chocolate is healthy; knowledge that chocolate has sugar means the chocolate is unhealthy; fact of chocolate's pleasant taste and health benefits overrides chocolate's containing sugar; move arm to pick up chocolate bar and bite into it. The resulting output is the eating of the chocolate. Computer programs are our kin, perhaps closer to us than monkeys.

There may be some limitations on which types of bodies can run your program. My HP, for example, can't run many programs that were designed for Apple computers. Neither can it run many programs that were made prior to 2000. So the program that is you might at least need a human body or brain similar to the one you have now. But, on the other hand, Apple computers can play many programs that were designed for Windows. So perhaps your mind could function in an artificially created body that is human software compatible. Star Trek's Data or Star Wars's C-3PO might do. But R2-D2 might not. The physicist Stephen Hawking once said: "I regard the brain as a computer that will stop working when its components fail. There is no heaven or afterlife for broken-down computers; that is a fairy tale for people who are afraid of the dark."[5] He might have been more hopeful had he thought of his mind as software instead of hardware.

Self-as-Psyche

The third possibility lodges your identity in what are called *psychological features*. These are the parts of us that we associate with our minds, such as memories, beliefs, desires, emotions, talents, and personality traits. Such features sometimes also include moral traits, such as moral virtues and vices. If you have a tendency toward bravery, then that is also one of

---

5. Sample, "Stephen Hawking," 21–23.

data stream: resurrection as re-creation 97

your *psychological features*. They may also include our relationships with others. Your role as father to Peter is also part of your psychology and thus identity as are your belonging to the Church and your friendship with God. So too are your tendencies to joke with John and weep with Wendy. Including such relationships nicely connects with the relational understanding of the human person that, as shown in chapter 3, many scholars take to be biblical. Self-as-Psyche is more popular than the last two views of the self, since we often think our *psychological features* are our most important ones.

> Self-as-Psyche: I am my psyche. I am the stream of memories, thoughts, beliefs, desires, emotions, talents, personality traits, moral traits, personal relationships, choices, perceptions, and experiences that make up my psychological life. Any future person is the same person as me as long as she has the same psyche, or consciousness, as me.

Some consider memory to be our most valuable *psychological feature* and believe that *personal identity over time* depends on memory alone. In fantasy and science fiction, characters often test another person's memories when that person's identity is in doubt. For example, in the Harry Potter series, Remus Lupin wants to know whether the "Harry" he sees before him is the real Harry or an impostor made to look like Harry by a potion of transmogrification. So he asks "Harry" a question that only the true Harry would know the answer to. This implies that memory determines *personal identity*—that I am the same person as the quiet eight-year-old boy who loved to watch the Smurfs precisely because I remember being that boy. I will live again after death just so long as in heaven some person or other has my memories. If he does, then he is me.

But memories are fickle. They come and go. Those that stay are often hazy and sometimes false. Do we really wish to bank our identities on such foggy features? In any case, which memories are crucial for one's survival after death? It cannot be those had at death, since some have lost all or most of their life's memories by then. Our midlife memories will not do either, because they would leave out our later grandparenting and globetrotting identity-forming memories.

Most of us do not remember anything about our lives prior to the age of four. Many of us will go senile and forget most of our memories before we die. If memory is the key to me then I did not exist until I was four. The three-year-old was either someone else or no one at all. So was the baby. It also means that if I go senile or comatose, then I will cease to exist before my body dies. But this does not seem right. Surely the baby and the boy were me. Surely the senile grandfather on the hospice bed is *numerically the same* person as the grandfather we always knew and loved even though he does not remember anything prior to yesterday.

Personal identity cannot depend on having the same memories. But it might depend on being part of a continuous overlapping chain of memories, like the continuous overlapping chain of atoms that we encountered in chapter 8. Recall the analogy of the rope, where the fibers overlap and no fiber runs throughout the whole rope's length. Memories are like those fibers and the rope is like our *personal identity*. We are the same persons over time, because all new memories overlap in our minds with older memories, which in turn overlap with even older memories, and so on back to the beginning of our lives. You are the same person as the baby you grew out of because you are connected to it by a chain of memories. The Alzheimer's grandfather is the same person as the grandfather we always knew because he is connected to him by a chain of memories, even if the overlapping is minimal.

But what happens when the rope ends, the chain is broken, and the last memory is gone? If we are a stream of memories, then we cease to exist when the last memory fades. That is one reason why *immediate resurrection* appeals to many who favor Self-as-Psyche. At death, one's psyche immediately jumps ship to a newly crafted body in heaven so that the memory stream, and thus the person, continues. But jumping ship only works by either being completely airborne for a few seconds or by stepping directly from one ship to another while the ships connect. Neither option is a case of Re-creation, in which the person ceases to exist and is then re-created from scratch. The former option is not that much different than Soul-Flight and faces many of the problems that it faces. Chapter 11 will explore the second option.

It is, however, difficult to reconcile Self-as-Psyche with the biblical belief that all will be raised together in the future at the Last Judgment. God might resurrect you at the Last Judgment with all the memories that you had at death. But it is hard to see how the newly resurrected chain of memories is a continuation of the original chain that ended back in 2014. The beginning of a rope may have exactly the same kind of fibers in exactly the same places as the end of another rope. But we still think them two separate ropes. Similarity at the ends is not enough to make them *numerically the same* rope. For that, we need to connect them.

In a sense, God's memory of our memories connects our original and resurrected selves. God's memory functions much like the computers in the teleportation example. It records the data and transfers it to the new body.

But there is good reason to think that our memories cannot survive the transfer. For one thing, if our memories necessarily depend on the brains that store them, then any memories placed in the new body could not be *numerically the same* memories. They may seem like them, but they would not be them. I do not merely want to remember watching punters in Cambridge with my kids. I want my memory to be the *actual* memory of that event. I want the memory I have in my mind to have actually, as a matter of historical fact, been caused by my physically being there in Cambridge by the River Cam. Otherwise, I would think the memory is only a replica of the true memory. It seems that memories are like documents. We can only fax copies of them to other minds. If the original document is destroyed then all we have left are copies.

Maybe God can store the true memory in his mind, so that the memory in God's mind is historically linked to my physically being in Cambridge. That would make it *numerically the same* memory. But how can the true memory be in anyone but me? The true memory is colored by a sense that it was *me* who watched the punters. But God is not me. The memory in God cannot be colored by me-ness. So it cannot be the same memory. Furthermore, according to this view, *I* am my memories. Thus, *I* would be stored in God, which is difficult to believe. So it seems that our *numerically the same* memories cannot cross the chasm between death and resurrection.

Philosophers who hold Self-as-Psyche usually broaden it to include all our *psychological features*, not just our memories. They also often argue that what matters is not the particular features themselves. What matters is the continuous overlapping chain of *psychological features*. Our beliefs, desires, and personality traits may change over time, but we are still *numerically the same* persons if our current beliefs, desires, moral traits, and personality traits are connected to previous ones through this overlapping chain. This solves the problem of Phineas Gage. His personality radically changed after his accident, but it was still continuous in some ways with his *psychological features* before the accident. So there is no difficulty in explaining why he is *numerically the same* person.

On this view, the resurrected person is *numerically the same* person if the *psychological features* she has when she is resurrected are sufficiently similar to those she had at death, thus continuing the chain where it left off. Died bitter and cranky? God can raise you bitter and cranky to provide the needed continuity, but then quickly remove the bitterness and crankiness.

But the same problems with memory apply to our other psychological features. God can remember all the *psychological features* we had at death. But his memory would only contain copies of those features. God's memory of your continuous desire for chocolate is not that desire itself because it is no longer *your* desire. God's memory of your super-human patience with autistic kids is not that patience itself, because it is no longer *your* patience. So he may give your resurrected replica a desire for chocolate and a superhuman patience but that desire and that patience would not be *numerically the same* as the desire and the patience you have now. So it is difficult to argue that the psyche of the resurrected person is a continuation of the psyche of the original person.

In the past, proponents of Self-as-Psyche were not worried so much about whether our psyches could exist in bodies that did not resemble the originals. British philosopher John Locke had no problem imagining that a prince and a cobbler could exchange their psychological features. He had no problem believing that the prince could inhabit the body of the cobbler and that the cobbler could inhabit the body of the prince. Much in fiction plays on the idea that we can inhabit different bodies, as in the first line of Kafka's story *Metamorphosis*: "One morning, when Gregor Samsa woke from troubled dreams, he found himself transformed in his bed into a horrible vermin."[6] We tend to accept that Gregor can become a bug and still remain Gregor.

But more recently, proponents of Self-as-Psyche more deeply connect mind and body. They suggest that our psyches are integrated with our bodies such that they cannot exist without a body. But they also often claim that our psyches cannot exist without having bodies much like the ones we have now. In this way, Self-as-Psyche gains an advantage over Self-as-Soul. It can explain, in a way that Self-as-Soul can't, why our bodies are important to our identities.

If this is correct then God must create a replica in heaven that is similar enough to your current body to support your particular psyche. You

---

6. Kafka, *Metamorphosis*, §1.

will need a brain with the right web of neuronal connections to support your particular memories, beliefs, and desires. You will need the right kind of fingers to support your skill at playing the piano. So not just any body will do. For you to be you, the body of a weasel or a Wookie will not work. Neither will a body like that of Einstein or Elizabeth. The only body that will do for you is a body that is similar enough to your current one.

This tight connection between psyche and body does not mean that our psyches are nothing but neurons arranged in certain ways. It does not mean that knowing everything that is going on in our physical brains—which neurons are connected with which and which neurons are firing when and where—will tell us everything there is to tell about us. It does not commit one to the *reductionism* we encountered in chapter 7. A person who holds Self-as-Psyche can believe that our *psychological features* are more than mere arrangements of neurons even though they believe these features can only exist in brains similar to our own.

The Problem of Replication

Re-creation has a lot going for it. It can successfully combine our intuitions that our *psychological features* are crucial to our personal identities with our intuitions that our bodies are also important. Neuroscience says that our minds can't exist without brains much like the ones we have now. Re-creation shows how one can take seriously the findings of neuroscience and still believe in life after death.

But Re-creation faces a serious problem. Catholic philosopher Brian Davies offers a counter-story to John Hick's:

Suppose you give me a lethal dose of poison. This, of course, does not make me very happy. But, you say: "Don't worry. I've arranged for a replica of you to appear. The replica will seem to have all your memories. He will be convinced that he is you. And he will look exactly like you. He will even have your fingerprints." Should I be relieved? Speaking for myself, I would not be in the slightest bit relieved. Knowing that a *replica* of myself will be enjoying himself somewhere is not to know that *I* shall be doing so.[7]

As Davies notes, we think much the same way about paintings. Munch's painting *The Scream* recently set a world record by selling for nearly $120 million. The art dealer who bought it would not have paid

---

7. Davies, *Introduction to the Philosophy of Religion*, 300.

that much for an exact duplicate of the painting because he would not have considered it to be *numerically the same* painting as the original.

Re-creation also faces the *duplication problem* from chapter 5. The Uralive Teletransportation Company's computer could re-create two of you at exactly the same time from the data sent to it from the spaceship. It could create thousands of you. Likewise, God could create two of you at exactly the same time from the information about you that he has stored in his mind. He could create an infinite number of you. But there can only be one of you at a time. None of these replicas would have a greater claim to being you than the others. So it seems that none of them can be you.

That means that your survival after death depends on whether or not God *happened* to create another replica of you at the resurrection. If God did, then neither replica can be you. But according to *the only X and Y principle* from chapter 5, your identity cannot depend on whether or not something or someone else happens to exist.

God is good and would not choose to create two replicas of you. But God *could* theoretically choose to create two or even more replicas of you and that is all that is needed to question Re-creation. In any case, Re-creation depends on either bodily structure, mental "software," or a psychological stream. DNA can be cloned, software can be copied and loaded onto different computers, and streams can be divided. Even if, for some reason, God could not theoretically create two replicas of you in heaven, perhaps we can someday create replicas of ourselves on earth. That possibility suggests that neither bodily structure, nor mental software, nor streams of consciousness preclude replication. That would mean that none of them guarantee personal identity. It would seem that Re-creation is a dead end.

But Re-creation has a fourth option that can't be so easily duplicated. According to this option, *personal identity* depends on having the same *first-person perspective*. I am able to think of myself as me. I am also able to think of my desire to roam the streets of Rome and eat gelato by the Trevi fountain as being my desire. I am also able to think of my six-foot middle aged body as being my body. My ability to think of myself in these ways is called my *first-person perspective*. It is the way in which I can think of myself as a someone, a self, and a subject. A future person is the same as me as long as he has the same *first-person perspective* as me.

I have been unconscious before and while unconscious, I do not think I was aware of myself at all. So if this view is correct, then I ceased to exist while my body was lying on the floor. Babies, and perhaps even toddlers, also do not yet have any sense of self. If this view is correct, then I did not begin to exist until I was a toddler.

Proponents of this view avoid this problem by instead claiming that, for a person to be a person, she needs to be the type of being that has the *possibility* of having a *first-person perspective*. Babies are persons because babies are human beings and human beings by nature usually develop a *first-person perspective*. The comatose and unconscious are also persons because it is still possible for them to regain consciousness and once again think of themselves as persons. It is only when it is no longer possible for them to do so that they cease to be persons.

> Self-as-First-Person-Perspective: I am my first person perspective, or my awareness of being me. A future person is the same person as me as long as she is the type of being that has the possibility of having the same first person perspective as me.

This view has important implications for cases like that of Terry Schiavo. Her brain stem, which controls things like her heartbeat and breathing, was the only part of her brain that continued to function. Her brain had deteriorated to the point where it was impossible for her to ever regain a *first-person perspective*. According to this view, Terry ceased being a person. Her body continued to exist as an organism, even though she was gone for good. But do we wish to claim that she died before her body did? If we hold to Self-as-First-Person-Perspective, then we will have to.

According to Self-as-First-Person-Perspective, I will be in heaven insofar as there will be a person in heaven who has my *first-person perspective*. It does not matter what kind of body I will have, so long as that body is the kind of body that can support my *first-person perspective*. Some who hold this view require that body to closely resemble one's current body. Some will not require much resemblance at all. A bionic body will do just as well.

The advantage of this view is that *first-person perspectives* are unique and unrepeatable. Two beings in two different bodies cannot both have my same *first-person perspective*. Even God can't simultaneously make two replicas that both have the same *first-person perspective* as the one that I have now. Neither can my *first-person perspective* split into two as happened to Riker's mind and body as described in chapter 5. The *first-person perspective* would have to go with one or the other. Only one of the two Rikers can have the original Riker's *first-person perspective*.

But what is it about a *first-person perspective* that can't be duplicated? Couldn't God theoretically create two replicas that both thought they had my *first-person perspective*? If so, then what is it about a *first-person perspective* that could distinguish the two from each other so that one of them could be the original *first-person perspective*?

For that matter, what is it about *a first-person perspective* that can make it the key to one's continued identity? How is a *first-person perspective* in 2020 the same as a *first-person perspective* in 2014? How is a *first-person perspective* the same in heaven as it is on earth? How can such a perspective be the same perspective if the original perspective ceased to exist at death? This view can only reply that it is just so. It is just a fact of the matter, like the fact that for every action there is an opposite and equal reaction. We can't really explain it, but we must accept it nonetheless. But such a response is unsatisfying to many.

Folding Time and Space

Re-creation claims that God can bring us back from nothing. The problem is that there is nothing from which to bring us back. There is also nothing to prevent God from re-creating many copies of us. But we are not faxes. It seems that our survival depends on more than God's memory of our minds and bodies and *first-person perspectives*. It seems that there must be something that provides continuity between me now and me in the hereafter. But how can that be if neither psyches, patterns, programs, nor *first-person-perspectives* can survive the deaths of their bodies?

Suppose though that you like the views of the self that Re-creation makes use of. You like the idea that you are your software, psyche, pattern, or first-person perspective. You also like the idea that you depend on a body to exist. You therefore favor *immediate resurrection*, in which you hop directly into your resurrected body. Yet you also like the idea of the *general resurrection*—that we are all raised together at the end of history. If so, then your best bet lies in the warping of time and space.

Imagine that our universe is a piece of paper with its timeline stretching along its length. The timeline begins on the left side of the paper and continues along the length of the paper. We each die at some point along that timeline. Our deaths will be relatively close to each other on the paper. The deaths of Peter and Paul are further to the left. Our great grandchildren are further to the right. Much further to the right is the *general resurrection* of the dead, the Last Judgment, and the beginning of the new creation. Now imagine that the piece of paper is folded so that the future time of the *general resurrection* touches the time of your death. Thus, when you die you can hop directly to your newly resurrected body. From your perspective, you will be immediately resurrected after you die. You will also be resurrected at the same time as everyone else at the end of history, because the time of the *general resurrection* also *touches* the time of everyone else's death.

The Time-as-Folded-Paper solution solves a lot of problems. It makes it possible for you to continue without any gaps in your existence, which avoids *the duplication problem*. It acknowledges that you cannot exist without being in a body, thus making neuroscientists and *holists* happy. It also combines *immediate resurrection* with the more biblical view of *general resurrection*. It shows how the thief will be with Christ in paradise today and also how that paradise is the future new creation.

This solution still has its problems. It undercuts one of the main advantages of Re-creation. It could explain, in a way that Self-as-Soul could not, how death is as bad as the Bible says it is. According to Re-creation, we really do die when we die. But if, at death, we immediately hop to our new bodies, then we do not really die when we die. Death is like walking directly from one train car to the next.

Furthermore, even if the time-warp solution solves the problem of multiple heavenly replicas, it still has not avoided the theoretical threat of fission. My psyche could, in principle, still split, either on earth or in heaven. Half of my stream of consciousness could flow into one body, while the other half could flow into another body. *The problem of duplication* would still apply to Self-as-Psyche.

The time-warp solution also needs to explain how you can jump directly from your current body to your resurrected body. Those two bodies would need to touch, since you cannot exist without a body. But is it even theoretically possible for them to touch? How does the touching of times bring about the touching of bodies when those bodies are both in the same physical dimension? In other words, how can two different bodies from the same dimension intersect with each other if they are not in the same slice of time? How can your future body at 7:42 a.m. on April 2, AD 77777 touch your earlier body at 10:11 a.m. on January 1, AD 2060 even if AD 77777 somehow intersects with AD 2060? It is easier to accept that some other brain from some other dimension intersects with your current brain than with another brain from a future time in the same dimension.

The problem of duplication poses the greatest problem for Re-creation. It makes the idea of the soul more appealing, because souls are not duplicable. Could there be a way to combine belief in the soul with a more *holistic* understanding of who we are than Self-as-Soul can offer? The next chapter explores that possibility.

10

Saved by the Soul: Resurrection as Re-formation

You push the fourth button. You feel your life slip away. Your memories fade. You try to focus on the memory of the moonlit walk on the beach but it disappears and you no longer even remember that you once had it. Your desires fade. The desire to reach the planet is gone. The desire to live dies. The desire to not cease ceases. Your feelings fade. The feeling of pain in your knee disappears as does the feeling of there being a knee at all. The feeling of imminent danger and the accompanying increased beating of your heart also fade. Your senses fade. All colors and sounds cease. You no longer see, hear, smell, taste, or feel anything—not even the air against your skin. You are no longer aware of anything outside yourself. You no longer know where you are in relation to the spaceship or the planet below, neither of which you even remember. In fact, you do not even sense yourself. It is as if you had ceased to exist and only a part of you has remained. All that is left are thoughts, but not thoughts about moonlit walks. Instead, you think only abstract thoughts—about mathematics, philosophy, and the essences of things. You think about the essence of a spaceship, but there is no longer any memory of any particular spaceship you have ever experienced.

Then you feel something—a connection, a sensation, a body! You feel blood pumping. You feel the presence of your knee again, but strangely, without any pain. You feel air against your skin. You feel the blood flow through your brain and the image of the moonlit beach resurfaces in your mind. Your desire to live returns, as does a feeling of joy that you survived. You sense that you are yourself again—that you have come back to life. Your body feels to you, from the inside, to be the same body as your original body. It is no copy, no replica. And so you feel as though you are truly you. Only now you are on the planet. And then, suddenly aware that you have eyes, you open them. Your body appears much the same, only without its scars and wrinkles.

You hear a humming sound. You turn and see a printer attached to a computer. It spits out a piece of paper which you read:

> Congratulations! You chose the correct button. The moment you pressed the button, the computer began to disentangle your soul from your body. But, as you found out, your soul can't do much without your body. How did you like only being able to think abstract thoughts? Interesting, isn't it? Anyway, the computer you see before you enabled your soul to shape a body from the matter on the planet here below. As you can sense yourself, it is the same body as the body you left behind on the spaceship. That's because your soul is what preserves the identity of your body. It can make your body again from new matter if need be. You need not worry whether you survived the journey. Same soul. Same body. What more could you possibly need to ensure your survival?
>
> Guaranteed by the
Uralive Teletransportation Corporation.

This scenario resembles the Soul-Flight scenarios of chapters 6 and 7. Our souls part from our bodies, maintains consciousness between death and resurrection, and then join with new bodies. But its view of who we are and how we are related to our bodies is closer to the views of the self that we encountered in chapters 8 and 9. The core idea of this view is that the soul is not a separate thing as *dualism* teaches. Instead, the soul is the structure or organization of living things. As a result, the disembodied soul is not the full person. It is the person's core. But it is still only a part of the person, as a computer's central processing unit is only a part of the computer.

This view is therefore more complicated than the previous views. For that reason, some critics think it incoherent. They claim that its attempt to take the best and avoid the worst of the other views is doomed to failure. It tries to have it all, but sometimes all just can't be had. But others believe that it holds great promise and will become more widely held once it is properly understood.

This view is prominent in Christian history. St. Thomas Aquinas held it and many consider him the brightest thinker that Christianity has ever produced and one of the greatest thinkers that humankind has ever produced. This view fell out of favor with the rise of modern science and the accompanying belief that science killed the soul. But many now believe that the kind of soul that science may have killed is not the soul that this view teaches. They believe this view is more compatible with modern science than either *traditional* or *emergent dualism*.

Scientists have taken notice. In 1982, John Polkinghorne, a Cambridge particle physicist, decided to become a priest in the Church of England. He returned to Cambridge in 1989 and became president of Queen's College. He has since written numerous books on science and religion and received numerous awards. But what is most interesting about this scientist-turned-theologian is that he proposes a view of the soul that is similar to that of Aquinas. Thus, Polkinghorne's more scientifically informed account serves as a helpful lead-in to Aquinas's.

Information-Bearing Patterns

As a particle physicist, Polkinghorne knows that one cannot explain a human being without explaining the particles that make her up. One will need to know about her atoms and molecules and how they interact according to the laws of physics and chemistry. One will need to know about her carbon, oxygen, and nitrogen atoms and her proteins, neurotransmitters, and DNA. But Polkinghorne believes that explaining all of that will not explain everything about a human person. In this, he resembles *emergent dualists*. He differs from them because he does not think we need an immaterial *thing* or *substance* to explain what science can't. He instead appeals to the idea that we each have an essential pattern or structure—an idea we encountered in the last chapter. That pattern carries information about the person's personality, moral traits, memories, desires, habits, bodily structure, and much else that we typically consider to be important to our personhood.

Polkinghorne equates this *information-bearing pattern* with the soul. He also believes that it is the self. In this, he resembles *traditional* and *emergent dualism*. This soul, or pattern, preserves the person's identity throughout her lifetime. The matter that makes up her body comes and goes. The carbon atoms and the protein molecules will change. But the pattern that organizes that matter remains.

> **Self-as-Information-Bearing-Pattern:** Any future person is me as long as he is the same information-bearing pattern as I am.

If Polkinghorne is right, then patterns naturally emerge when matter is arranged in complex ways. He describes an experiment that supports such emergence:

> Consider an array of electric light bulbs. Each bulb can be in one of two states, "on" or "off." The system develops in steps and there are simple rules . . . which tell how this happens. Each bulb is correlated with two other bulbs somewhere else in the array. What that bulb does at the next step is determined by what states those two other bulbs are in now, on or off. The system is started up in some random configuration of illumination, some bulbs on and some off. It is then allowed to develop according to the rules. I would have guessed that nothing very interesting would happen and that it would just flicker away haphazardly for as long as you let it do so. I would have been quite wrong. Very soon the array self-organizes itself into an amazingly orderly behavior, settling down to cycling through a very limited set of patterns of illumination. The degree of order spontaneously generated in this way is astonishingly great. If there are ten thousand bulbs in the array, in principle there are 10^{3000} (a one followed by three thousand zeros—an immense number in anyone's book) different states in which it might be found, but it turns out that it will soon cycle through only about a hundred![1]

We do not yet know what is going on with the light bulbs. Any explanation will need to involve more than the bulbs, the wires, the electrical currents, and the rules that governed whether the bulbs would be on or off. It seems that an orderly pattern of behavior has emerged. Any adequate explanation of what is going on will need to involve that pattern.

The bulbs, wires, and electrical currents are like the atoms and molecules that make us up. The rules that determine whether they are on or off are like the laws of physics and chemistry that govern our atoms and molecules. This experiment supports the idea that complex entities, like

---

1. Polkinghorne, *Quarks, Chaos, and Christianity*, 73–74.

amoebas, amethysts, auks, and ecosystems, consist of both matter *and* pattern. Any adequate account of them will need to involve the latter.

Polkinghorne implies that something similar happens in the development of each human person. The complex pattern that is the person emerges from a particular complex arrangement of atoms and molecules and the physical laws governing their behavior. It emerges when the egg and sperm unite or at some other point in the development of the fetus in the womb.

Our essential patterns are not static, however. They, like the matter they organize, are always changing. Our personalities, interests, and desires change as we gain new life experiences. Teen rebels become disciplined writers. Shy bookworms become corporate executives. A rod through the brain can remove one's sense of responsibility, as happened to Phineas Gage. But Polkinghorne suggests that each pattern has a signature pattern within it—a sub-pattern that is unique to each individual and never changes. An *information-bearing pattern* is more like a city with suburbs in flux and a downtown that always stays the same.

Our signature pattern could also change from one moment to the next. But it would remain a core unchanging pattern if its changes occur as part of a repeating pattern. We tend to think of the soul as the static unchanging essence of who we are. But if the soul is a pattern then no part of it needs to be exactly the same at every moment in time. One could agree, with the Buddhists, that every part of us changes every moment. My memory of walking the dog on Halloween night will be slightly different a nanosecond later. As will my whimsical mood and my thoughts about two plus two. Even the core of who I am changes every moment. My essential personality traits, or whatever it is that makes me unique, are slightly different from one moment to the next. The Buddhists could be right that there is nothing about me that stays the same throughout my entire lifespan. The Christian could still be right that I have an unchanging essence, so long as the changes occur according to a larger pattern. That pattern, stretched out over time, is my soul.

Perhaps the soul is like a musical theme that repeats throughout a musical score. That theme is never the same from one moment to the next, because a different note is played at each moment in time. Yet the theme exists and gives the score a unity it would not otherwise have. We may be more like a passacaglia than a painting—defined by repeating rather than static patterns. Our signature patterns are the ground bass that keeps repeating. Those patterns may themselves slightly change, just as the recurring theme of a passacaglia can be transposed to higher or lower levels. The ever-changing accompanying polyphony makes up the rest of our patterns. We may notice our polyphonic patterns more, but if we listen to our lives more closely we will also hear our ground bass.

Scottish philosopher David Hume is famous for saying that he could not find a self when he looked within his mental life. Perhaps he did not look long enough to notice any recurring patterns. Perhaps we need to reflect back on an entire lifetime to notice it. The same may be true for persons who experience radical personality changes during their lifetimes. There may be more polyphony at some moments than others and so it may sometimes be harder to hear the ground bass. Or the ground bass may have shifted to a lower level, making it harder to hear.

Our essential patterns also include our relationships to God, other people, and creation. Each particular relationship has its own pattern. That pattern is part of who you are—part of both your pattern and that of the other person or being in the relationship. This pattern includes your roles with regard to others—father to Joseph, member of the Church, adopted son of God, and such. It also includes your patterns of interactions with others. Consider a relationship with a close friend. You and your friend's patterns create tendencies in the way that you give and exchange gifts, joke, argue, converse, share inmost thoughts, and make decisions together. These tendencies will slightly vary for each person you relate to. You may laugh about the inanities of politics with Paul while avoiding the topic altogether with Susan. Our patterns, and thus our souls, are intricately tied to the patterns of others.

Our personal identities therefore extend beyond the confines of our skin. They extend into God, others, and our environment through our relationships with them. Our personal identities are not like marbles in a bag, completely independent one from the other as the traditional view of the soul implies. They are more like webs interlinked one with another, where some strands of the web extend into other webs. Polkinghorne's view takes into account the importance of our relationships to who we are in a way that *dualism* can't. That makes it a good choice for those who believe that the Bible teaches a relational understanding of the human person, as discussed in chapter 3.

The Problem with Patterns

The problem with patterns, however, is that they do not outlive their material. Some of you may remember those oval-shaped swirl rugs in which you could trace a line from the edge as it swirls inward and ends at the center of the rug. That swirl is a pattern. Unwind the rug so that the swirling line becomes straight and both the rug and its pattern are destroyed. "Unwind" our bodies so that they die and our patterns are destroyed. It seems that Polkinghorne's attempt to rescue us from *reductionism* has not rescued us from death.

Yet Polkinghorne believes there is a way for our patterns to survive death. He considers two possibilities, without fully committing to either. According to one possibility, God remembers the person's essential pattern, storing it in his mind. Then God uses it to create her again at the resurrection, by using it to organize new matter into a new body. The resulting person is *numerically the same* person as the original because she has the same pattern. Our patterns are ever-changing, so presumably the key is to use the person's signature pattern and then add in whatever else from her pattern that God chooses.

This option is really another version of Re-creation, similar to the Self-as-Structure option discussed in the last chapter. It faces the same *problem of duplication* that Re-creation views face. God remembers the rug's swirl in his mind and then uses it to create that rug again out of new material. But God could use that same pattern to create yet another rug and another and another. He could instantaneously create an infinity of such rugs. None would have a greater claim to being *numerically the same* rug. So none can be *numerically the same* rug. Likewise, God could use your pattern to re-create multiple persons all at once at the resurrection. None have a greater claim to be you. So none can be you.

The other possibility is that God somehow preserves the pattern apart from the body. God keeps it in existence, perhaps in his mind. He then rejoins it with a new body at the resurrection. This pattern would likely be unconscious—resulting in a version of Soul-Sleep. Or it might be conscious—resulting in a conscious *interim state* in which the self is at least minimally aware of being in the presence of God. But Polkinghorne does not explain how it is possible for God to preserve one's pattern in existence, even in God's own mind. Patterns do not generally exist disembodied—at least not the kind of material patterns of which we are familiar. Can you imagine the rug's pattern existing by itself without being in anything patterned after it?

Polkinghorne also does not explain how it might be possible for a disembodied pattern to be conscious. We normally do not think of patterns as being conscious. Naturally, we would think that the person as a whole is conscious, but that her consciousness was made possible by her brain's being shaped by her pattern.

Like *emergent dualists*, Polkinghorne believes that the resurrected body will need to be sufficiently similar to the original body. After all, the soul is a pattern according to which the matter of the body is organized. Thus, the matter of the resurrected body will need to be organized in a way consistent with the way it was organized in the original body. The resurrected body's organization does not need to perfectly match the original body's organization. But it does need to faithfully express the person's signature pattern. The resurrected Gandalf will not necessarily have a beard, but he will have a tallish body that glows with magic and intelligence. The resurrected Churchhill may not be bald or old, but he will have Churchhill's commanding face. Polkinghorne's view more closely knits soul and body than *emergent dualism*. *Emergent dualism* requires a sufficiently similar body because the emergent mind emerged from a particular body and can only properly function in bodies like it. But Polkinghorne's view requires a sufficiently similar body because the soul is the body's pattern and thus the body an expression of it.

Polkinghorne has achieved a more scientific account of who we are by making the soul into a pattern rather than a substance. But that account has trouble explaining how we survive our deaths. Again, the more scientific an account becomes, the more difficult it is to square it with life after death.

Polkinghorne acknowledges the similarity between his view and Aquinas's. They both view the soul as more like a pattern than a thing. But there are important differences—differences that make Aquinas's view a clearer example of Re-formation rather than Re-creation.

My Soul Is Not Me

Aquinas's view is important because it is central to much Catholic teaching. There is nothing *necessarily* Catholic about it, as it also appeals to other Christians. As we will see, it has many advantages over the other views we have considered so far.

Like Polkinghorne, Aquinas believes that the soul is like a pattern. It is the principle of organization for the matter of the body. Unlike Polkinghorne, Aquinas does not believe that the soul is the person. He says, "But soul is not the whole human being, only part of one: my soul is not me."[2] The person, he believes, is the combination of both soul and body. More exactly, he believes that the person is a living body, an ensouled body, a body that consists of both soul and matter. I am my body, but my body includes a unique organizing pattern or structure, which is my soul. Aquinas thus more closely knits soul and body than either Polkinghorne or the *emergent dualists*.

I continue to exist so long as my living body continues to exist. At this point, Aquinas's view sounds much like Reassembly. But it is different because, for Aquinas, my living body continues to exist only insofar as my soul continues to exist. To be me, any future person must also have the same soul as me. For such a person cannot even have the same body as I have unless that person has the same soul as me. I am my body, but being my body necessarily means having a particular soul.

> **Self-as-Ensouled-Body:** Any future person is the same person as me as long as he is the same ensouled body as I am and thus has the same soul and body as I have.

For Aquinas, the soul actively shapes the matter of the body, organizing it into the particular kind of body that it is. The soul thus makes your body a human body. It organizes your neurons into a human brain. It organizes your muscles and bones into human legs. It makes possible all your abilities by organizing your body's matter in the right way for those abilities to exist. It organizes the bones of the legs in such a way that walking upright on two feet becomes possible.

The soul also organizes the matter of your body in such a way that it has the abilities associated with being alive. The soul is thus the principle of life, which means that all living things have souls. Plants have the kind of soul that organizes the matter of their bodies so that they can digest food, grow, and reproduce. Animals have the kind of soul that organizes the matter of their bodies so that they can move and sense the

---

2. Aquinas, "My Soul Is Not Me," 192–93.

surrounding world. Higher animals have the kind of soul that organizes the matter of their bodies so that they can also have desires, emotions, memories, and primitive levels of cognition. We humans are unique in having the kind of soul that also makes possible thinking abstract thoughts and making choices.

As principles of organization, souls are not substances. They do not normally exist by themselves as complete things in themselves. They are more like hands or leaves than clocks or trees. A hand by itself, whether from a human or a clock, is not a complete thing in itself. It is a part that has been removed from its whole. The same goes for the soul.

Yet souls are not quite parts either—at least not in the way that hands are parts of bodies. Souls are not material. They are more like immaterial *aspects* of ourselves. If Beauty were real, it would not be some material part of a beautiful painting. It would not consist in particular blotches of paint in the corner. It would rather consist in the overall pattern or organization of a painting. That pattern is a part of the painting, but in the sense that it is an immaterial *aspect* of the painting. The soul is more like Beauty than a hand.

Normally, patterns and structures cannot exist on their own. Aquinas seems to face the same problem as Polkinghorne in accounting for how the soul can survive the death of the body. He tries to solve it by making the human soul a special sort of soul. Plants and non-human animals depend on their matter for everything they do. There is no digestion without physical mouths and stomachs. No sight without eyes or hearing without ears. No emotions without neurons.

But humans can do something that does not require matter. Humans can think. Aquinas believes that thinking about abstract thoughts like the nature of God and the essence of sheep is an immaterial activity and thus can occur without the brain. I will not go into the full argument for why Aquinas thinks this but I should note that many today find it unconvincing. He does, however, believe that we more naturally acquire knowledge of abstract concepts through our sense perception. He also believes that we more naturally think about abstract thoughts through using images which we can only access through our brains. We have difficulty thinking about the essence of a sheep without the image of an actual sheep in our minds. So he does not think much of our ability to think without our bodies. He merely wants to show that thinking in itself does not happen in them. That is enough, he believes, to show that our souls can exist without our bodies. He believes that something that can act by itself can exist by itself. Human souls can think by themselves without their bodies. Therefore they can exist by themselves without their bodies. If the soul can think outside its box, then it can exist outside it too. But it will exist as incomplete, as a part that has lost its whole. Although whether or not the soul will continue to exist after the body dies depends on whether or not God chooses to keep it in existence. So the soul is not naturally immortal in the sense of *necessarily* surviving the death of the body.

Thus, Aquinas believes our souls can continue to exist after our bodies die because they are able to continue to think after our bodies die. That means that they are conscious after we die. How then is Aquinas's view different from *dualism*? First, as mentioned earlier, Aquinas believes that the soul is not me. It is only a part of me. I am not conscious apart from my body. Only a part of me is.

Second, for Aquinas, the soul's consciousness apart from the body is not that exciting. The disembodied soul is only capable of thinking about the essences of sheep and other such abstractions. It cannot imagine any sheep when it thinks about sheep. Imagine thinking about the essence of a rose without being able to picture its shade of red or imagine its sweet smell or the gentle touch of its petals. The disembodied soul also cannot picture the faces of its loved ones here on earth. It still loves them in the sense that it wishes them well. But it cannot *feel* any love for them, for it cannot *feel* anything. It certainly cannot see or hear what is happening on earth or anywhere else because it cannot see or hear. Aquinas believes that God somehow gives the disembodied soul knowledge of its loved ones and events on earth. But it is highly questionable whether this is possible given his understanding of the intricate relationship between soul and body. Souls cannot even think about *individual* persons or things without brains with which to do such thinking. Happily, however, the disembodied soul more greatly experiences God after death. But that experience is not "happy" in the warm fuzzy sense since a disembodied soul can feel no warm fuzzies.

Lest its unnatural disembodiment lasts forever, Aquinas assures us that the soul will get its body back at the resurrection. Then the person will be complete and exist again. But Aquinas believes this requires the resurrection of our very same bodies that died. The original body must be raised, for is not that what resurrection means? If I am an ensouled body, then how can any future person be me if he does not have *numerically the same* body as I have now? If my soul gets an altogether new body at the resurrection then that body would not be me. In any case, the soul cannot join with a significantly different body since it is fitted for a particular body. My soul cannot be in the body of a bee, a wookie, or a George Clooney. Nor can it be in your body.

As a result, Aquinas's view seems to require the reassembling of our bodies.[3] If the resurrected body must be the same body that died, then it will have to consist of the matter of that body. God will need to collect my ashes or my atoms from the corners of the earth and reunite them with my soul. But we have seen that Reassembly has a lot of problems. Surely there is a better way to get our bodies back. Many recent interpreters of Aquinas believe that there is.[4]

The soul, after all, is what makes the body to be the body that it is. The soul therefore carries the body's identity. Your body is the expression, externalization, incarnation, and flowering of your soul—of your signature pattern or structure. That means that your body is your body because your soul is its organizing pattern. Any future body will be the same as your current body if it is organized and structured by your soul. That is good news, because it means that any future body does not need to have any of the matter of your current body to be *numerically the same* body as your current body. The soul can shape whatever matter is at hand into *numerically the same* body as your current body. Resurrection is the re-formation of your body and not its reassembly. Your same body will rise again at the resurrection even though it may consist of *numerically different* atoms altogether. The cannibals can have their day, for we need no longer worry about who is eating our atoms.

Some may object to Aquinas's view because they feel that their bodies do not match their souls. A tall person, for example, may feel like his soul better fits a small body. But this world is imperfect. Our bodies are also shaped by factors other than our souls. Perhaps he got a tall gene, when he should have got a short one. Such factors may block the body from being able to perfectly express the soul. Also, our souls may better fit our bodies than we realize. Perhaps the tall person has not yet realized that he also has a "tall" soul. At the resurrection, our bodies will perfectly express our souls. The world will no longer have its imperfections. Short souls will have short bodies.

---

3. See Davies, *Thought of Thomas Aquinas*, 218–19, and Geach, *God and the Soul*, 26–28. Also see Langley, "Aquinas, Resurrection, and Material Continuity," for an examination of the problems and possibilities of this view.

4. See Brown, "Aquinas on the Resurrection of the Body," 190–91; Bynum, *Resurrection of the Body*, 259; and Stump, "Non-Cartesian Substance Dualism," 516.

Getting the Best of Both

Aquinas's view has many advantages. It seems to avoid the *duplication problem* faced by Re-creation. God cannot even in principle resurrect two bodies that have equal claims on me. I have got only one soul and it can shape only one of those two bodies. So the one that it shapes will be mine—will be me. The soul continues to exist between death and resurrection so it cannot itself be duplicated. And it makes no sense to split a soul in half despite what *Harry Potter* author J. K. Rowling might have us believe. She may have Voldemort's soul split in seven, but immaterial aspects are not the sorts of things that can be split.

Re-formation takes the best of each of the other views. *Traditional dualism* is attractive because it affirms the existence of the soul. Soul Sleep is attractive because it keeps the soul but yet accommodates the science that suggests that we need brains to be conscious. Reassembly is attractive because it affirms the central importance of our bodies to who we are. *Emergent Dualism* and Re-creation are attractive because they maintain a tight connection between our minds and our bodies without reducing us to our atoms. Re-formation does it all. It keeps the soul yet says that we are our bodies. It links mind and body more tightly than both *emergent dualism* and any of the Re-creation views. It also approximates Soul Sleep. Re-formation's disembodied soul may be awake. But its cognition is diminished.

Re-formation has a hint of *dualism* since it allows for the soul to exist apart from the body. Yet it avoids some of the major problems with *dualism*. Interaction between mind and body? No problem. The soul is the body's organizing principle. Interaction between the two is therefore as natural as the ecology of a tide pool influencing a crab's behavior. Neuroscience and the mind? Re-formation holds that nearly all our thinking depends on the brain. Remove the brain and that thinking stops. It does allow for some thinking to take place without the brain, but far less than *traditional dualism*. Continuity between humans and animals? According to the Re-formation view, we are animals. I, my very self, am an animal. As are you. We both have souls, but then so do all animals. So the continuity with them is great. The difference is that our souls make it possible for us to think about the essences of sheep. According to *traditional dualism*, we are not animals for animals do not have souls.

Re-formation also gives us everything we want biblically. Soul-Flight cannot explain why death is an enemy, why the resurrection is necessary for life after death, and why the Bible's view of us seems so *holistic*. Reassembly and Re-creation, on the other hand, explain them well. But they have trouble explaining those biblical passages which suggest that we are conscious between death and resurrection. Re-formation makes sense of all of the above.

Death has a sting because we really do die. It is true that our souls survive our deaths, but they are only a part of us. The house does not survive its collapse when one wall is still standing. Thus without the resurrection, death would mean our permanent extinction. Our hope lies in God's raising us from the dead, just as the Bible suggests.

Re-formation is thoroughly *holistic*. We are our bodies. As such, we have two aspects, an immaterial spiritual soul and a material body—a description of who we are that would satisfy many a biblical scholar. It is more *holistic* than the Re-creation views of the self which identify us more with our minds or psychological features. If we are our software, psyches, or *first-person perspectives*, then we are not our bodies even though we may depend on them to exist.

Yet Re-formation also has an *interim state*. Our souls are conscious between death and resurrection. "Today you will be with me in Paradise," says Jesus to the thief (Luke 23:43). The thief's soul will literally be present with the Lord in paradise right after he dies.

Despite their similarity, Aquinas's view is more biblical than Polkinghorne's. By equating ourselves with our souls, Polkinghorne diverges more from biblical *holism*. Polkinghorne is also caught in a biblical bind. If he claims that the soul exists between death and resurrection then the person does not die at death. Thus, our hope for eternal life would not depend on resurrection as the Bible suggests. Death would still have a sting but it would be a lesser one. The person would still long for resurrection because life without the body is impoverished. But resurrection would not be *necessary* for our eternal existence. But if he claims that the soul does not survive the body's death and is merely remembered by God, then he denies the *interim state* and has difficulty explaining those passages which seem to support it.

Aquinas's view, like Polkinghorne's, can also incorporate a more relational understanding of *personal identity*. If my soul is an organizing pattern, then it is also the pattern of my relationships to God, others, and nature. My soul's relationship with God survives death and then perhaps renews its relationships with deceased friends and loved ones in paradise. But death cuts off its bodily relationships with the living. Since I am a living body, then I am also the network of relationships with others that is centered in my body. My relationships with my sons involve feelings of love, memories of playing with toy boats in a Parisian park, and tendencies to lovingly pat them on their backs. All of which, for Aquinas, occur in and depend on our bodies. Only the pattern of these relationships survives my death. Their substance, their existence, dies with my body.

I am also the network of relationships with nature that partly constitute my body. We tend to think that our bodies end at the edge of our skin. But our bodies are constantly taking in food, oxygen, and water from the surrounding environment and constantly giving back bodily waste to the surrounding environment. Our bodies are themselves parts of larger natural processes, such as the water, carbon, and nitrogen cycles, which connect our bodies with each other. If I am my body, then I am not fully me when I am extracted from natural cycles. That does not mean that these cycles must be the same in heaven as they are on earth. We should hope that they will be somewhat different so that we no longer age or die. But it does mean that we require being enmeshed in some natural environment to be fully ourselves.

If my identity as a person includes my relationships with others, then death destroys that identity. I cannot be fully me if I am not in relationship with other bodies, both human and non-human. Resurrection restores those bodily relationships and thus restores my full identity. Aquinas would never put it this way. His resurrected bodies were static and boring, existing in a natural environment but no longer woven into larger natural cycles.[5] But a more relationally minded thinker could adapt Aquinas's view to stress the way that bodies enmesh us in nature.

Re-formation seems too good to be true. It is like having a gilled swimmer that can also breathe air and walk on the land or a mammal that can lay eggs. It is like having a fish with lungs and legs or a lizard with fur and milk. But such things can't happen, can they? Re-formation, it seems, wants the impossible. Yet frogs and platypi exist. So why can't our souls be amphibians? Why can't our souls breathe both on earth and in the realm of God and the angels? Sometimes we can have it both ways. Sometimes we can get everything we want. Yet, as the Rolling Stones aptly remind us, we can't always get what we want. The question is whether or not we can in this case.

---

5. See Lindsay, "Thomas Aquinas's Complete Guide to Heaven and Hell," 38–39, for a humorous look at Aquinas's conception of the resurrected life in heaven.

Neurons, Patterns, and Persons

Re-formation has much going for it. But it also has some problems. The first problem has to do with the nature of the disembodied soul. Re-formation affirms an *interim state*. But not for me or you. Jesus tells the thief, "*You* will be with me in Paradise" (Luke 23:43). He did not say that only his soul will be there. When Paul says, "We would rather be away from the body and at home with the Lord" (2 Cor 5:8), surely he is suggesting that we ourselves would be present with the Lord. The story of the rich man and Lazarus suggests that Lazarus himself is in heaven. Re-formation, it seems, is not so biblical after all.

But it is if Jesus and Paul are using synecdoche. More commonly, synecdoche means using a part to refer to a whole, as in "One does not live by bread alone" (Matt 4:4). "Bread" is only one type of food, but here it is meant to represent food as a whole. Synecdoche can also mean using the whole to refer to a part of the whole. You say, "The world is against me." But you don't mean the *whole* world. You mean only a part of it. We complain about Capitol Hill. But our complaint is not against the whole hill. We mean only a part of it, the US Congress. Likewise, when Jesus says, "You will be with me in Paradise," he means only a part of the thief, his soul. "We would rather be away from the body and at home with the Lord" does not mean "when we are away from the body, we are at home with the Lord." It means "when our souls are away from our bodies, our souls are at home with the Lord." Similarly, the story of Lazarus and the rich man refers to Lazarus, the whole person, to make the story flow better. But it refers to only a part of him. It refers to his soul.

Re-formation's conception of the *interim state* has other problems. If *we* are not in the interim state, then why should what happens in it matter to *us*? Jesus comforts the thief by telling him that a part of him will be in paradise that day. To which the thief could rightly respond, "So what?" Why should Paul long to be "away from the body" when only a part of him will then be "at home with the Lord"? My soul may enjoy God between death and resurrection. But why should I care, since it will not be *me* enjoying God? My soul may become purified in purgatory between death and resurrection. But *I* will not become purified. None of what happens to my soul in purgatory is happening to *me*.

Furthermore, the soul is supposed to be conscious between death and resurrection. But only persons can be conscious and the soul is not a person. How can a being that is not a person be conscious and have thoughts?

These objections seem to require a reformation of Re-formation. We tend to assume that personhood is all-or-nothing. One either is or is not a person. But perhaps there are quasi-persons—not quite persons and not quite not persons. Why not? The universe is a complex place. Perhaps disembodied souls are quasi-persons rather than non-persons.[6] Perhaps quasi-persons can be somewhat conscious, since they are somewhat persons. My soul then is not fully me, but it is quasi-me. I still die when my body dies because I cease to exist as a full person. But quasi-me survives. Whatever happens to quasi-me in the *interim state* matters to me because quasi-me is, after all, quasi-*me*. When the thief died on the cross, quasi-thief went to paradise. So Jesus's words are still a comfort to him. Paul longs for a post-body presence with the Lord, since quasi-Paul will enjoy it. I will exist again as a full person at the resurrection. When I do, I, the complete me, will absorb all that quasi-me experienced in paradise or purgatory. Quasi-me's experiences will become *my* experiences when quasi-me rejoins my body. All of quasi-me's purgatorial growth will become *my* purgatorial growth. Quasi-Paul's post-body enjoyment of the Lord will become Paul's own post-body enjoyment of the Lord once Paul is raised again from the dead.

Finally, many, if not most, neuroscientists would object to even Aquinas's understanding of the *interim state*. Aquinas allows for disembodied consciousness and disembodied thinking. But, as we have seen, there is mounting evidence that consciousness depends on the brain or something physical like it. We are connecting more and more of our thinking with particular regions and processes of the brain. We may one day be able to locate which neurons are involved in thinking about the essence of a sheep. Aquinas, along with *traditional* and *emergent dualists*, can always reply that neuroscience only proves that brain activity is correlated with our thinking—that certain regions of the brain are active when certain thoughts are thought. It cannot prove that the thinking itself happens in or requires the brain. Yet the mounting scientific evidence makes it harder to believe that the thinking does not happen in and require the brain or something physical like it.

Re-formation's second problem has to do with the soul's origin. Aquinas believed that God individually creates each human soul. He

---

6. See Pasnau, *Thomas Aquinas on Human Nature*, 387–89, for this suggestion.

creates it when the embryo has developed enough to sustain it, which he believes to be about three months into the pregnancy. Chapter 4 showed that there are many problems with this claim. When, for example, in the evolutionary line did God create the first human soul? There seem to be no good answers.

Many today therefore reject Aquinas's view that God creates the soul. They believe instead that the soul naturally emerges from the embryo. It is, after all, the essential organizing pattern or structure of the human being. It arose and arises just like any complex structure in nature. But this belief has a cost—a cost that may be too high for many believers. The belief in God's special creation of each soul is the kind of belief you want to write on a birthday card. It shows why each individual person is precious and unique. It grants dignity to each individual in a world that too often denies dignity. We today are commercialized and technologized. We are increasingly replaceable by robots. But if God specially created you, me and every outcast on every dismal street, then every one of us has a special irreplaceable dignity. That is why many cling to the idea that we have souls and that God specially created them. On the other hand, arising from the earth has its own appeal. If we naturally arose from the earth, then we belong to the earth. We are connected with not only all other human beings, but also with all other creatures. We will return to these themes in chapter 15 when we draw out the implications of these views for how we treat each other and the earth and its creatures.

Re-formation's third problem is that science seems to have killed the soul, and not just the *dualist*'s "escape from the earth" kind. Aquinas's view of the soul as the body's structure was once popular. But the Scientific Revolution of the 1600s changed that. One either became a *traditional dualist* or a thoroughgoing *physicalist* of the-everything-can-be-explained-in-terms-of-atoms type. Scientists increasingly leaned toward the latter. Science denied any place for structure, pattern, or organization in explaining nature. If atoms explained everything, then organization explained nothing. In fact, atoms explained organization. Whatever structure anything had was due solely to the activities of its atoms following the laws of physics and chemistry. Many scientists today believe this to be good science. If so, Re-formation is doomed. Even its understanding of the soul as a pattern must be rejected.

But science is changing. More scientists are taking seriously the idea that structure or organization are real components of living things—that we cannot fully explain you or a ewe without explaining the activities of the atoms of which you or the ewe are made *and* explaining the structure that is organizing those atoms. The structure is much more than the arrangement of the atoms and science should take note. According to one such scientist:

> The physico-chemical picture of the living organism is only half the truth. The missing half concerns the nature of the organizational relationships that make the behavior of obviously living systems uniquely different from that of obviously non-living systems . . . In many ways this is the more important half. For here lie the differences between life and death, and between the higher and lower forms of life as they affect us most . . . Even if we knew down to the last molecular detail what goes on inside a living organism, we should still be up against the fact that a living system is an organized whole which by virtue of the distinctive nature of its organization shows unique forms of behavior which must be studied and understood at their own level.[7]

Many other respected scientists have made similar claims.[8] They are not reaching these conclusions by applying Aquinas to biology. They are reaching them through their own observations of the way the world works. Science may be heading in Aquinas's direction. The Re-formation soul is far from dead.

The biggest problems for Aquinas's' view are similar to those for Polkinghorne's. First, if the soul is the body's structure or pattern, then it should not be able to exist without the body. The structures of two separate houses are separated from each other because one is in these walls and roofs and the other is in those walls and roofs. If the soul is like a structure, then my soul is separated from yours because it is in my body and your soul is in your body. Remove the bodies and what keeps them apart? Aquinas would answer that they remain distinct because they are fitted for the two different bodies. My soul is fitted for my body and your soul is fitted for yours. That is enough to maintain their distinction when separate from the body. Still, does it make sense to speak of structures, even of the soul-ish organizing kinds, in this way? How do the two disembodied organizing patterns exist in connection with each other? Do they exist side by side? But there is no side by side apart from matter. Do

---

7. Sommerhoff, "Abstract Characteristics of Living Systems," 147–48, as quoted in Jaworski, *Philosophy of Mind*, 284.

8. See Jaworski, *Philosophy of Mind*, 283–85.

they exist far or near from each other? But there is no far or near apart from matter.

Second, how can disembodied patterns be conscious, since patterns are not the sorts of things that are conscious? Third, if the whole person, and not the soul, is what thinks, then how can the disembodied soul think? For the above reasons, some contemporary Christian philosophers consider Aquinas's view incoherent.[9]

Deep problems, it seems, lie at the heart of the-view-that-is-too-good-to-be-true. They center on the view's requirement that the soul can exist without a body. If only there were a way for the soul to have a body between the original body's death and resurrection. Perhaps there is . . .

---

9. See Corcoran, *Rethinking Human Nature*, 39–40, and Hasker, *Emergent Self*, 167–70.

11

Surfing in Slipstream: Death and Other Dimensions

You push the fifth button and feel a jolt. The world around you instantly disappears. You no longer see the button or the spaceship or anything familiar. You see colors and clouds slipping by and hear a swooshing sound. You can neither see nor hear as well as you used to, which is just as well since the world around you is confusing enough as it is.

At the same time, your body feels lighter. You look at it and instead see the body of a ghost—whitish, ephemeral, and translucent. You feel that you are made of fog. Yet your body has the same structure—the same hands and legs. Your fingerprints, though foggy, are the same. You feel wind whoosh your ghostly skin, but the feeling is duller than you are used to. It is pleasant, but barely—like being nearly numb. Your memories become as foggy as your ghostly body. You remember a moonlit walk but none of the details. The whole experience reminds you of something you once read in Dante, but you can't recall what it was.

You feel another jolt. The world dims to nothing. Then it reappears with solidity. You see grassy hills and a blue sky, but with a vibrancy and clarity that exceeds even your pre-button experience. You feel a breeze on your skin. It feels good, better than you have ever before experienced. You look at your body. It is solid and fleshly again. The same arms, legs, and fingerprints. It reminds you of that moonlit walk, which you now remember more clearly than ever—down to the exact shades of blue of every shell you encountered on the beach. You feel that you are you again, but now more you than you were before.

You hear a buzzing sound and turn to see a printer attached to a computer. It is printing out a piece of paper. You take it and read:

> Congratulations! You chose the correct button. The moment you pressed the button, the spaceship's computer instantly slipped you into slipstream, which is a subspace tunnel. It gave you a body made of air and fog so that you could survive while in slipstream, for we all know you can't live without a body. Your original body immediately died and blew up with the spaceship. We hope you enjoyed slipstream but apologize that we couldn't give you a body that allowed you to enjoy it more. A familiar fleshly body couldn't survive it. But our wonder-working technology has enabled the planet's computer to bring you back into our dimension right here on the planet. It also gave you a fleshly body back, but enhanced its abilities. We think you will like it much better than either your original or slipstream bodies. You are still you because you never died. You never died because you had a body all along.
>
> Guaranteed by the
> Uralive Teletransportation Corporation.

Surfing in Slipstream

In the television series *Star Trek: Voyager*, the crew of the starship *Voyager* were trapped in a quadrant of space far from earth. It would take a lifetime for them to get back by traveling through space. So they created a subspace tunnel in front of the ship that allowed their ship to slip into subspace so that they could get to earth more quickly. In one of Gene Roddenberry's lesser-known series, *Andromeda*, the crew of the starship *Andromeda Ascendant* enter and exit slipstream tunnels to hop from one part of space to another.

We have looked at four different views for how we might get from death to resurrection. Each of them has problems. Perhaps science fiction can come to the rescue. If we can't get from our body's death to our future resurrection through time and space as we know it, then perhaps we can get there through slipstream.

Slipstream is science *fiction*, not science. So how can it help us? But, as it turns out, it may or may not be science and it may or may not be fiction. The science of the past centuries dismissed subspace and other bodily dimensions of existence. The only real world was this material world and perhaps also a completely bodiless spiritual realm. But today's science is more open now than ever to the existence of such things. Today's science is more willing to side with Hamlet than Horatio. To rephrase Hamlet, "O Horatio, there is more to this world than past science has ever dreamt of." That is good news for life after death, because it opens up possibilities that past science denied. It also may not matter what science says, because such dimensions could be completely undetectable by the science of our dimension. Perhaps God could slip us into them without science ever noticing those dimensions or our slipping into them.

The core idea of the fifth view, Slipstream, is that neither you nor any part of you can exist disembodied. You, or a part of you, can only survive death with a body of some kind. Since that body cannot be in this dimension—we'd notice it and we don't—then it must be in some other dimension. Perhaps it is in subspace. Perhaps it is in another dimension altogether. At death, God slips you into a body in that other dimension. Then, when the time is right, God slips you back into this dimension with a newly resurrected body from this dimension.

This chapter unleashes the imagination. It invites us to develop creative solutions to the problem of how we get from death to resurrection. Its motto: "Think Dimensionally." Think Sphereland, not Flatland. Think outside/inside/beyond the box. Think Star Trek or Doctor Who. There may be boundless afterlife possibilities waiting for an Einstein to discover.

This chapter will cover five ways we might travel dimensionally from death to resurrection: via body-snatching, body-morphing, body-splitting, body-hopping, or soul-storing. There may be others not yet dreamt of, but the following five are already.

Nearly all the views of the self that we have considered have a vested interest in Slipstream. Even Self-as-Soul might welcome it. One of that view's biggest drawbacks is that it typically claims that we can think without a brain or something physical like it. But if the soul could have a body between death and resurrection then it could use that body's brain to think. Even Soul Sleep might welcome a temporary body because it is questionable whether something such as the soul can exist without doing anything at all. A temporary brain would allow it to dream. Many are skeptical that Self-as-Emergent-Soul can justify the soul's disembodied existence. If the soul is like a magnetic field then it should die when its body dies just as a magnetic field ceases with the destruction of its magnet. But give the emergent soul a body in slipstream and it will continue to have a base to generate it.

Self-as-Body and Self-as-Brain would both benefit more from Slipstream than Reassembly. If the body or brain somehow continues in another dimension then it no longer matters what happens to the corpse's atoms.

Self-as-Structure, Self-as-Software, Self-as-Psyche, and Self-as-First-Person-Perspective all depend on bodily existence. Many would argue that Self-as-Information-Bearing-Pattern also ought to. But if the self has a body immediately after death, then the self continues to exist. God does not need to re-create the self from scratch at the resurrection, thus avoiding the *duplication problem* discussed in chapter 9.

Finally, Self-as-Ensouled-Body has difficulty explaining how the soul, as the body's structure or pattern, can exist disembodied. But if the soul has a body immediately after death, then it never needs to exist without a body. Slipstream thus solves some of the major problems of each of these views.

Body-Snatching

It is a fact that our bodies do not slip into another dimension when we die. The corpse is there for all to see. Our slipping into slipstream at death cannot be the same as it is for *Voyager*'s crew in Star Trek or *Andromeda*'s crew in Andromeda. Their very bodies slip into and out of slipstream. They do not leave corpses behind every time they make the jump. But, when we die, our bodies stay right here on our hospital beds. But things may not be as they seem. The body left on the hospital bed is not necessarily the deceased's body. It is possible that the body on the bed is a perfect simulacrum.

Suppose that, at death, God snatches the person's body and substitutes a perfectly identical corpse. God could do this in an instant so that none of our scientific instruments could record it. Science could neither affirm nor reject it.

Peter van Inwagen, a contemporary philosopher from the University of Notre Dame, first proposed this idea as a possibility in a famous journal article.[1] He did not think it was necessary to snatch the whole body though. He thought that just the brain and nervous system would

---

1. Van Inwagen, "Possibility of Resurrection," 114–21.

do. God preserves them in another dimension while perfect replicas of them lie inside the corpse. Then God rejoins them with a resurrected body back in our dimension at the *general resurrection*. The result is not much different than a Neanderthal who was frozen to death and then thawed out and revived by modern science, or a person who was revived from cryogenics.

This view could help many of the views of self that we have discussed since it provides a continual bodily basis for the self, whether the self be a soul, an *emergent* field, a software program, a psyche, or an *information-bearing pattern*. But it especially helps Self-as-Body. It preserves the same body without needing to collect one's atoms from the four corners of the earth. It also helps Self-as-Brain, because the person's brain will have continued to exist between death and resurrection in some other dimension.

Van Inwagen, however, has in mind another view of the self. This view, called animalism, equates the self with a living organism.

> **Self-as-Living-Organism:** I am a living organism. Any future person is the same person as me as long as he is part of the same ongoing biological life as I am.

I continue to exist only as long as my *life* continues. I might survive an interruption of that life if that same life could be resumed again after the interruption. But that would require that my body is preserved in stasis during the interruption—or at least, as van Inwagen suggests, that my brain and nervous system are preserved in stasis.

Body-Snatching suggests that the self is unconscious between death and resurrection, as the brain and central nervous system are stored in some heavenly vault. But it need not be. The brain could be in a heavenly vat, stimulated by divine electrodes to have conscious experiences between death and resurrection. It could perhaps have a dim awareness of God's presence or have dreams as if it were asleep.

Body-snatching sounds far-fetched. But it is possible. God could do this. Science has no way to rule it out.

Yet it makes God into a body-snatcher. Worse, it makes God into a deceiver. God fools us all by making it look like our dead bodies remain on earth. Would a good God do that? Some young earth creationists propose that God created the world six thousand years ago. But he made it look like it was billions of years old. Van Inwagen's proposal sounds similar, making it also highly suspect. There is an important difference though. God has no reason to fool us with fossils. But he has a good reason to snatch our bodies.

God could only avoid deceiving us by removing our bodies at death without leaving fake copies behind. That would be more honest, but it would also throw science in disarray. God has otherwise created a world that we can count on because it consistently follows the laws of science. God may work miracles here and there, but not too often so that the world remains predictable. We cannot count on a world where dead bodies always magically disappear for no scientific reason. Perhaps God chooses to leave fake bodies behind not to deceive us but to keep the world scientifically reliable and to remind us of what would happen to us if Christ had not conquered death.

Ghostly Bodies

Surely God could find a better way than body-snatching to get us from death to resurrection. God could instead give us a temporary body in some other dimension. Such a body could not be as good as the resurrected body. Otherwise the resurrection has no point. So God might give us instead the body of a ghost. For a time, we could join the ranks of Casper, Nearly Headless Nick, and the Ghost of Christmas Past.

The idea has literary appeal. It is found in Homer, Virgil, and Dante. In Homer's *Odyssey*, the Greek hero Odysseus visits the realm of the dead and encounters the fallen heroes of the Trojan War. They have shadowy insubstantial bodies—the kind that makes one really wish one were still alive on earth. Achilles is there and he tells Odysseus that he "would rather be plowman to a yeoman farmer on a small holding than lord Paramount in the Kingdom of the dead."[2] In Virgil's *Aeneid*, the Trojan hero Aeneas also visits the kingdom of the dead and likewise encounters the deceased with shadowy bodies.

But Dante, in his *Divine Comedy*, populates all of hell, purgatory, and heaven with such ghostly bodies. He has the Roman poet Statius explain them while climbing Mount Purgatory. Once the soul leaves the body at death, it goes to purgatory and immediately shapes the air around it into a body that resembles its original body. This new body is made of air and condensation. It is therefore insubstantial. Statius tells Dante: "This airy body lets us speak and laugh; with it we form the tears and sigh

2. Homer, *Odyssey*, 134.

the sighs that you, perhaps, have heard around this mountain."[3] But what these ghostly beings desire most is to get their earthly bodies back at the resurrection. Until then, their senses are dimmed, their pleasures dulled, and their activities limited.

The Bible also speaks of shadowy bodies. The Old Testament dead are in *Sheol*, where they have shadowy insubstantial bodies like those in Homer and Virgil. Their hope lies in the resurrection because then they get livelier more substantial bodies.

Ghostly bodies are both scriptural and part of a long literary tradition. They may also be the key to solving thorny philosophical problems about how to get us from death to resurrection. What's not to like?

The trick is to explain how we might make the transfer from the original body in this dimension to the ghostly body in the other. It requires the intersection of two dimensions. But how do we get from one to the other? Imagine two flat dimensions existing side by side like two pieces of paper lying one on top of the other. A body in one world, perhaps a two-dimensional human-shaped body, can touch a body in the other world if the one is on top of the other. A person in one body in one world could conceivably transfer to the body of the other world. No one would notice because no one can see beyond her own flat dimension. Perhaps our three-dimensional world can connect with another three-dimensional world in the same way so that we could similarly transfer into another body in that other dimension. The next three options explore three ways that we might make such a transfer.

Body-Hopping

According to the first option, we hop from our dying bodies into other bodies in another dimension. What makes the jump depends on what you are. If you are your soul, then your soul simply hops from one body to another. If your soul is an emergent field, then it would need to hop into another body sufficiently similar to its original. If you are your psyche, then your stream of consciousness flows directly into the other body in the other dimension.

Body-hopping might also work via information transfer. Self is software? Then you can be transferred to another body as information can be transferred from a computer to a flash drive. Self is *information-bearing*

---

3. Dante, *Purgatorio* 25.103–5.

pattern? Then your pattern can be transferred to another body. A passacaglia is a pattern. Yet *numerically the same* performance of a passacaglia would continue even if all the musicians and instruments were instantly and miraculously replaced by musicians and instruments sufficiently similar to the originals.

Such transfers would need to be scientifically undetectable. Otherwise, the fact that we do not detect them scientifically would be a major strike against their happening. But science only detects the transfer of matter or energy. It cannot detect the transfer of either information or immaterial entities. So each of these views are scientifically possible, assuming that our psyches are either immaterial or a kind of information.

But the problem with transferring information from one body to another is that we generally think that the transferred information is not *numerically the same* as the original. We are inclined to think that it is a copy of the original. The software program that is saved on the flash drive is a copy of the original program. The original still remains in the computer. If you press the pattern of a picture of a rose onto another piece of paper, then you have made a *copy* of that pattern. The original remains on the piece of paper on which it was first designed. We would still think it a copy even if the original was destroyed right when the copy was made.

We could also have, at least in theory, instantaneously saved the computer program to two different flash drives. Imagine that the passacaglia's musicians and instruments are instantly replaced by two sets of musicians and instruments, both of which equally resemble the originals. Or imagine that at death our own patterns were instantaneously transferred to two different bodies in two different dimensions. Due to the *problem of duplication* discussed in chapters 5 and 9, we are compelled to say that the original has been copied in each of these cases.

A similar problem applies to Self-as-Psyche. Suppose that half your psychological traits jump to one body in the next dimension and the other half jump to another. Which one is you?

For body-hopping to work, the self cannot be like a flame passed on from one candle to another. The same flame can light two other candles at once. To avoid the duplication objection, patterns and programs will need to *themselves* transfer to the new bodies. Streams of consciousness will need to be inherently un-splittable and yet also transferable to new bodies. Perhaps there is something about our patterns and our psyches that make them inherently non-duplicable. But it is unclear what that something is.

Body-Morphing

The second option is more a morphing of our current bodies than a hop into different bodies. But how can that be, given that our corpses are buried in St. Vincent's? It can be, if our souls are the organizing structures or patterns of our bodies. This option thus depends on the Self-as-Ensouled Body view of the last chapter. Our souls continue to shape matter into a body after we die, only now it is the matter of another dimension. Thus, the soul creates a body that looks much like the earthly one, but now made up of something less substantial. That something could be air, condensation, quantum particles, or something not from this world. The same pattern then that makes up our current bodies also makes up these ghostly bodies. The pattern, or the soul, is what makes the body into the body that it is. Same pattern, same body. In a way, our souls have transformed our earthly bodies into ghostly ones, even though we leave earthly corpses behind.

The process is much like the way Dante describes it. In fact, Dante held something like Self-as-Ensouled Body. He too saw the soul as an organizing pattern. It organized the air around it in the afterlife to create its aerial body.[4] Dante though did not believe that the aerial body was a morphing of the earthly body, since he believed that the true body lay in the grave waiting to be resurrected by reassembly.

Typically, however, those who hold Self-as-Ensouled-Body believe that souls are matched to their earthly bodies. They cannot inform other kinds of bodies. Aquinas, for example, would not go in for aerial bodies.

But perhaps souls have latent powers that only become activated when the conditions are right.[5] We may be unaware of these latent powers because they are never activated in this dimension. Perhaps they could be activated in another. All along, the soul had the ability to shape aerial, quantum, or slipstream matter. It never had the chance until it met the Grim Reaper and slipped into subspace. As long as the pattern is the same and the material is amenable to being so shaped—and perhaps God has the power to make it amenable—then the pattern should be able to shape the material.

---

4. We do not know whether or not Dante intended his aerial bodies as purely literary devices. His intentions aside, his concept of the aerial body is a useful image for understanding the body-morphing option.

5. See Ross, "Together with the Body I Love," 6–9, for this suggestion and an interesting account of the Body-Morphing option.

Our souls may have still other latent powers. The souls of caterpillars do. The caterpillar's body morphs into that of a chrysalis, which in turn morphs into that of a butterfly. Yet it remains the same insect species and the same individual animal. If it has got a soul, then its soul persists through these changes and is partly responsible for them. That means that the caterpillar, chrysalis, and butterfly stages are all expressive of the same underlying pattern or structure. A biologist would say that the insect has the same genome throughout the changes. But certain genes, such as those of wing production, are not activated in the caterpillar stage. The same can be said for the underlying structure or pattern of the caterpillar and the butterfly. It remains the same, but parts of it are not activated until the butterfly stage. The caterpillar and the butterfly are thus *numerically the same* individual animal with *numerically the same* soul and *numerically the same* body. That soul at first has latent powers to structure wings but they are not activated until the conditions are right. Might not we human beings also have later stages that can express the same underlying pattern or structure even though they look as radically different as that of a butterfly and a caterpillar—even though they might, for example, use slipstream matter for their bodies?

The soul's encounter with the other dimension's matter might activate its latent powers to form something like a chrysalis. Bodily resurrection in this dimension might activate still more latent powers to form something quite different—as different as a butterfly from a caterpillar. The *interim state* could be our chrysalis stage from which our new forms will emerge and take flight at the resurrection. The chrysalis body could even be made of other-dimensional earthly atoms like carbon rather than of insubstantial slipstream matter. That would make us more substantial than ghosts and yet still maintain our ultimate hope in the resurrection. Who wants to be a chrysalis forever? To paraphrase Achilles, "Better a plowman to a yeoman farmer than lord Paramount in the Kingdom of the chrysalides."

Some may object that our DNA contains no traces of radical development. We find, for example, no un-activated genes waiting to grow us wings. But those who hold Self-as-Ensouled-Body believe that souls lie deeper than DNA. Our essential patterns are more profound than combinations of A, G, C, and T. Some latent powers can be hidden.

If this view is correct, then death is a natural part of human life, for it marks a natural stage in human development. This idea is popular today. The body-morphing option gives Christians a way to accommodate it.

The challenge, however, is to square this with Scripture, which seems to treat death as unnatural. What sense is there in Christ's conquering death if death is but a natural stage in our transition to resurrected bodies?

Body-morphing solves Re-formation's central problem of how a body's essential pattern can exist disembodied. With this option, that pattern has always got some other-dimensional matter to shape.

But body-morphing has a problem that caterpillars do not have. According to Self-as-Ensouled-Body, the body is *numerically the same* body if it is organized by *numerically the same* soul. Therefore, the interim body, be it of a ghost or a chrysalis, must be *numerically the same* body as the original earthly body. Yet the original lies under the gravestone at St. Vincent's. Two simultaneously existing bodies cannot be *numerically the same* body. But it seems that the body at St. Vincent's has a greater claim to being the original body. It is, after all, made of the same material particles as the original living body. It is, after all, its corpse. So whatever the interim body is, it is not the same body as the original. If so, then neither can it be the body of the soul that shaped the body now lying at St. Vincent's.

Self-as-Ensouled-Body has an answer—an answer that is not ad hoc. According to it, the corpse is no longer a human body. It no longer has an organizing pattern or structure. It has become a soul-less mass of material particles. It therefore has no claim to be *numerically the same body* as the original. There is only one possible candidate, and it is either a ghost or a chrysalis. For sameness of body, having the same soul trumps having the same matter.

Body-Splitting

The third option splits the body into two resulting bodies. One is the corpse at rest at St. Vincent's. The other is alive and well in another dimension. But if you do not hold the Self-as-Ensouled-Body view, then how is the other-dimensional body a continuation of the body that a moment ago was dying in the hospital? The answer lies in a novel understanding of what it is that makes a body the same body over time.

My forty-year-old body is *numerically the same* body as my four-year-old body because it is part of the same ongoing life. The atoms of my current body are completely different than the atoms of my four-year-old body. But the body is the same because the atoms of my current body are part of the same life as the atoms of my four-year-old body. But what is it that makes my current atoms part of that same ongoing life? What makes a life a life?

Reassembly suggests that the bodies are the same because of the continual overlap of atoms. But God could suddenly wipe out all the atoms of my body and instantly replace them with completely new atoms such that no one would even notice. God would not do that, but that is beside the point. The point is that we would say that the body with the new set of atoms is still the same body even though there is no material overlap whatsoever. But then continual material overlap cannot be what makes a future body *numerically the same* as a past one.

According to the body-splitting option, future bodies are *numerically the same* as past ones because they are linked together by a causal chain. My blood flows through my aorta because my heart just pumped it. My blood absorbs oxygen in my lungs because my lungs just breathed it in. My bladder stores waste products and excess water because my kidneys just sifted them out. My leg muscles contract because my neurons told them to. Much of what happens in my body right now is caused to happen by processes occurring in my body just prior to this moment. And those processes in turn were largely caused by processes occurring in my body just prior to that moment, and so on all the way back to my four-year-old body. That is what is meant by a causal chain.

We normally think that that causal chain ceases at death, for death is the cessation of life. But that is uni-dimensional thinking. Perhaps the chain continues in slipstream, tunneling its way to the *general resurrection*. We cannot rule it out. The activity of the particles of my body at the moment of my death could cause the particles in some new body in some other dimension to do what they do. We can imagine a lifeless human body premade by God and readied in the other dimension to be activated and energized by the particles of my body at death. Thus the causal chain continues. Thus my life continues. Thus my body continues. Thus I continue.

The genius of this option is that it concocts a way for one's ongoing life to continue after death that does not involve divine deception. Neither one's body nor one's brain is snatched away by God and replaced by an identical fake. The corpse at St. Vincent's really consists of the same material particles as the body that died. But that corpse is not your real body because it is dead. Its particles are not part of your body's ongoing life. The particles of the corpse have not been caused to do what they do by anything in the previous living body because they are not doing anything at all. The real body must be the one in the other dimension—the one whose activities were directly caused by the processes of the living body at the moment of death.

Kevin Corcoran, a contemporary Christian philosopher, advocates this option because he believes that we are purely material beings.[6] He does not think we have a soul or anything like it. He adopts something like Self-as-First-Person-Perspective but also believes that our continued existence requires having our same bodies. He believes sameness of body requires a continuing causal chain. Some may hold another view of the self and still believe that their continued existence requires that they have their same bodies. The body-splitting option may help them too.

This option is compatible with science. It does not require a disembodied consciousness. No scientific measurement can rule it out because we cannot scientifically measure whether the life processes of our bodies at death are causing activity in particles in another dimension. If the inter-dimensional causation involves a transfer of energy, however, then it might violate the law of the conservation of mass and energy that was discussed in chapter 6. But the causation might be the sort that transfers information instead of energy—information, for example, about whether a neuron should or should not fire. As we have seen, such transfer, if it is possible, involves no transfer of energy.

Body-splitting's greatest challenge is instead the *problem of duplication*—the same problem faced by many of the other views discussed in this book. Suppose that your ongoing life processes activated two different bodies in the other dimension. Then your life would continue in each one. But neither of them has any greater claim on being the continuation of your body. Thus neither can be the continuation of your body. Your life could even continue in two different bodies in two different dimensions or even in many different bodies in many different dimensions.

Suppose that the life processes of your body at death do only continue in one body in one other dimension. That body, we think, must be your continuing body. But if your life processes happened to also continue in another body, then neither body could be your continuing body. Thus, whether or not your body continues as a body in another dimension depends on whether or not there is another body that has a better or equal claim to being your continuing body. But a thing's identity, as

6. Corcoran, "Constitution View of Persons," 167, and *Rethinking Human Nature*, 132–33.

we saw in chapter 5, cannot depend on whether or not some other thing happens to exist.

Perhaps living processes can't split. Perhaps they must go with one body or another, but not both. But it is hard to see why that must be so. Perhaps Body-Splitting needs to be combined with a view of the self that is immune to splitting. Corcoran's choice, Self-as-First-Person-Perspective, might qualify.

Soul Storage

The Bible seems to teach that death is real and bad. But if body-morphing, body-splitting, and body-hopping are true, then death is neither real nor bad. The Bible also teaches that our hope for life after death depends on the resurrection of the body. But, according to these views, we have bodies before the resurrection of the body. We can see, hear, and touch. We can see the faces of the dearly departed we have missed. We can still feel the pleasure of the gentle breezes of subspace. Body-morphing and body-splitting also suggest that we have *numerically the same* bodies between death and resurrection as we do before death and after resurrection. That seems to take the resurrection out of resurrection. How can the body be raised from the dead when it never in fact died?

Ghostly and chrysalide bodies give death some sting. Ghostly bodies are limited and insubstantial. Who wants the dimmed vision and dull pleasure of a ghost? Better a lowly janitor at Hogwart's School of Magic than the ghost of Moaning Myrtle. Ghosts look forward to once again seeing fifty shades of blue and feeling the full warmth of a hug. Chrysalide bodies are more substantial than ghostly bodies but they are also more limited. They may be made of carbon. But a person with them will have a more minimal consciousness than those with ghostly bodies. In one sense, the caterpillar dies when it becomes a chrysalis. So too with us if we were to have the human equivalent of a chrysalis body. Even though we may yet live with these bodies and not truly die, we are still much worse off than we were before. Ghosts and chrysalides have good reason to long for resurrection.

Yet, for biblical reasons, it would be nice to have a kind of bodily interim existence that more closely approximates a cessation of our existence. Body-snatching is a death of sorts, but only in the way that a person is killed when cryogenically frozen. The person's body continues to exist in the meantime, waiting to be revivified. Can Slipstream involve an option more akin to death? It can—in the heavenly equivalent of a hard drive.

Suppose that another dimension contains physical storage units capable of storing whatever it is that makes us us. Perhaps they are part of an infinitely complex other-dimensional hard drive specially made by God. If the essence of who we are is like a software program or an information-bearing pattern, then God could take our programs or patterns from our dying bodies and store them in this heavenly hard drive via information transfer as in the body-hopping option. But, unlike body-hopping, they are stored in something like a computer rather than an animate body. Eventually they will be transferred into new resurrected bodies. Presumably, our patterns or our programs would be unconscious during this time. In this, Soul Storage resembles Soul Sleep, except that here, the "soul," understood as program or pattern, exists in something like a computer rather than on its own.

God could store multiple copies of our programs or our patterns on his heavenly hard drive, making Soul Storage also vulnerable to the *problem of duplication*. An omnipotent God wouldn't need to make multiple copies, since he could guarantee that the hard drive would never lose its memory. But, as we have seen before, that God *could* make other copies is enough to question this option. Here, too, our programs or our patterns would need something that makes them intrinsically incapable of duplication.

Soul Storage could also benefit Self-as-Ensouled-Body. That view holds that the self is both soul and body. The soul alone is not the self, for it is the self's underlying pattern. One of the main objections to this view is that it seems incoherent for the soul, as an organizing pattern interwoven with its body, to exist apart from that body between death and resurrection. Body-snatching, body-morphing, and body-splitting solve this problem by giving the soul a body between death and resurrection, or rather by making it possible for our *current* bodies to continue after death in a transformed and truncated state. But then the person does not really die and resurrection is less a conquering of death. Soul Storage makes it possible for the person to really die and for her essential pattern to survive death without existing on its own. God stores the pattern in his hard drive. But the person really dies since her body does not continue.

Many proponents of Self-as-Ensouled-Body would argue that a structure cannot be stored in something material that it is not structuring.

So the soul cannot be in some material that it is not organizing. But why not? A song is a structure that shapes a material medium such as air into sound waves. Yet it can be stored in CDs, cassettes, and computers. There its pattern remains inert, waiting to again make sound waves when someone presses play. The song itself does not exist when stored. But its pattern does. The song only exists when it is making sound waves. Likewise, God can store the soul in silicon that it does not structure. There it waits to again shape carbon when God presses play. Then the person will be resurrected.

Consider the holodeck from *Star Trek*. It is a virtual space where three-dimensional life-like objects are created from photons. Some of these objects are characters, made to look and act like persons. But in one episode, one of them, Moriarty, becomes conscious. Like all holodeck objects, his pattern is stored in the holodeck computer. That way, his pattern is preserved when his character is deactivated. When reactivated, the computer uses his pattern to again shape photons into his body. The pattern is the same, whether it is shaping protons or stored in silicon and not shaping anything. Moriarty exists when his photonic body exists, ceases to exist when his body is deactivated, and exists again when his body is reactivated. He remains *numerically the same* Moriarty when reactivated because his pattern continued to exist when he was deactivated. The major difference between us and Moriarty is that our patterns themselves actively structure our bodies, whereas the computer uses Moriarty's pattern to actively shape Moriarty's body. Even so, Moriarty shows how it might be possible for our patterns to be similarly stored.

Interestingly, Moriarty's pattern gains consciousness while stored in the holodeck computer. If we can grant that, then perhaps we can also grant that our patterns could gain consciousness in God's heavenly hard drive. Those who believe that the self is an ensouled-body tend to want the soul to be conscious between death and resurrection. But persons, not patterns, are conscious. An omnipotent God could, however, conceivably create a storage device that was complex enough to allow a minimal dream-like consciousness to emerge from a stored pattern. It might be just enough for the person's pattern to be peacefully aware of God's presence and what its loved ones on earth are up to. God could even splice some actual neurons into that device. The pattern would not itself be structuring the neurons and the wires, but it would be connected with them enough to have at least some awareness. This solution does not necessarily reduce consciousness to the mesh of neurons and circuits in the hard drive. It does not require that there is nothing that it is like to be that pattern from the inside. It does, however, require that a quasi-person, and thus a quasi-person's consciousness, can somehow emerge out of a stored pattern.

Immediate Resurrection

At this point, you may wonder, why wait? If we can skip dimensions, then why can't we skip right into the resurrection when we die? Enough of ghostly bodies, subspace tunnels, and heavenly hard drives. Whether snatched, morphed, split, or bumped, our bodies could be immediately resurrected in another intersecting dimension right when we die. We could get to heaven in a heartbeat.

So God is a body-snatcher. Then take our brains and put them in newly resurrected bodies right away. So our souls can shape new matter. Then let them shape heaven's matter right away. Why not go straight from a caterpillar to a butterfly? So God is a body-splitter. Then split the body right into heaven. Let life's causal chain flow directly into resurrection. So our souls can hop. Then let them hop right into heaven. Why would a good God make us wait around as ghosts when he could resurrect us right away?

An immediate hop to heaven though would seem to place the resurrection in another dimension rather than at the end of the history of this one. It seems to mean giving up the traditional Christian belief in the *general resurrection*. Chapter 9 discussed the possibility of folding time and space to make it possible for us to be raised immediately into the *general resurrection* at the end of history. So why not fold time and space so we can hop, morph, or split directly there?

The folding of time and space is great for science fiction. But it may be meaningless techno-babble. If it is logically impossible, then not even God can do it. In which case, we will need a route to the resurrection. Slipstream provides it.

Immediate resurrection via snatching, hopping, morphing, or splitting also removes the gap between death and resurrection. If we are immediately raised, then we continue without interruption. There is no moment in time at which we either cease to exist or experience a diminished or truncated existence. We would not die in any respect. Death would no longer have its biblical sting and resurrection would look more like reincarnation or rebirth.

Finally, the folding of time and space would diverge from the traditional Christian understanding of death, resurrection, and the *interim state*. Many biblical passages also seem to suggest an *interim state*. Slipstream provides a way to hold on to the traditional Christian understanding of those biblical passages.

This chapter has covered different ways to slip into slipstream to solve the problem of how we can have a personal afterlife. There probably are more ways. It is worth letting our imaginations roam about. Who knows what we might think of? Science fiction, it turns out, is a boon to Christianity.

So far, this book has covered five main options and their variations for how to get from death to resurrection. Many of them square with Scripture, science, and philosophy, although some better than others. Does it make a difference which one you choose? It does. The last section of the book explains the difference.

Processing the Puzzle: Implications of the Five Options for the Here and Now

12

Dealing with Death: Remembering the Dead and Preparing for Death

My mother's Christmas tree is a memorial to the dead. On it are ornaments specially chosen to represent family and friends that have died. It started with an ornament for my father who died when I was twelve. He got a rainbow with an angel sitting on it. Others followed. Sadly, we had to add a new ornament to the tree this year. It was an ornament for my uncle who died in his early sixties. It is an Almond Joy. The Almond Joy expressed how, as a boy, he always concluded the family prayer with "Amen-d Joy." Every year, my mother gathers her now-grown-up kids together for an ornament hanging ceremony. Each ornament is hung as a reminder that the dead are there with us, watching over us, waiting for us to join them in heaven.

The idea that the dead are watching over us is widely held. But some views of death and resurrection rule it out. This chapter explores the implications of the five views of death and resurrection for how to remember and speak about the dead, how to handle their bodies, and how to approach our own deaths.

The Communion of the Saints

Most Christians throughout history believed that the dead in Christ are watching over us and that the living enjoy a kind of fellowship with them. This idea is called *The Communion of the Saints* and is in the Apostle's Creed.

The Communion of the Saints is important for Catholics, because important Catholic practices depend on it. What use is praying for the dead if they are asleep or nonexistent? What use is praying to the saints if they are asleep or nonexistent? This idea is also important for many Protestants too, who take comfort in the belief that their deceased loved ones are watching over them and maybe even praying for them.

Whether or not we believe that we have communion with the dead also changes the nature of ceremonies that involve the dead, such as funerals and All Saint's and All Soul's Day remembrances. Every year, churches light candles on All Soul's Day to remember those that have died in the church. But how do we understand this ceremony? Do we believe that the dead we are remembering are present with us so that they are aware of the ceremony and perhaps in special communion with us during it? Or should we be careful to exclude from the ceremony any mention of the dead being present with us? The same considerations apply to funerals. Should the ceremony incorporate the idea that the deceased is present too, with us in our grieving? Or should it focus only on his future resurrection from the dead and avoid any references to his currently being in heaven?

Latin American base communities will sometimes read aloud the names of the martyrs. Their members then cry out, "*Presente.*"[1] The practice implies that the martyrs are presently in existence and in communion with the living. If they are not, then this practice will need to be abandoned or reinterpreted to mean that the martyrs are present only in our memories.

Such beliefs depend on the existence of the *interim state*—a state in which the dead exist between death and resurrection. The Catholic doctrine of purgatory, in which some of the dead are purified of their sins before entering heaven, also depends on the existence of the *interim state*. Of the five main views discussed in this book, Soul-Flight provides the simplest explanation for this state. The soul parts from the body and exists in the *interim state* until the resurrection of the body. Since the person is her soul, she exists and is conscious in this Interim. She is fully aware of what we are doing now. Perhaps she is in purgatory. Then, our prayers can help her soul be cleansed of its sins. The saints also exist as souls separated from their bodies during this Interim. So we can pray to them and they can pray for us.

But the soul needs to be awake during the *interim state* for this to work. Soul-sleep keeps the soul in existence. But it does not keep it

---

1. Moltmann, "Is There Life after Death?," 254.

dealing with death: remembering the dead and preparing for death

awake. It therefore denies any understanding of the *Communion of the Saints* which requires that the dead be consciously in communion with us. A sleeping soul cannot know about the hanging of its Christmas Tree decoration.

All Slipstream views support an *interim state*. But some, such as body-snatching, body-morphing, and Soul Storage, may deny consciousness to the dead in that state. Slipstream views that do allow consciousness during the interim, however, require us to reimagine the way in which the dead are present with us. They are not present as disembodied spirits "hovering" in our midst. Instead, they exist bodily in another dimension. We might also imagine some of our ceremonies creating special meeting places between the two dimensions allowing the dead to somehow be present in our dimension at least temporarily. Perhaps somewhat like the way that many Christians believe that Christ's body becomes present in the communion bread—as a physical presence that we cannot sense.

Re-formation can also support the *Communion of the Saints*. Aquinas, for example, believed that the soul, the body's organizing pattern, exists separate from the body between death and resurrection. Thanks to God's help, it is aware of some of what happens on earth. But we have seen how he has a hard time explaining how the soul, as an organizing pattern, can have consciousness without its body. In any case, Aquinas himself believes that the disembodied soul can only think abstract thoughts. It cannot remember the faces of those it loved on earth. It seems that, to be consistent, Aquinas cannot claim that the disembodied soul knows much of what happens on earth. The *Communion of the Saints* would be limited, at best.

Aquinas also believes that the soul is not the person. It is only part of the person. So he does not think that an organizing pattern can be a person. We do not then commune with the dead themselves in heaven. We instead commune with their souls. We pray for Susan's *soul* in purgatory and not for Susan herself. We pray to St. Simon's soul, but not to St. Simon himself. We believe that dad's soul is present when we hang the ornament, but not dad himself. We may say that we pray for Susan. But we are using synecdoche, the kind in which we use the term that applies to the whole when we really mean just a part of that whole.

As we saw in chapter 10, it may be more helpful for the Re-formation view to think of personhood as something that comes in degrees. The disembodied soul is a diminished person rather than a part of a person. Full personhood requires embodiment. But the soul by itself is partly that person, unlike a severed arm that was once part of the person but is no longer partly that person. The disembodied soul can be conscious because it is still partly a person. When we pray for Susan, we pray to a diminished Susan. When we pray to Simon, we pray to a diminished Simon. A diminished dad is present when we hang the ornament.

Re-formation requires that the deceased have a reduced consciousness. They are at peace. They do not suffer. They are with God. But their thoughts and desires are abstract, lacking emotions, sense perceptions, memories, and images. We look on them longingly because we desire to be with God and no longer suffer. But they also look on us longingly, though without emotion. They desire to once again feel joy, remember moonlit walks, listen to Bach, smell mint, and see our faces. We have pain and also vitality. They have peace but lack vim. Re-formation supports the *Communion of the Saints*, but changes the typical understanding of it.

Reassembly and Re-creation, however, must reject the *interim state*. For both, we do not exist between death and resurrection. There can be no *Communion of the Saints*.

Yet Re-creation can preserve something of it, but not in the way we normally think of it. Some Re-creationists believe that we are immediately resurrected into heaven, conceived as a separate dimension. That would mean that the dead currently do exist, but as already resurrected. It also means that they are alive as much as we are, only somewhere else. If so, then the *Communion of Saints* is no longer a communion between the living and the dead, or unraised, but a communion between those who live on earth and those who live in the material heavenly dimension. *Immediate resurrection* also rules out purgatory and the practice of praying for the dead, at least as we usually think of it. They do not need help in reaching their goal because they have already reached it. One might, however, pray instead, as N. T. Wright suggests, that they may be more fully "filled with God's joy and peace."[2]

Re-creation also rules out the distinction between All Saint's Day and All Soul's Day. All Saint's Day, celebrated on November 1, remembers the dead who either skipped purgatory or passed beyond it to attain the vision of God in paradise. All Soul's Day, celebrated on November 2, remembers all the departed, including those still in purgatory. Catholics and some Anglicans make this distinction. Re-creation erases this distinction and is thus unlikely to appeal to Catholics and some Anglicans.

---

2. Wright, *For All the Saints?*, 39–40.

Re-creationists might also adopt the time-warp option discussed in chapter 9. According to it, the dead are immediately raised at the *general resurrection*, which is at the end of the history of this dimension. But that means that we are resurrected at the same time as those who died before us. This could establish a communion between us and those who have already died, but that communion is also between our pre and post-resurrection selves. Dad is watching the hanging of his ornament. But my own resurrected self is watching too, standing right next to him. That is neither how we usually think of it nor perhaps how we wish to think of it. Nor is it how Christians have historically thought of it. But that is what the time-warp option entails.

Each of the five options, with the exception of Reassembly, can accommodate something of the *Communion of the Saints*. But some of them require altering our conception of it, perhaps more than some would like.

Burial or Cremation?

We spread my father's ashes in a lake high in California's Sierra Nevada Mountains. We did this because he wished it. We gathered with family and friends and took scoopfuls of the ashes and poured them in the lake. It was a beautiful moment, even for a boy of twelve as I was then. But it was not a traditional moment. Christians, throughout history, have tended to bury their dead, preferably in coffins.

There is good reason to reevaluate the practice of burying the dead. Burial takes up a lot of space and space is running out. It also harms the environment since it uses many harmful chemicals. It is also more expensive than cremation. But can a consistently Christian theology support cremation?

Each of the five views on death and resurrection can support either burial or cremation. But each view makes a difference in how we understand them. Some views also more naturally support one or the other.

Reassembly, for example, naturally supports burial. If we are our bodies and if we need these same bodies back at the resurrection, then what we do with the corpse matters. On this view, the very body that is laid in the grave will rise up out of it when Jesus returns. We ought then to bury the body so that it will be there when Jesus returns. Cremation destroys the very body that will rise again.

Most Christians throughout history who believed in Reassembly knew that the corpse will likely decompose before Christ's return. But they believed that God can collect whatever particles made up our corpse at death and put them back together again at the resurrection. The point of burial for them is more symbolic than necessary. It honors the person by honoring the body that that person is or has. It reminds the living that that same body will rise again. Cremation dishonors the person by destroying her body, suggesting perhaps that her body need not rise again. Reassembly therefore does not require burial, but it fits it well.

On the other end of the spectrum are those views which suggest that it does not matter what we do with the corpse. If Soul-Flight is true, then the body has little to no bearing on our identities. No hermit crab worries about what has happened to its previous shell. Many modern Christians hold this view. Yet many of them still insist on burying their dead.

Soul-Flight does not rule out burial. But it does change the way we look at it. Burial becomes not so much an honoring of the dead as a comforting of the living. But today, the most consistent option for Soul-Flight would be to choose the cheapest and easiest means of disposal. It logically leads to cremation. The burning of the body perfectly symbolizes the idea that this body is not our home—that the body is like the eggshell that needs to be cracked so that the chick can move into a fuller life.

None of the other views place as much emphasis on burial as Reassembly. But those that require the resurrected body to be similar to the original body may appreciate the symbolic value of burial. The body's particles may not be crucial to identity. But its appearance is. Burial preserves the body's face and fingerprints, at least temporarily, as a reminder of their importance to the deceased's identity. The Emergent form of Soul-Flight, Re-formation, and many Re-Creation and Slipstream views require some similarity between the original and the resurrected bodies. But many Slipstream views, such as body-snatching, body-morphing, and body-splitting, do not believe that the corpse is the person's body. Body-snatching does not believe that it was ever the person's body, since it is a fake. These Slipstream views may de-emphasize burial, and body-snatching, like Soul-Flight, has good reasons to reject it.

Each of the five views and their variations can also support cremation, although for different reasons. Soul-Flight may support it as symbolic of the *unimportance* of our bodies to our identities. But the other views can support cremation as an expression of the *importance* of our bodies to our identities. But how does that work, given that cremation destroys our bodies?

It all depends on the story that we tell, as can be seen in our attitudes toward compost. Some view compost as rot and as a convenient means to dispose of waste. But others view compost as a beautiful expression of the transformation of orange peels into healthy summer soil. Compost also symbolizes the interconnections between plants, soil, worms, and microorganisms.

We can similarly view cremation as an expression of the interconnection between our bodies and the earth. Our bodies are part of the earth and belong to it. Cremation symbolizes that belonging by reducing our bodies to ashes that can then provide nutrients for the earth. We are a part of the earth insofar as we are our bodies. We need the earth insofar as we need our bodies. Reassembly, Re-formation, and some Slipstream views can support cremation insofar as it expresses that we are our bodies and are therefore part of the earth. Re-creation and other Slipstream views can support cremation insofar as it expresses our need for our bodies and therefore our need for the earth.

Chapter 3 suggested that the Old Testament understands the person holistically and relationally, as an integrated whole that is in relationship with others. The body represents the dimension of a person's existence whereby she relates to the physical world, thus making her relationship to the physical world an important component of who she is. If cremation symbolizes our connection to the earth, then it expresses a biblical understanding of who we are. We can have good theological reasons to spread ashes in gardens, streams, and forests. My family's ceremonial spreading of my father's ashes in Huntington Lake is a practice amenable to a Christian interpretation.

According to Reassembly, our very ashes will be restored in our resurrected bodies. The journey of those ashes through lakes and streams and fish and bears and forests and fruits and flowers is the journey of the very particles that will make us up in the resurrection. In a sense, my father became one with the lake, at least for a while. Medieval Christians treasured the relics of the saints because they believed that their very bones would rise again as a necessary component of the resurrected saint. Cremation with a Reassembly spin makes lakes and streams and forests into something like relics, perhaps worthy of some of the veneration once given to bones.

Non-reassembly views hold that God does not need to form our resurrected bodies from our ashes. Yet they may still hold that God will choose to form them from the ashes of the earth as an expression of our oneness with it. Some sense must be made of Jesus's resurrected body as consisting of the matter his body had when he died. Perhaps it makes the theological point that our own resurrected bodies will come from the matter of this earth.[3] In which case, the whole earth is the garden from which the dead will sprout, even though they may not sprout from the "seeds" that were their original bodies. Veneration extends to the whole garden and not just to the "seeds" and the lakes and fields where they were planted. Non-reassembly views can also interpret cremation as a symbol of the linking of the destinies of the self and the earth.

Suppose you still feel that cremation does not properly respect the body. You are also concerned that cremation has an environmental impact, since it involves energy and the emission of carbon into the air. Yet you are concerned about the greater expense and environmental impact of modern burial. You have another option. You can choose what most Christians have done through history. You can bury the dead with decomposable wooden caskets and use no chemicals on the body or the wood. There is a growing progressive movement called "Green burial" which advocates for this traditional practice. This option balances both burial's honoring of the importance of the body to personal identity and cremation's emphasis on the interconnections of our bodies and the earth, while minimizing any environmental damage.

Approaching Death

The five views also have implications for how we approach death. Oscar Cullmann, a twentieth-century biblical scholar, is well-known for contrasting the different ways in which Socrates and Jesus approached death.[4] Socrates, he says, represents the unbiblical Greek approach, while Jesus represents the biblical Hebrew approach.

Socrates faced death calmly. He showed no terror or fear. Why? Because he believed that death was just a transition. At death, the soul, the true self, is finally freed from the body and able to transition to a happier heavenly existence. Death is therefore friend, not enemy. Much in

---

3. See Polkinghorne, *Quarks, Chaos and Christianity*, 112.
4. Cullmann, *Immortality of the Soul or Resurrection of the Dead?*, 19–27.

dealing with death: remembering the dead and preparing for death

the Christian tradition agrees. Death is the transition to heaven. It is the end of bodily suffering and a release from this painful sometimes hellish world. St. Francis spoke of "Sister Bodily Death" in his famous "Canticle of Brother Sun."[5]

Jesus, on the other hand, faced death with a great deal of anxiety. He sweat blood. He prayed to the Father that "this cup could pass from him" (Matt 26:39), that he would not have to die. Why? Because for a good Hebrew, argues Cullmann, we are our bodies. Death is the destruction of our bodies and therefore the destruction of our selves. It is enemy, not friend. It destroys life. It severs relationships as we can no longer be physically present with those who die. Paul stated that "death is the last enemy" (1 Cor 15:26).

The circumstances of Jesus's and Socrates's deaths are different. We can only read so much into the different ways in which they faced death. Socrates knew that he would die by drinking hemlock, a relatively pain-free and quick form of death. Jesus knew that he would die by crucifixion, a painful drawn-out miserable way to die. Socrates was around seventy when he died. Jesus was thirty-three. Almost anyone would wish to skip the torture and early death that Jesus faced. For some, that Jesus showed such anxiety is a testimony to the incarnation—that Jesus is fully God *and fully human*.

We all must choose how to face our deaths. Do we approach it as friend or as enemy? Do we embrace it or do we fear it? Do we wish its coming or do we resist it? The five views have different implications.

But none of these views see death as only an enemy to be feared, since they all affirm an afterlife. They all hold that after death comes resurrection. So death is a transition. But it is not a natural or welcome transition for those who view death as an enemy. It is a violent disruption of God's intentions for the good of his creation and for our own individual goods. Life is good and death destroys it. To such views, death is an enemy we would prefer to avoid. But we need not fear it because Christ has conquered it. God has brought great good out of something inherently evil. So the difference is not so much whether or not death is feared. The difference is whether or not death is welcomed.

Death is no enemy for Soul-Flight. It might even be a friend. The adherent of Soul-Flight, like Socrates, faces death calmly and happily. For some, death might even be more a cause for celebration than for mourning.

---

5. St. Francis of Assisi, "Canticle of Brother Sun," 39.

Some versions of Slipstream also look on death more kindly. If the person fully survives the transition into Slipstream, with all selfhood intact, then the person never really died. Her very life processes continue on in both body-splitting and the "caterpillar-to-butterfly" version of body-morphing. For the latter, death may be a natural transition rather than a violent destruction of life. Does the caterpillar view the chrysalis as enemy?

According to Reassembly and Re-creation, we completely and totally die. Death is indeed an enemy. Preparing for death is more like preparing for falling off a cliff even though you know you will eventually fully recover from it and even become more vigorous than you were before. You do not wish to go through with it and would avoid it if you could, but you at least have the comfort that things will be better on the other side. The funeral is cause for mourning, not celebration.

Re-formation and some versions of Slipstream combine elements of them both. According to Re-formation, either only a part of the person survives death or only a diminished version of the person survives death. According to the former, the person dies completely, but at least a part of her survives. According to the latter, she both does and does not survive death. So this view lends itself to viewing death as both friend and enemy. On the one hand, something of the self continues through the transition. On the other hand, death does destroy personhood. But not completely. An Aquinas faces death as both a Socrates and a Jesus.

Similarly some of the Slipstream views hold to a diminished view of the person between death and resurrection. To them, the bodily being that journeys through the Slipstream is more like a shadow of the person than the full and complete person. The result also makes death both friend and enemy. Death is indeed an enemy if it makes you into a ghost. But being a ghost is still better than being nothing at all. It is also better than having your "soul" stored in a heavenly hard drive. Soul Storage still sees some friend in death since one's pattern survives. But it sees more enemy in death than other Slipstream views since it holds that the person really dies. Slipstream views view death as less violent than Re-formation, since they involve some kind of bodily survival, but they still view death as violent. Re-formation and Slipstream are your best bets if you neither welcome nor fight death and if you view funerals as cause for both mourning and celebration.

This chapter explored the implications of the five views for how we deal with death. The next chapter explores their implications for whether and how we might communicate with the dead.

13

Near-Death Experiences, Ghosts, and Speaking with the Dead

PAM REYNOLDS HAD AN operation at the age of thirty-five. The surgeons stopped her heart. Her brain functions ceased. She then felt herself leave her body and saw the operating room as if from above. She saw the surgeon holding an electronic instrument. She heard a female voice worrying about the small size of her blood vessels. She had the impression they were operating on her groin, which was unexpected given that it was a brain surgery. Then, she felt that she was in a tunnel moving toward a light. When she got to the light, she saw her deceased relatives and friends. But her deceased uncle said she needed to return to her body. So she did. She came to. She learned that the surgeon was using an electronic saw to open her skull. They were indeed concerned about her small blood vessels. And they did operate on her groin since they needed to send a catheter through her groin to her heart. The surgeons were baffled by her account.[1]

Pam's story is not unique. Many have had similar experiences. Common to them is a meeting with lost loved ones. But what are we to make of stories like these?

The last chapter explored the question of whether we ought to think of the dead as alive in heaven and perhaps also "present" with us. But can they also communicate with us before we have completely left this life? Is it possible for Pam's uncle to have really met her at the light at the end of the tunnel? Is it possible for mediums to convey messages to us from our long-lost aunts? Is it possible for us to see our grandmother's ghost? This chapter explores how our understandings of death and resurrection bear on whether or not it is possible to speak with the dead.

---

1. Bartholomew, "After Life," 124. Also see Evans, *Is God Still at the Bedside?*, 46.

Experiences of speaking with the dead, whether real or not, are often profound and meaningful. They bring emotional comfort. They turn sinners into saints. They transform values, making God and others more important than possessions and fame. It is therefore worthwhile to consider which views of death and resurrection are compatible with these experiences.

Our take on these experiences must not contradict our views on death and resurrection. If we wish to affirm these experiences as real, then we need a view of the afterlife that fits them. Otherwise, our views do not make sense and skeptics are right to challenge them.

Near-Death Experiences

Pam's story is an example of what is called a *near-death experience*. We do not know whether these experiences are before, at, or after death. We do not, for that matter, know when death occurs. Is it when the heart or the brain stops or when there is no longer any possibility of revitalization? On some accounts, *near-death experiences* occur before all brain activity ceases. On other accounts, they occur after all brain activity ceases. If death occurs when the brain stops then *near-death experiences* may happen after death. But if death is the point at which there is no longer any possibility of revitalization, then *near-death experiences* happen before death.

Near-death experiences involve two distinct phases. Sometimes they involve both. Sometimes they involve only one. In the first phase, the patient has the sensation of leaving her body and then looking down on her body and its locale as if from above. While "disembodied," she can see and hear, as Pam saw the surgeon and his saw and heard a nurse speaking. Sometimes, the patient sees and hears what she could not have known before. In one case, a man experienced leaving his body and seeing and listening into a neighboring room where relatives were praying for him. After he was revived, he accurately recounted the prayers that were said and that a pastor had arrived in the middle of them.[2]

In the second phase, the patient experiences going to another place altogether. Almost always, the patient feels as if she, like Pam, is in a tunnel heading toward a bright light. She feels profoundly serene and joyful. She then meets deceased loved ones who tell her she needs to return to earth. In one case, a man met an acquaintance whom he thought was still

---

2. Cooper, *Body, Soul, and Life Everlasting*, 232–33.

alive. But it turns out that his acquaintance had actually died a day earlier thousands of miles away. Many others have similarly reported meeting relatives and acquaintances whom they did not know had already died.

These views, on the face of it, support Soul-Flight. The patient leaves her body because she is her soul and her soul can leave her body. She goes to heaven and meets the souls of her other loved ones who have already died and left their bodies.

Yet she "sees" and "hears" what is happening around her dead body. If real, *near-death experiences* not only support the soul's existence but also the soul's ability to perceive while separate from the body. That claim, as discussed in chapter 6, is hard to sustain. How can a soul look at its dead body "from above" if it is not a physical object in space? As a purely immaterial being, it can have no "angle of vision" into the physical world. The soul also sees its loved ones in heaven. But if they are souls, then they are invisible and cannot be seen. Perhaps instead the soul, in encountering the deceased loved ones, perceives remembered images of their bodies. Yet that is not how the patients experienced it. So Soul-Flight still has difficulty explaining *near-death experiences*.

How do the other options fare? *Near-Death experiences* are incompatible with Soul Sleep, Re-creation, Reassembly, and *immediate resurrection*. These options allow no conscious experiences between death and resurrection.

Immediate resurrection might work if the *near-death experience* is an experience of the resurrection itself. But that would radically alter the traditional understanding of resurrection. Resurrected bodies are permanent and incapable of death. But if the person returned back to her earthly body when it was revivified, then her resurrected body would have had to die when she left it.

Re-formation may be able to support *near-death experiences* since it agrees with Soul-Flight that the soul separates from the body at death. But it also holds that the soul is not the whole person. So the soul, not the patient, has the *near-death experience* where she meets only the souls of her deceased loved ones. She remembers it as her experience when she revives, because she then makes her own whatever it is that her soul experienced. But, according to Re-formation, the soul cannot have actually seen or heard anything. Nor could it have felt any emotion. The person, when revived, would have reinterpreted her *near-death experience* as involving sights and sounds, when in reality her soul had gathered information about what was happening through some other means, such as, for example, mental telepathy. She would have reinterpreted her soul's encounter with her loved ones in terms of seeing their bodies, when in reality it had not. She would have reinterpreted her soul's clarity of mind in heaven as a feeling of peace, when in reality it was not a feeling at all. Such reinterpretations would be the only way she could make sense of her *near-death experience* once back in her body and brain.

Slipstream fares better. According to some of its versions, we survive our deaths by having ghostly bodies in some other dimension. The patient could see her body in the hospital in this dimension with the eyes of her ghostly body. She can see her deceased loved ones because she sees their ghostly bodies. The tunnel she experiences might even be a slipstream tunnel to heaven.

But, according to some Slipstream views, your body also slips into slipstream. The body you leave behind is the corpse that was once your body, but your real body continues in ghostly form. But how can that be if your corpse is not yet a corpse—if you are only "mostly dead" like Wesley in *The Princess Bride*? If the body on the operating table is not yet completely dead, then it, and not your ghostly body, should be your real body. Your real body cannot enter another dimension until the body left behind is completely dead and thus no longer has the greater claim to being your real body. For these views, a *near-death experience* cannot be real if it happens before complete and total death, which it does if death is defined as that moment at which revivification is no longer possible. Thus, Slipstream is the best option for taking near-death experiences at face value, as long as it does not require that the dimensional body be a continuation of the original body.

Most views, therefore, do not easily accommodate *near-death experiences*. But they can if these experiences happen in the dying person's brain instead of in some other heavenly dimension. Perhaps God gives the dying person a vision of meeting with loved ones and a sense of peace. This would satisfy both neuroscience and each of the views on death and resurrection. The cost is that they are no longer genuine experiences of the afterlife and cannot tell us anything about it.

Some take *near-death experiences* to be evidence for the soul's surviving the death of the body. They could also provide evidence for various Slipstream options and against views which are incompatible with *near-death experiences*. If we have good evidence for *near-death experiences* happening outside the brain, then we have good evidence for and against various views of death and resurrection. If we already experienced something of what would happen to us on our journey from the ship to the planet, then we would have a better idea of what button we should push to get us there.

But the evidence is mixed. Much of it is anecdotal, which is not generally very good evidence. Not everyone honestly reports their experiences. I suspect that most do. Even so, many unconsciously make mistakes in reporting them. Ask different people what happened when they saw the Pathfinder hit the Prius and you will hear conflicting answers. We tend to read our expectations and biases into events. That is why the best reporting will involve careful detective work using good scientific and/ or historical reasoning. We cannot easily apply that kind of reasoning to something as private as *near-death experiences*.

Many neuroscientists also claim to be able to explain some of the common features of *near-death experiences*. Deprive the brain of oxygen and the person experiences tunnel vision and floating feelings. No wonder that the patient experiences floating above her body and being in a tunnel as her brain is dying and losing oxygen. Drugs often used in trauma cases cause hallucinations. Stressed bodies, like those that are dying, produce endorphins which cause peaceful easy feelings. We should expect that extremely stressed brains will cause persons to have unusual experiences. According to one theory, our brains draw from our memories to construct images that seem real to us as a way of dealing with the stress of being near death. None of these more naturalist explanations prove that the person did not actually have an out-of-body experience. But they do show that we ought to be careful before concluding that they did.

But what about the patient's ability to know what could not otherwise have been known? The patient could have unconsciously picked up some of this information before going unconscious. We unconsciously absorb more than we realize from our surrounding environment. The patient could also have unconsciously picked up some of this information while unconscious. There is evidence that comatose persons can hear people talk. It is possible that Pam, for example, heard the nurse talk about her blood vessels with the very ears of her "mostly dead" body, even though those ears were taped shut. It is possible that she heard the surgeon's electronic instrument and constructed an image of it in her brain. Might it also be possible to hear, while unconscious, people praying in a neighboring room?

Coincidences are also bound to happen given large enough numbers of people. It could be a coincidence that the patient experienced meeting a deceased loved one whom he did not know was deceased. It could even be a coincidence that Pam thought she heard the nurse complain about her veins when the nurse in fact did. This is even less remarkable if we consider that Pam may have known from previous doctor visits that her veins were small. It could even be a coincidence that a patient knew what was prayed in a neighboring room, especially if he knew that such prayers follow a typical pattern. His seeing of the pastor's arrival could also be coincidence, especially since pastors typically arrive at deathbed scenes.

We need to know whether patients report such incidents to a greater degree than is statistically likely and if other unconscious influences have been ruled out. We also need to know how often patients get details wrong or how often they encounter loved ones who were not in fact deceased. We may only hear about the "amazing" cases, which bias our understanding of what is going on. We cannot accept such reports as offering strong evidence one way or the other until we have a more widespread systematic scientific study of such cases.

Finally, even if we could eliminate coincidence and unconscious influence, it does not mean that the person had an out-of-body experience. The person could have "seen" and "heard" through clairvoyance or "remote viewing." God, angels, demons, or other supernatural beings could also have caused the person to gain such information.

We really do not know at this point what to make of *near-death experiences*. Therefore, they cannot in themselves provide strong evidence for or against the different views of death and resurrection. In the meantime, we can make sure that our understandings of *near-death experiences* are consistent with our understandings of death and resurrection, whether in preaching, teaching, official church statements, or our own personal beliefs.

Mediums and Séances

Near-death experiences offer the possibility of speaking with the dead when one is near death. But could there be a way to speak with the dead in the prime of life? Many think so. Some claim to be in tune with the other world—like radios that pick up distant signals. They are called mediums.

King Saul once disguised himself to ask a medium to summon the prophet Samuel, who was dead. God considered it wrong for Saul to do this. Thus, Christians have traditionally believed it wrong to consult mediums. But do Christians believe it even *possible* to summon the dead?

Today, mediums are known for holding séances. In them, many people gather together and close their eyes. Then the medium speaks to them as if she were conveying messages from deceased family or friends. Mediums seem convincing because they sometimes say things that only family members would know. Only you and your deceased granny know about the key that is buried beneath the kitchen floor. So if the medium mentions the key, it seems she could only have known about it through speaking with your deceased granny. Séances were popular in the late nineteenth century. Even the creator of Sherlock Holmes, Sir Arthur Conan Doyle, was convinced that mediums could speak with the dead.

As with *near-death experiences*, our beliefs about mediums and séances must be consistent with our views on death and resurrection. Soul Sleep, Re-creation, and Reassembly rule them out. If the dead do not exist or are unconscious, then we cannot communicate with them.

Soul-Flight, Slipstream, and Re-formation allow it because they believe that the dead exist in the *interim state* and are conscious. According to Re-formation, however, the medium speaks with granny's soul and not with granny herself. Her soul may also have limited memories of her earthly life and limited awareness of what is happening on earth. Even if a medium could speak with the dead, she may not be able to get much information out of them. In which case, we would have no good reason to believe the medium really was communicating with the dead.

Immediate resurrection might permit communication with the dead. But the medium would be communicating with the already bodily resurrected person. The time-warp version of *immediate resurrection* might also permit it. But, according to it, we all immediately rise together at the same time. Your resurrected self could be standing right next to granny as you are communicating with her through the medium. For that matter, you could just as easily communicate with your future resurrected self through the medium. If you find that weird, then watch Star Trek, where things can get even weirder than Portland, Oregon. The question is whether we believe that weird can happen and, more importantly, whether weird can be biblically, scientifically, and philosophically sound.

If we had good reason to believe that mediums really do communicate with the dead, then we would have good reasons for choosing one of the views on death and resurrection that support it. But, at this point, we do not have good reason to believe that mediums really do. Many mediums are proven frauds. They gather information about clients through normal investigative means or by informal chatting prior to the séance.

They also make vague statements that clients can interpret as applying to them. James Randi, a well-known skeptic and magician, has issued a million-dollar challenge to anyone who can prove a paranormal claim.[3] No medium has met the challenge. That does not mean that no mediums are genuine, but it is cause for suspicion.

Ghosts

Ghosts work well in fiction and other dimensions. But do they work so well in our reality? Can the dead visit us as ghosts? Many have thought so. St. Augustine tells the story of St. Felix, who appeared after he had died to comfort the people of Nola while barbarians besieged them.[4] Aquinas, noting that story, argues that it is possible for the dead to appear to the living.[5] Many today continue to claim to have seen ghosts. Some try to find evidence of ghosts using video cameras, tape recorders, metal detectors, electromagnetic radiation detectors, and even coffee pots. So far I do not think they have found any.

Some views on death and resurrection support ghostly visits and some do not. Soul Sleep, Re-creation, and Reassembly do not. Slipstream most easily supports it because, according to many Slipstream views, the dead already have ghostly bodies. They need do nothing special to make their appearance here, except, of course, intersect with our dimension. Soul-Flight and Re-formation can possibly support ghosts, although, according to them, the dead do not have bodies. These views would have to explain how the dead can take on a ghostly appearance in our dimension. Perhaps they could temporarily shape the light and air of our dimension so that they appear as ghosts. Perhaps they take some other-dimensional matter into our dimension and use it to make their appearance. Such things may not even be scientifically possible.

Immediate resurrection might allow the dead to visit us, but not as ghosts. The dead would have to visit us with their already resurrected bodies. These bodies would be more earthly than airy and more human than ghostly. Jesus, after all, visited us with his resurrection body since he rose from the dead here on earth and not in some other dimension. But I

---

3. James Randi Educational Foundation Staff, "One Million Dollar Paranormal Challenge," line 2.

4. Augustine, *On the Care to Be Had for the Dead*, §19.

5. Aquinas, *Summa Theologica*, suppl. 69.3, 2820.

have not heard of anyone who claimed to see any other fully resurrected body here on earth.

If we could confirm ghost sightings, then we would have strong evidence for one of the above views that support ghostly visitations. But we have not confirmed any. We also have reason to suspect any ghost sightings. We humans have a tendency to see what is not there, and not only when we are hallucinating. We tend to see familiar patterns when confronted with something that reminds us of them. We are fooled into seeing Big Foot or the Loch Ness Monster. We sometimes find faces where they are not, such as the face of the Virgin Mary in a tortilla or the face of a man on Mars. We may do the same when we think we see a ghost. This does not mean that we did not see a ghost. But it does mean that we need to be careful before concluding that we did.

If you are inclined to believe that *near-death experiences*, mediums, and ghosts really do put us in touch with the dead, then you will want to choose Soul-Flight, Slipstream, or Re-formation. But, at this point, we cannot use *near-death experiences*, mediums, or ghosts as good evidence for these views.

14

Inward or Outward? On Saving, Healing, Caring, and Communing

You are now reading this book. You may be thinking that your view on death and resurrection will help when at a funeral, near death, or when you seem to see a ghost. But you may think that it has little to do with what you will do after you finish reading this book—with what you will do today, tonight, or tomorrow. Soul-Flight or Slipstream? Reassembly or Re-creation? No matter. So you plan to put the views aside and do something else. But these views have everything to do with that something else. This chapter shows why.

Each view on death and resurrection supports one or more views of the self. But none of them support every view of the self. Each view of the self can be placed on a continuum between identifying the self with something about us that is internal, private, and invisible and something about us that is external, public, and visible. One extreme views the self as solely something internal such as the soul and the other views the self as solely something external such as the body. If you think that you are something "inner," then you will tend to care more about your own "inner" life and the "inner" lives of others. If you think that you are something "outer," then you will tend to care more about your own "outer" life and the "outer" lives of others. Each view of the self naturally, but not necessarily, leads to a different degree of emphasis on these two kinds of lives. So does each view on death and resurrection insofar as it supports more external or internal views of the self.

We can wear many different sizes of pants, but only if we have a belt. Only one size fits naturally and needs no belt. Buy that size and your life is blissfully belt-less. You can believe that you are solely your soul while

inward or outward? on saving, healing, caring, and communing

preferring gardening to prayer. But the preference does not fit so well. Prefer the prayer and your preferences will better fit your beliefs.

Chapter 2 quoted a conversation between *Seinfeld* characters Jerry, George, and Elaine about how not to waste one's life. Elaine asks: "Is this a waste of time? What should we be doing? Can't you have coffee with people?"[1] Elaine and her friends are right that thinking about death helps one think better about how to live more fully. But they still have little to go on in thinking better about it. Beliefs about death and resurrection provide that help. They show us what we think ultimately matters about ourselves and others. Living life fully will mean spending our limited time and energy on cultivating and nurturing what we have thus discovered to matter most. This chapter explores some of the implications of our views on death, resurrection, and the self for how to live our lives.

Well-being. What does it mean to thrive, to flourish, to be well? If your self, the essence of who you are, is something internal, then well-being is primarily internal. Your thriving has to do with inner states of your mind or your heart, such as inner peace, happy feelings, or freedom from guilt. If your self is something external, then well-being is primarily external. Your thriving has to do with something physical and visible, like your body, and something public, like your relationships. Well-being is having good friendships, a thriving community, a healthy body, a life in touch with nature, and enriching bodily experiences like hiking through the Cascade Mountains, picking blueberries, or drinking pinot noir.

If you are something internal, then you will seek well-being by focusing on inner healing. First achieve inner peace and then outer peace will flow. First get your sins forgiven by God and then you will be better able to forgive the sins of others. Believe that your soul or your psyche is the key to your survival after death? Then it makes sense that your well-being primarily depends on the state of your soul or your psyche.

If you are something external, then you will seek well-being by focusing on healing your body and your relationships. Cultivate healthy communities and ecosystems and inner peace will follow. Get in touch with nature and some friends and a healthy mind will follow. Forgive the sins of others and you will find that you feel forgiven. An hour in the woods does more for the soul than an hour on the knees. Do you believe that the resurrection of your body is the key to your survival after death?

---

1. "Pony Remark," http://www.youtube.com/watch?v=AzMlbDCNkdQ.

If so, then it makes sense that your well-being primarily depends on the quality of your interactions with the world and other people.

Lifestyle. What is the best kind of life to live? If your essence is something internal, then the best kind of life is one focused on cultivating your inner life. Develop your heart and mind, through prayer, meditation, or study. Become a mystic, seeking oneness with God. Or become a scholar, devoted to learning as much as you can. Seek what Christians have traditionally called the contemplative life.

As for your body, treat it as a beast to tame. Discipline it so that it becomes more like the soul. Turn away from the pleasures of the senses—whether sex or pinot noir. Socrates said that we ought to spend our lives preparing for death.[2] Death, for him, was the soul's final release from the body. The best way to prepare for our future disembodied life was to live now as best we can as if we were disembodied. Study, meditate, and skip the pub.

Or treat your body like a disposable camera. Take whatever pictures with it that you will because you know that you will one day throw it in the trash. Since you are not your body, what happens to or in your body does not affect you. So indulge. Eat, drink, and be merry, for tomorrow you will be without your body.

If your essence is something external, then the outer life is best. The life of art, music, nature, hiking, gardening, yoga, and chatting like Jerry and Elaine at the coffee shop. The life of family, friends, and community. But the best life is not a life of indulgence. Eat, drink, and be merry, but in a way both pleasurable and health-giving. For you are your body, so your health means your body's health.

It might seem that introverts prefer the inner life and extroverts prefer the outer. But we are much more complex than that. Introverts are musicians, hikers, and gardeners. Introverts often thrive best in community. Extroverts are scholars and mystics too. Being an introvert is not a logical expression of belief that the self is inner in the way that being a contemplative might be. Being an introvert has more to do with being in the world in a quieter way than with withdrawing from the world.

You may, like me, think that the best life is the balanced one. *Both* inner *and* outer, not either/or. If that is your inclination, then it may lead you, in the end, to gravitate toward a view of self, death, and resurrection that combines them. If both body and soul or psyche are the

---

2. Plato, *Phaedo*, 64a, 12.

inward or outward? on saving, healing, caring, and communing 169

keys to our survival after death, then it makes sense to live well in both body and soul.

Experiencing God. How and where do we experience God? If you are soul and psyche, then soul or psyche is where you meet God. With head bowed and eyes shut—alone in prayer or meditation. Or you will encounter God through study—through reading the Bible or studying theology. The bread and wine of communion are reminders of the true experience of Christ, which takes place in your soul.

But if you are your body or deeply interwoven with it, then you meet God in your body and the world. You experience God in exploring a forest, planting a garden, playing the violin, or fellowshipping with friends. The bread and wine of communion are the very means by which you experience God.

Worship. If the self is inner, then worship is about the individual's inner states and her private relationship to God. Worship is about emotions and beliefs, feeling God's presence, and hearing the preaching of the Word. Hymns and choruses use "I" instead of "we," as in "*I* know whom *I* have believed" and "*I* believe in Jesus."

Rituals are at best symbolic of inner states and at worst distractions to be avoided. Communion is only a symbol of Christ's death for us. The important thing in baptism is what the baptizee *believes* when being baptized. Church buildings are best when uncluttered, stripped of all art and imagery. Just four walls, a podium, and pews. Souls without bodies.

If the self is outer, then worship is public and bodily. Worship is more about what we do together in praising and experiencing God and less about what we are feeling and thinking. It involves the body, with kneeling, standing, clapping, foot-washing, and maybe even dancing. Hymns and choruses use "we" instead of "I," as in "Now thank *we* all our God" and "They'll know *we* are Christians by our love."

Sacrament is more central than sermon. The bread and the wine are not just symbols. They convey God's spiritual gifts to us. They inspire, heal, rejuvenate, and cleanse. In baptism, God is cleansing us through the water.

Outer-oriented worship appeals to all the senses. From the sound of harp and drum to the smell of swinging incense, the taste of communion wine, and the beauty of the painting on the church wall. Take pleasure in them. In doing so, you also take pleasure in God who comes to you through them. Critics though may reply that all body and no soul results in gaudy buildings with gaudy art.

Salvation and Evangelism. If our true selves are our inner selves, then salvation is solely between the individual and God. You are saved if your internal states are right—if you, for example, *believe* that Jesus is God or if you *feel* that your sins are forgiven. Salvation is a matter of the inner self being right with God so that it can go to heaven after the body dies. Evangelism is about saving souls or psyches. It involves sharing the good news and preaching the Word. All else is a means to that end.

But if our true selves are our outer selves, then salvation involves our bodies too. The word "salvation" derives from the Latin word *salvus*, which means "safe" and "sound" and "well." From it comes the Latin word *salus*, which means "health." Salvation involves the healing of our bodies, which will come at their future resurrection. Evangelism involves giving bread and medicine for the purpose of healing bodies and not as a means to saving souls.

Salvation also has more to do with our relationships than our inner states. We are saved through reconciliation with God and with each other. Evangelism is about healing relationships and restoring and cultivating face-to-face community.

Care/Harm. How do we care for others? If the true self is the inner self, then we help others have the right beliefs and feelings. We preach, teach, hand out Bibles, and share the gospel. If the true self is the outer self, then we attend to bodily needs. We give food and drink. We provide shelter and medicine. Giving water bottles and blankets to hurricane victims is an end in itself and not a means to the end of helping them believe the gospel or feel God in their lives.

Our view of who we are also affects our understanding of what it means to be harmed. St. Augustine tells the story of his friend Alypius who attended a gladiatorial game in Rome. Alypius decided to close his eyes so that he would not be exposed to the violence on display. But the crowd roared when a gladiator was wounded. Alypius opened his eyes and saw the blood. It excited him and he became addicted to attending gladiatorial games. Augustine writes, "He was struck in the soul by a wound graver than the gladiatorial in his body, whose fall had caused the roar."[3] Augustine considered Alypius's wound greater than the gladiator's, because it wounded his *soul* rather than his body. If we are more closely identified with our souls, as Augustine believed we were, then what harms the soul harms us more than what harms our bodies. But

---

3. Augustine, *Confessions* 6.8, 101.

inward or outward? on saving, healing, caring, and communing

if we are more closely identified with our bodies then what harms the body harms us more. If we are an integration of psyche and body, then wounding the soul wounds the body and wounding the body wounds the soul. The gladiator's wound is also a psychic wound and Alypius's is also a bodily wound.

Our understanding of self also affects our understanding of how to treat wounds. If we are our souls, then bodily wounds are not important in themselves. We fix those wounds in the way that we would fix a broken shovel, as making repairs to a tool for the sake of the tool-user. The real healing work occurs within—in the transformation of hearts and minds. But if we are our bodies, then we treat bodies for their own sakes, as having their own dignity and worth. If instead we are a mixture of both soul and body, then we heal wounds by healing both mind and body. Bodies better heal when the mind is healed or healing. Believe that the medicine will ease the pain and it more likely will. Minds better heal when the body is healed or healing. Remove the pain, ease the mind. If the self is holistic, then medicine ought to also be holistic.

Suppose you believe that we are souls and not bodies and that therefore the state of the soul matters more than the state of the body. If you do, then you have a good *justification* for harming bodies to save souls. You may be tempted, as some medieval Christians were, to torture heretics to get them to *believe* the right things so that their souls could be saved. You may be tempted to force conversion at the end of a bayonet. You may also be tempted, as some modern Westerners have been, to kill the bodies of another country's soldiers and civilians to bring its people "enlightenment" and "freedom."

You may also be tempted to suicide. I mention this carefully. But the logic must be made clear so that we can deal with it. If the goal of life is to free one's soul from its bodily prison, then why not expedite the goal? If we are our souls and our bodies merely shells that we do not ultimately need, then why not be rid of them? Why not cast them aside like extra cars that are no longer needed? *Dualist* philosophers like Plato rejected suicide because it violated one's duty to the gods. Violation of duty harms the very soul one seeks to save. *Dualist* Christians also reject suicide because it violates God's commands and rejects the bodies that God has given to us. Most Christian *dualists* throughout history have never been extreme *dualists* who deny all importance to our bodies. They still view them as God's good creations. Gardeners, after all, appreciate their shovels. Thus, while *dualism* can suggest suicide, it does not necessarily do so, for there are reasons why it is ultimately harmful to both one's soul and the souls of others.

Dualism's downside is its tendency to support violence. But that downside is matched by an upside—an upside that many *dualists* point to as one of its greatest attractions. If we are souls, then we are beings that are more than just material machines, or even extremely complex organic creatures. We are also heavenly beings like God and the angels. We are also unique individuals. Every soul has its own unique personality that sets it apart from all others. Every person thus has an inherent and eternal dignity and worth. Every person is worthy of love and respect. No innocent person ought to be sacrificed for the betterment of society. Souls are safeguards against the denigration of individual persons.

Furthermore, *dualism* may bring comfort to those who suffer. Imagine a heretic being examined by a late medieval inquisitor. The inquisitor jabs a screw into the heretic's thumb and the heretic cries out, "You can harm my body but you can't harm *me*." Or imagine that your back throbs with pain. One way to cope with the pain is to repeat the mantra, "The pain is in my body, but it is not happening to *me*." Distancing one's self from the pain makes it easier to cope with it.

If, however, we are our bodies, then our pains truly wound *us*. Violence harms the *person* herself. Torture cannot save souls because it harms *persons*. War cannot spread "enlightenment," because it harms the very persons it aims to enlighten. Furthermore, if another person's body is destined for an eternity with God, then it has dignity. If the very body you see before you will be raised, then the very body you see before you is worthy of love and respect. Harming other bodies counteracts the very resurrection that God has planned for those bodies. If you are your body, then you have dignity also because your body has dignity. When combined with belief in resurrection, body-based views of the self can also grant us dignity and worth.

Praise/Blame. If we are identified with our souls or our psyches, then we might be more inclined to believe that we have free will. If we are just our bodies, then we might not. Whatever happens in our bodies would have to result from previous happenings in our bodies. The arm twitches because the muscles contract. The muscles contract because electro-chemical energy moves through the neurons. Our bodies function according to ongoing chains of cause and effect. But free will interjects energy or information into the chains from outside of them, thereby redirecting them. The arm raises because we, through our free

inward or outward? on saving, healing, caring, and communing

will, interjected energy or information into the chain of cause and effect that redirected it to cause the arm to raise instead of twitch. But where did that extra energy or information come from? No part of the body could have caused it without having been caused to do so by previous factors. Some part of us that transcends our bodies, such as our souls or minds, must have caused it. Belief in the soul therefore makes it easier to explain the source of our free will. Deny the soul and it is not clear where our free will comes from.

If we do not have free will, then we are not the cause of anything that we do. *I* did not cause my hand to grab the candy and walk out of the store without paying for it. *I* did not cause my hand to give the bag of almonds to the homeless man standing at the street corner. Chemicals in my brain's neurons caused my hand to grab or give and those chemicals were shaped by my previous experiences. The experience of the despair of poverty shaped my neurons to be prone to cause my hand to steal. The experience of hearing sermons in church shaped my neurons to be prone to cause my hand to give to the poor. But there is no *me* causing anything. My experiences alter my neurons, which move my hand.

If I have a soul then my soul caused my hands to hand over the almonds. If I am my soul, then *I*, through my own free will, caused my hands to hand them over. If I am just my body then my neurons made me do it. If I am my *psychological features* and these features are intricately embedded in my neurons, then it still seems that my neurons made me do it. As integrally tied to my neurons, it seems that they are still largely shaped by my previous experiences.

But if *I* did not cause my hand to give or grab, then how can *I* be responsible for what my hand does. I could always blame it on my neurons and I would be correct. So neither you nor anyone else can blame me for stealing the candy. It's not *my* fault. You might still need to punish me because you want to reshape my neurons into not wanting to cause my hand to grab again. Neither can you nor anyone else praise me for giving almonds to the man on the street. It's not *my* doing, so you would be wrong to honor me. You might still want to say, "Good job," and pat me on the back. But that is because you want to reinforce my neurons so that they will give again. The denial of free will also affects our relationship with God. Not even God can praise or blame me for my actions. That would not be fair of God. I may be a sinner, but it's not my fault.

Some philosophers say that we are still responsible for our actions even if we do not have free will. They say that we still *wanted* to do these actions, so we are responsible for them. But others such as me are not convinced. I may have wanted to grab the candy, but that is only because my neurons and past experiences made me want it. I may have wanted to give the almonds, but that is only because my neurons and past experiences made me want to. To me, if I haven't got free will, then I am not responsible for anything I do.

Clarence Darrow, the lawyer who defended the teaching of evolution in the Scopes Monkey Trial, defended a teenage killer in another famous court case. He argued:

> Nature is strong and she is pitiless. She works in mysterious ways, and we are her victims. We have not much to do with it ourselves. Nature takes this job in hand, and we only play our parts... What had this boy had to do with it? He was not his own father; he was not his own mother... All of this was handed to him. He did not surround himself with governesses and wealth. He did not make himself. And yet he is to be compelled to pay.[4]

If we do not have free will, then it seems that Darrow's troubling conclusion is right. Yet it seems to give an incentive to be immoral. We can always blame our neurons. Belief in free will empowers us to act for the better. Yet denying free will also has its advantages. It makes us more sensitive to the ways in which factors beyond our control influence our behaviors. That can make us more compassionate toward those who are driven to immoral acts by their past experiences—by the way that poverty, war, or other traumas have shaped them. If we come from the perspective that everyone always chooses their actions, then we are inclined to blame everyone for their actions regardless of their circumstances. That might be unfair to those who truly are victims of their neurons.

Whether or not we have free will also influences our view of society. If we have no free will, then it is possible to make people good by providing the kinds of experiences that will make them good. Educate morality. Make sure everyone has a good life. Change the environment, change the person. B. F. Skinner's *Walden Two* imagines such a society and how the denial of free will plays into it. But if we have free will, then it is impossible to create a perfect society. Anyone can always freely choose to be bad, even if they have been trained by their society to be good.

If we believe that we are our souls, then we are more inclined to emphasize our free will and to hold each other responsible for our actions.

---

4. Linder, "Leopold and Loeb Trial," lines 67–70.

If we believe that we are our bodies and that we do not have souls, then we are more inclined to emphasize the ways in which our experiences make us into who we are. Alternatively, perhaps we have *limited* free will. Sometimes we make free choices. Sometimes our neurons make us make them. Some complex actions may result from a complex combination of both our free will and our neurons. Sometimes we are right to praise or blame. Sometimes we are not. Sometimes we are right to praise or blame a little but not a lot. Each situation is different. Views of the self that combine both soul or psyche and body, or that deeply root our souls or psyches in our bodies, would best support such a view.

Forgiveness. Our views of the self also affect important Christian practices. Whether or not we are more identified with something inner or outer changes our understanding of what forgiveness amounts to. If we are our souls or psyches, then forgiveness is a matter of our inner states. It has to do with our feelings of guilt and shame and our inner well-being. Forgiveness makes us *feel* well again. It gives us *inner* peace. Forgiveness is complete when our insides are cozy. But if we are our bodies or deeply rooted in them, then forgiveness is more a matter of our relationships to others. It restores the relationship between the forgiver and the forgiven. It brings *outer* peace. Forgiveness is complete when the relationship is right.

Death, Resurrection, and the Inner-Outer Continuum

Each view of death and resurrection connects with particular views of the self that emphasize internals, externals, or both. Views of the self lie on a continuum between internal and external, depending on the degree to which they emphasize either one.

Soul-Flight favors inner views of the self because it identifies the self with the soul. *Emergent Dualism* and Soul Sleep versions of Soul-Flight are closer to the middle of the continuum but are still on the internal side of it. Reassembly, on the other hand, favors outer views of the self since it identifies the self with the body.

The other three views are more complicated. Re-creation generally favors outer views of the self, although to varying degrees. That is because Re-creation believes that the self cannot exist without a body. But some varieties of Re-creation, such as Self-as-Information-Bearing-Pattern more closely connect soul and body than others. Self-as-Psyche and Self-as-First-Person-Perspective are closer to the middle or even internal end of the spectrum since they identify the self with *internal* mental states. Even here, Self-as-Psyche views vary. Some also include personality traits and relationships with others, which are more external. Some believe that the self does not require a certain body type and can thus have a body of any kind. That places them closer to the internal end of the spectrum since the true self is even more distanced from the body. Re-creation therefore tends to support outer views of the self, but can also support inner views depending on the view of self that it uses.

Slipstream also tends to favor external views of the self, since it requires the self to be embodied at all times. But it, like Re-creation, can support a variety of views of the self. If used to support a Self-as-Psyche or Self-as-First-Person-Perspective view that more greatly dissociates self from body, then it will be closer to the internal end of the spectrum.

Re-formation normally views the self as an ensouled body. The self *has* a soul which survives death, which places it on the internal end of the spectrum. But the self *is* a body, which places it on the external end of the spectrum. Re-formation is therefore more external than any of the Re-creation views, since none of them identify the person with this body that we have right now. Re-formation is therefore a both/and view. The self is *both* soul *and* body, *both* inner *and* outer. It transcends the continuum. That gives it a distinct advantage. I will return to this point in the conclusion.

Believing and Doing

How then to decide whether to choose more internal or external views of self, death, and resurrection? Perhaps we should let our practices be our guide. What have been the Church's traditional practices concerning how we experience and worship God, evangelize, heal, praise, blame, and forgive?

Suppose our practices reflect a tendency toward the externals. Then we ought to either align our beliefs about the self with those practices or we ought to change the practices so that they align with our beliefs. We ought to similarly align our beliefs and practices if our practices reflect a tendency toward the inner. Believing and doing should naturally suggest and mutually reinforce each other. Inconsistency is always a sign that something is wrong, that tweaking is required.

inward or outward? on saving, healing, caring, and communing

We tend to think that our beliefs ought to guide our practices. First get the beliefs right, then alter the practices accordingly. This is often the best approach to take. Our practices sometimes derail and we need to get our beliefs straight in order to realign our practices.

But sometimes we ought to work in reverse. Why? Because practices contain unarticulated insights and intuitions that are passed on tacitly. As the Hungarian philosopher-scientist Michael Polanyi famously said, "We know more than we can tell."[5] When we eat the bread of communion or when we wash each other's feet, we may be showing in our actions that we know that our bodies are an important part of who we are. Why else would the physical act of eating bread and scrubbing toes become conduits of God's grace? We may consciously believe that we are souls and not bodies. But the eating and the washing may suggest that we know better, somewhere deep down.

Which way do we go? From beliefs to practices or practices to beliefs. We will need to make that judgment in each case. The important thing is that they are consistent with each other. That is what this chapter helps us do.

---

5. Polanyi, *The Tacit Dimension*, p. 4.

15

Animals and the Earth: Toto, Dirt, and Eternal Life

WE HUMANS NATURALLY WONDER whether we will survive our deaths. Traditionally, Christians have focused on that question. But that kind of focus gives the impression that we humans think that life is all about us. Maybe it's not. Maybe we are part of something larger and life is about that something larger. Maybe we are not the only earthly creatures destined for eternity. Maybe animals are too. Maybe the whole earth is. If so, then perhaps we should also preach the resurrection of the animals and the resurrection of the earth. That would lead us to think beyond ourselves and grant greater importance to and respect for animals and the earth. It would also lead us to see ourselves as a part of that something larger—to see that our destiny is tied to the destiny of the earth. It would lead us to believe that this world is our home and we are not just passing through. Whether we are right to include animals and the earth in the afterlife has momentous implications. This chapter explores which of our views on death and resurrection can support such ideas and their implications. First, we will consider the animals. Then we will consider the earth.

Many Christians hesitate to talk about what the afterlife may be like. Many Christians would rather leave heaven a mystery. They worry about wild speculations about things that we don't really know much about. They have good reason for this, since some people do speculate about heaven as if they know what they are talking about when they really don't. But I think we need to talk about heaven, for three reasons.

First, we need to be sure that our conception of the afterlife makes sense—that it involves no inconsistencies. Scripture teaches that we will have bodies in heaven. But what does that mean? It's inconsistent to say that heaven is a purely spiritual realm and that there are bodies in it. So heaven can't be a purely spiritual realm. Furthermore, heaven is by definition good.

But, for it to be good, our resurrected bodies can't get sick, die, or have serious pain and discomfort. But for that to be true, our bodies will have to be different from how they are now and that means that scientific laws will need to operate differently in the afterlife. So we have already established some things about the afterlife just by thinking about it. This is not speculation. It is fleshing out the logic of heaven, based on Scripture and good theological and philosophical reasoning. If we do not flesh out that logic then we risk believing things that can't be true.

Second, our beliefs about heaven bear directly on what we should do in this life. The last chapter explored how our beliefs about what part of us makes it to heaven have implications for how we are to live right now. This chapter explores how our beliefs about whether heaven includes animals and the earth have implications for how we treat animals and the earth in this life.

Finally, if we don't talk about heaven, then we risk being completely uninspired by it. Let's heed the challenge by contemporary Yale philosopher Shelly Kagan: "It's a striking fact that even those religions that promise us an eternity in heaven are rather shy about the details. Why? Because—one might worry—if you actually try to fill in the details, this wonderful, eternal existence ends up not seeming so wonderful after all."[1] I find a heaven with animals and the earth to be more inspiring than one without. So, for me, it's worthwhile to think about such a heaven. In *The Last Battle*, which is the last book of the *Chronicles of Narnia* series, C. S. Lewis imagines an inspiring heaven of infinite exploration. We need more of C. S. Lewis's imagination to help us see how eternity can be wonderful.

Animal Immortality and the Christian Tradition

Christians today do not talk much about whether animals will be in heaven, despite the Psalmist's claim that God "save[s] humans and animals alike" (Ps 36:6). Pastors often dodge the issue. Much of the Christian tradition denies the possibility. Aquinas, for example, envisioned a heaven without animals or plants—one of his less inspiring moments.[2] But he does not speak for all the great thinkers, or even for the Bible.

Here is Isaiah's beautiful vision of the Messiah's coming reign:

---

1. Kagan, *Death*, 238.
2. See Lindsay, "Thomas Aquinas's Complete Guide to Heaven and Hell," 39.

> The wolf shall live with the lamb, the leopard shall lie down with the kid, the calf and the lion and the fatling together, and a little child shall lead them. The cow and the bear shall graze, their young shall lie down together; and the lion shall eat straw like the ox. The nursing child shall play over the hole of the asp, and the weaned child shall put its hand on the adder's den. They will not hurt or destroy on all my holy mountain. (Isa 11:6–9a)

Isaiah even includes predators in his paradise. The asps and adders are there, living peacefully with infants. This passage also symbolizes peace between nations. Predators like lions, leopards, and bears represent oppressive nations who cease being oppressive. Cows and kids represent the oppressed peoples who now become equal to the oppressive nations. That vision is also beautiful. But the passage can be both literal and symbolic. That seems to me to be the most natural and meaningful way of reading it.

The book of Revelation also puts animals in heaven:

> Around the throne, and on each side of the throne, are four living creatures, full of eyes in front and behind: the first living creature like a lion, the second living creature like an ox, the third living creature with a face like a human face, and the fourth living creature like a flying eagle. And the four living creatures, each of them with six wings, are full of eyes all around and inside. Day and night without ceasing they sing, "Holy, holy, holy, the Lord God almighty, who was and is and is to come." (Rev 4:6b–8)

According to N. T. Wright, these living creatures represent the animal kingdom.[3] If so, then animals are capable of worshipping God in their own way and will be in heaven praising God. They are surely not emotionless automatons!

Now skip Aquinas's lifeless heaven and fast forward to Martin Luther:

> You must not think that heaven and earth will be made of nothing but air and sand, but there will be whatever belongs to it—sheep, oxen, beasts, fish, without which the earth and sky or air cannot be . . . Ants, bugs and all unpleasant stinking creatures will be most delightful and have a wonderful fragrance.[4]

---

3. Wright, *Revelation for Everyone*, 47–48.
4. Quoted in McDannell and Lang, *Heaven*, 153.

John Calvin agreed. So did John Wesley. How else, thought Wesley, could God be just if he does not make such "amends to them [the animals] for all they suffer while under their present bondage."[5] In the twentieth century, C. S. Lewis argued that our pets, at least, might show up in heaven.[6]

Nice sentiments. But is it even possible for animals to show up in heaven? More to the point, is it even possible for *numerically the same* animals to show up in heaven? Is it possible for my pet dog Jasmine to show up in heaven? That depends on your view of death and resurrection.

Animals and the Soul

Traditionally, whether or not animals can survive their deaths depends on whether or not they have souls. Much in the Christian tradition suggests that they do. Aquinas, for example, believed that animals had souls that made it possible for them to have emotions, pleasures, pains, memories, and primitive thoughts. But much in the Christian tradition also suggests that animals do not have the kinds of souls that survive death. Aquinas, for example, believed as such. Having a soul does not guarantee life after death.

But what makes our souls so different from those of the animals? If Soul-Flight is correct that we are our souls and that therefore we exist *as full persons* after the death of our bodies, then we are not really animals. It means that neither you nor I are animals. The concept of "animal" does not make sense without an animal body, without being a biological organism. If an animal could survive death because its soul could survive death then it would not really be an animal. Being an animal is incidental to it—like a prince who is reborn as a frog only later to be reborn as a pauper. The frog's body was just a temporary shell for the prince. Being an animal was just a temporary phase of the prince's existence and so was not an essential part of his identity. We are much more inclined to think that we are not animals because our mental capabilities are so much greater than those of animals. It is much more difficult to think that Jasmine the Chihuahua is not essentially an animal.

Some in the modern period, like the philosopher Descartes, denied that animals have souls. They equate having a soul, or mind, with being

---

5. Wesley, "Sermon 60: The General Deliverance," §3.5.
6. Lewis, *Problem of Pain*, 139–40.

able to think. To them, animals are mere machines, with no real emotions, pleasures, or pains.

Dolphins are highly intelligent and seem to be able to think. Philosophers like Descartes might be willing to grant that they are more like us and not really animals either. Soul-Flight can thus potentially extend the afterlife to dolphins, and maybe also intelligent apes. But the cost is to deny that they are essentially animals. That cost may be too high.

The *Emergent Dualist* version of Soul-Flight fares better. According to it, our souls are deeply connected to their bodies because they emerge from them and normally require them for their activities. They survive death not because they can think but because "emergent souls" are the sorts of things that God can sustain apart from bodies. They are like fields and fields are, in theory, sustainable apart from what gave rise to them. Insofar as an animal generates such an emergent field, then there is hope that God can sustain that field after the animal dies.

It is less of a stretch to say the animal remains an animal once its soul, or field, separates from its body at death. Its emergent field emerged from and was shaped by its animal brain. It also needs its animal brain and body back to properly function. The animal's soul when separated from its body looks much more like the soul of an animal than the soul of a prince that temporarily inhabited the animal's body. Some, however, may feel that this still stretches the concept of "animal" too far.

Re-formation is also more promising. In Polkinghorne's version, the soul is an information-bearing pattern. If God can preserve our patterns in existence between death and resurrection, then presumably God could also preserve the patterns of individual non-human animals.

According to Aquinas's version of Re-formation, the soul is the form of the body and the person is not the soul. Therefore, the soul without the body is either only part of the person or a severely diminished person. On this view, the person is essentially an animal, requiring an animal body. In the same way, any animal soul that survived the death of its body would be incomplete without that body. That soul would be only a part of the animal or a diminished version of the animal. So the Re-formation view does not claim that an animal soul apart from an animal body is a full and complete animal. Nor does it claim that the animal which has the soul is that soul and can therefore exist full and complete without its animal body. Thus, Re-formation makes it possible for the animal's soul to survive death without making the sketchy claim that the animal ever exists without its body. That gives Re-formation an edge over *emergent dualism*.

But traditionally, Re-formation only allows human souls to survive the deaths of their bodies. That is because only human souls are capable of doing something that does not require a body or a brain. They can think about abstract things like the essence of apes. That makes it theoretically possible for them to exist apart from their brains and bodies. Animals are only capable of sense perceptions, emotions, memories, pleasures, pains, and simple thoughts. Such things require brains. So their souls cannot survive the deaths of their bodies because their souls cannot in any way function without them.

If it could be shown that some of the higher animals, such as dolphins and apes, could think abstract thoughts then the traditional Re-formation view could make room for them to survive the deaths of their bodies. Or if it could be shown that some other animal activity does not require a brain, such as consciousness, then maybe it could make room for more animals to survive the deaths of their bodies. Re-formation thus stretches the concept of "animal" less than *emergent dualism* but it also more strictly limits the variety of animals that have a shot at immortality.

Animals and Resurrection

It would seem that non-soul-based views of death and resurrection have a better shot at extending the afterlife to animals. God can resurrect non-human animal bodies from the dead as well as he can resurrect human bodies from the dead. According to Reassembly, God collects all the particles that made up our bodies at death to reassemble those same bodies again at the resurrection. God could do the same for the particles that made up the bodies of animals when they died. But that would only add to Reassembly's problems. Most humans eat animal meat, which means that most of us, this vegetarian author excepted, have the particles of dead animal bodies making up our own bodies. If we died, then who gets those particles at the resurrection? In addition to billions of human particles to sort out, God now has trillions of animal particles to sort out. An omnipotent God can sort them out. But he would have to miraculously intervene in the paths of these particles through history so that every animal he plans to resurrect will have enough particles unique to their original bodies with which he can resurrect those original bodies. Given such complications, Reassembly may not be the best option for those wishing to defend animal immortality.

God can also presumably re-create an animal from scratch just as well as he can re-create a human from scratch. But, as we have seen, Re-creation depends on some view of *numerical identity* that makes it possible for the resurrected person to be *numerically the same* person as the original person. If God re-creates an animal, then something must make that animal *numerically the same* animal as the original. If that something is the animal's pattern or structure, then God could re-create an animal just as well as he could re-create a human person. But what if sameness of psyche is required? God would then need to re-create the animal's same psychology to re-create the same animal. The re-created Lassie would be *numerically the same* Lassie as the original because she has the same personality traits, memories, and such as the original. That might work for Lassie, but it might not work for a goldfish with little memory or personality.

Self-as-Psyche is usually based on the idea that our personal identities in this life are preserved by psychological continuity. Our psychologies change over time, but there is enough overlap from one moment to the next that makes it possible for the same person to persist throughout the changes. Such continuity requires overlap and many animals may not have any overlap. Something has to stay the same. But if animals go through life from one perception to the next—see yellow flower → smell pollen → feel breeze → see green leaf → smell green leaf—then nothing of their psychologies persist from moment to moment. For such animals, psychological continuity cannot be what preserves their identities over time. The re-creation of their psychologies at the resurrection would not guarantee that they themselves have been raised.

The *first-person perspective version* of Re-creation further limits the scope of animal immortality. According to it, the resurrected person is the same as the original because she has the same *first-person perspective*. That presumes self-awareness. But how many animals are self-aware? This view may limit the resurrection to Koko the gorilla and other such animals who have acquired self-awareness through interacting with humans. C. S. Lewis suggested that our pets might attain immortality through their interactions with us.[7] This could be the means by which that happens, at least for more intelligent pets. But if you want your pet tortoise to go to heaven, then this view is not for you.

---

7. Lewis, *Problem of Pain*, 139–40.

Animals and Slipstream

Slipstream views offer the best hope for animal immortality because they make it possible for animals to survive death without becoming disembodied. The animal body survives, although it may be diminished or ghostly between death and resurrection.

Body-snatching poses no extra problems for animals than it does for humans. God can as easily snatch the brain and nervous system of a dog at death as he can snatch the brain and nervous system of a human at death. This option is in any case based on the idea that human persons are essentially animals. We never cease being an animal in the *interim state* because the core of our animal body is preserved. Ditto for a dead dog.

Body-morphing also works for animals. We can imagine animals transforming cocoon-like into newer intermediate forms that have enough continuity to preserve sameness of species. Caterpillars do it. Why not cats too?

Body-splitting option also works as well for animals as for humans. The chain of cause and effect that preserves the ongoing life of the human person splits in two so that the living chain continues in slipstream while the now deceased chain persists on earth. The same can happen for the causal chain of a parrot's life.

Soul Storage also works. Given its reduced complexity, the animal's essential pattern can more easily be stored in God's dimensional hard drive than ours can.

Body-hopping also works. But which animals it works for depends on which view of identity body-hopping is using. If it uses Self-as-Soul, then the animal's soul can hop as well as the human's. If it uses Self-as-Psyche, then only those animals whose psychologies continue from one moment to the next can hop into another body. If it uses Self-as-First-Person-Perspective, then only those animals with *first-person perspectives* will make it.

The Implications of Animal Immortality

Much more is at stake than our desire to see our pets again. If animals are present in the kingdom come, then we will need to rethink our treatment of them in the here and now.

If our bodies are raised into eternity—and especially if they are integral to our very selves—then we ought to treat the bodies of ourselves and others with a great deal of respect. God values them enough to grant them eternity. So too we should value them enough to heal them rather than harm them. The same reasoning applies to the bodies of animals. If they are raised, then we ought to respect their bodies and work for their healing.

In practice, respecting the bodies of animals means ending factory farms. Crowding animals into small pens and pumping them with hormones and chemicals that make them neurotic surely qualifies as disrespect. It also means ending at least some animal testing. If God intends to redeem the mouse's body, then how can we splice genes into it to mimic Huntington's Disease? How can we inject neurotoxins into a rabbit's body to mimic Parkinson's? We disrespect both the animal's body and the God who intends to redeem it.

Respecting the bodies of animals may also mean not eating them. If you will spend an eternity in fellowship with Bessie the cow, then would you eat Bessie here and now? If God values Bessie's body enough to grant it eternal life, then how can we eat her beef?

If we take seriously the idea that animals will be raised, then we might want to give animals a more prominent place in our churches and their ceremonies. Some churches already invite pets and farm animals into the sanctuary for an annual blessing of the animals. But why not also have pet funerals at church? Why not add some candles for our pets in All Soul's Day celebrations? Why not name our deceased pets during the All Soul's Day service as we do for humans who have died? Why not extend "the great cloud of witnesses" to include our deceased dogs and cats? Perhaps they too are also among the saints in glory with whom we commune.

The Resurrection of the Earth

Many Christians today are rethinking traditional Christian views of the earth's destiny. Heaven is traditionally depicted as either an unearthly spiritual realm or a material realm completely disconnected from this earth. But there is much in the Bible that suggests otherwise.

For one thing, the Bible teaches the resurrection of the *body*. Bodies, however, do not exist in vacuums. They interact with material environments. With our eyes, we see red and blue. But red and blue are light and light is material. With our ears, we hear sounds. But sounds consist of the motion of material particles, whether of air, water, or some other suitable medium. Our heavenly cantatas will remain silent without any matter to convey them to our ears. Our hands have no point if they cannot pick anything up. Our feet have no point if there is no earth to walk upon. What is a body if its skin cannot feel a breeze? The logic of the resurrection suggests that heaven will also consist of a material environment for our bodies to interact with.

The Bible also seems to suggest that the resurrected world will be related to this earth in some way. Revelation 21 speaks of the new heaven and the *new earth*. The question then is whether the *new earth* is a resurrection and transformation of the original one or an entirely new one completely made from scratch. As we saw in chapter 3, Paul seems to think that God will one day redeem this very earth, and indeed all of God's creation: " . . . in hope that the creation *itself* will be set free from its bondage to decay" (Rom 8:21; italics mine). Colossians reinforces the same idea: " . . . through him God was pleased to reconcile to himself *all* things, whether *on earth* or in heaven, by making peace through the blood of his cross" (Col 1:20; italics mine). It would seem that we and the earth share a similar destiny—that this world is our home and we are not just passing through.

The traditional doctrine of the *general resurrection* also supports the idea that the *new earth* is linked somehow to the old one. According to that doctrine, all are raised together on this earth at the end of its history. Presumably, once resurrected, we could then ditch this earth for a completely different material realm. But combining the *general resurrection* with the verses from Paul quoted above suggests that we will continue to inhabit this creation.

The earth, of course, would be transformed. No more death and decay. No more pain and suffering. No more serpents biting babies. The *new earth* is not an eternity of "the vale of suffering" we now experience. It is oceans, mountains, and flowers without tsunamis, quakes, and allergies.

Some may object. How can all the humans who are saved, and perhaps also all the animals, inhabit such an earth? But that is no problem for an omnipotent God and a lively imagination. The laws of science will be transformed. Perhaps the earth will become the size of Jupiter without the added gravity. Or the earth will exist simultaneously in multiple dimensions that we can hop between, much like the premise of the 90s sci-fi hit, *Sliders*.

The more serious problem is whether it is possible to raise *numerically the same* earth. What makes it the same earth? That problem ties in directly with the question of what makes it possible for *numerically the same* person to re-exist. If reassembly is required, then God can easily reassemble the earth from its ashes. If re-creation preserves identity, then God can re-create the earth as well as he can re-create one of us. Re-formation would work if the earth itself has a pattern. Its pattern could be transposed into another dimension where it reshapes altogether different matter into *numerically the same* earth. Or, if the earth itself has no pattern, then perhaps the patterns of its systems, ecosystems, and creatures could be transposed into the other dimension where they reshape altogether different matter into *numerically the same* systems, ecosystems, and creatures. Perhaps that is enough to claim that it is *numerically the same* earth. Slipstream might work if combined with Re-formation. God could store the earth's pattern or patterns in an appropriate storage medium until the time of its future resurrection. Otherwise, it is hard to conceive of the earth temporarily slipping into another material dimension.

There is no problem though if the earth does not perish. Its identity is not in question if it persists through its transformation into the new earth. Whatever makes the earth *numerically the same* earth over time would continue without interruption.

The New Earth, the General Resurrection, and the Difference They Make

The idea that the *new earth* is a resurrection of the original has important implications for how we treat the earth. For one, it gives the earth eternal value. It also means that our destinies are linked with the earth's. We had better learn how to care for it, because we will spend eternity with it. Whenever we learn how to care for the soil or clean up our rivers, we develop the virtues of earth-care that will guide us in the *new earth*. We also develop the proper affections for the earth that will be with us in eternity. If the *new earth* gives us a vision of what the earth is meant to be and will be some day, then we are also inspired to move earth here and now closer to what it is meant to be. An otherworldly or extra-dimensional heaven saps energy from caring for this earth.

There are still good reasons to care for this earth, however, even if it is not destined for eternity. If you are given a gift, you still care for it while you have got it even though you know it will someday break. It shows respect to the gift-giver. It is also part of properly enjoying the gift.

But eternity does make a difference. If you know that you will live in a city for a long time, then you are more energized to try to improve it. You will make the effort to vote for better libraries. You will advocate for better public transportation and cleaner air. You will invest more in developing relationships with other people in the city. But if you know that you will be moving away in a few years, then you will put your efforts into preparing for that move. You still care about the city, but you are not going to put that extra oomph into making it a better place. To vote or not to vote on Measure B? Maybe you will not make the extra effort to go to the polling station if you will not be around for the new downtown library building. You are also less willing to make new friends in the city. You will be thinking about how to make new friends in the new city. The difference is not in the caring. It is in the energy and priority put into the caring.

The combination of the idea of the *new earth* and the doctrine of the *general resurrection* has further implications for history, culture, community, and all our efforts to further God's kingdom here on earth. If the resurrected world is a transformation and continuation of the history of the earth and human activity on it, then that history and activity will be redeemed. We should therefore care deeply about what happens in this world's history. God's kingdom will come in history as it is in heaven. This is not "pie in the sky" spirituality that discourages action for the betterment of this world. If we know that we ultimately belong in this world then we will work for its healing.

If we are all raised together in the future of this timeline and this earth, then everything we do now to help build God's kingdom matters. We are not like islanders who build beautiful buildings on an island that will eventually sink. What is the point of working for God's kingdom on earth if the earth is doomed and we hope to find God's kingdom in a heaven in some other dimension?

Whatever we have done in history to promote truth, goodness, justice, and beauty has eternal value because it has contributed to furthering history towards its fulfillment in heaven. That which is true, good, just, and beautiful in human culture and society has eternal value. That is something to remember when gazing at a Monet, listening to Vivaldi's *The Four Seasons*, admiring a Gothic cathedral, or savoring a bite of chocolate cheesecake. It is especially something to remember when working with the poor to help them build better homes and communities for themselves. N. T. Wright, one of the more prominent contemporary New Testament scholars, puts it well:

> You are not oiling the wheels of a machine that's about to roll over a cliff. You are not restoring a great painting that's shortly going to be thrown on the fire. You are not planting roses in a garden that's about to be dug up for a building site. You are—strange as though it may seem, almost as hard to believe as the resurrection itself—accomplishing something that will become in due course part of God's new world. Every act of love, gratitude, and kindness; every work of art or music inspired by the love of God and delight in the beauty of his creation; every minute spent teaching a severely handicapped child to read or to walk; every act of care and nurture, of comfort and support, for one's fellow human beings and for that matter one's fellow non-human creatures; and of course every prayer, all Spirit-led teaching, every deed that spreads the gospel, builds up the church, embraces and embodies holiness rather than corruption, and makes the name of Jesus honored in the world—all of this will find its ways, through the resurrecting power of God, into the new creation that God will one day make. That is the logic of the mission of God. God's recreation of this wonderful world, which began with the resurrection of Jesus and continues mysteriously as God's people live in the risen Christ and in the power of his Spirit, means that what we do in Christ and by the Spirit in the present is not wasted. It will last all the way into God's new world. In fact, it will be enhanced there.[8]

Wright envisions an ultimate and eternal intertwining of heaven and earth where all that we do for God's kingdom will find its completion. Even *Time* magazine has picked up on Wright's vision and used it as one of its cover stories.[9]

Albus Dumbledore is the wisest wizard in the Harry Potter series. But if he believed in the *general resurrection* then he would have given Harry Potter different advice when they spoke in the place between the living and the dead. Harry must choose whether to go on to the peaceful place of the dead or to return to the troubled world of the living. If he returns then he will need to face the evil wizard Voldemort in a final battle to save the Hogwart's School of Wizardry and England's entire wizarding world from his evil reign. Dumbledore tells Harry: "By returning, you may ensure that fewer *souls* are maimed, fewer families torn apart. If that seems to you a worthy goal, then we say good-bye for the present."[10] But is

---

8. Wright, *Surprised by Hope*, 208–9.
9. Meacham, "Heaven Can't Wait," 30–36.
10. Rowling, *Harry Potter and the Deathly Hallows*, 722; italics mine.

that all that matters in the history of the world? If the *general resurrection* were true in the wizarding world, then the final battle at Hogwarts matters because it is part of a history to which the dead will return when they are raised. The *general resurrection* suggests that what we do in history matters not just because our actions protect some *souls* but because they also protect the *bodies* of those souls. Our actions in history also matter because they protect the earth and promote the communities and cultures of history that we create and belong to. Protecting souls goes hand in hand with redeeming the bodies, communities and causes to which they belong. Hogwarts matters. England matters. The earth matters. The real action is in the land of the living. Harry chooses to return to that land, which implies that he agrees.

If the *general resurrection* is true, then our redemption is intertwined with the salvation of the earth and the completion of its history. It is intertwined with the healing of our nations, our cities, and our institutions. It is intertwined with Christ's reign of peace and justice here on earth. It is God who will ultimately heal the world. So the *general resurrection* and the *new earth* do not imply that we can usher in God's kingdom ourselves or that we will necessarily be able to move history closer to it. But we should think that everything that we do now, in this world, in this history, matters, because it will be completed in the future, in this world, in this history.

The *general resurrection* also implies that we are communal beings who need each other rather than self-sufficient and isolated individuals. The idea that we are all raised together at the same time sends the message that we are all in this together. Individuals do not stand alone before God for judgment. Whole communities and peoples stand together. Salvation is also communal. Ultimate healing is in community, not apart from it. We are only fully healed when our relationships with others are fully healed.

Such ultimate healing is not just within community, but also *between* communities. Imagine the mass of freshly resurrected humanity standing before God on Judgment Day. Our "enemies" are standing there too. They were resurrected together with us, as *one* with us. Many of them will likely join us in the *new earth* for all eternity. We do not know which of our "enemies" will and which will not. Depending on your beliefs about heaven and hell, you may believe that most or even all of them will be saved. Scripture speaks of God "reconciling himself to all *things*," which implies "all *persons*" (Col 1:20; italics mine). This is not, of course, to minimize God's rightful wrath against the great evils and injustices committed by humans throughout history. But it seems to imply that Judgment, whatever that means, is followed by forgiveness and reconciliation. If so, then how can we now treat our enemies as enemies? Understood this way, the *general resurrection* is an incentive to seek peace and reconciliation with all others, insofar as it is possible. Combined with the idea of the *new earth*, this incentive to peace also extends to animals and the land.

Assessing the Options

Suppose that you, like me, are inspired by the implications of the *new earth* and the *general resurrection* for creation, community, history, and peace. If so, then you will want to choose one of the views of death and resurrection that support the *new earth* and the *general resurrection*. If these implications really matter to you, then you may wish to choose the view of death and resurrection that *best* supports them.

Immediate resurrection, as traditionally understood, does *not* support them. According to it, we are immediately raised in some other dimension altogether and with matter that is not part of this physical universe. That dimension may have carbon atoms, but they are not from this dimension. This view implies that the healing of the earth is incidental to and not integral to the healing of ourselves. Perhaps God will eventually heal the earth and perhaps we will someday return to it, but we can be perfectly happy and complete without it. The redemption of our bodies at the resurrection would occur in another dimension, entirely disconnected from the redemption of the earth. Our destinies may both be eternal, but they are not interwoven. We would still have some extra incentive to care for the earth and its history, but not as much as if the resurrection of the body itself coincided with and depended on the resurrection of the earth.

According to *immediate resurrection*, we are all resurrected at different times in another dimension's timeline. That makes it more individualistic, ahistorical, and other-worldly. We are resurrected as isolated individuals and outside of history. Gone is the *general resurrection*'s linkage of resurrection and reconciliation. Gone is its emphasis on the importance of the history of this world and the furthering of the kingdom in it. The important thing is to prepare ourselves as individuals for another world.

But *immediate resurrection* has other options. Suppose that we all arrive at the other dimension at once. Suppose its timeline is so different from ours that one millisecond of its timeline intersects with all of human history in ours. We die at our different times, whether Bronze Age or Fourth Millennium, but we are each immediately resurrected at the same time into the other dimension. That could make *immediate resurrection* as community-oriented as the *general resurrection*.

Immediate resurrection can support a *general resurrection* at the end of history by folding time and space, as discussed at the end of chapter 9. Suppose the moment of the *general resurrection* in earth's future folds back on earth's history so that it somehow intersects with every moment of history up to that point. Thus we are all *immediately* raised at the general resurrection at the end of this history. Philosophers and scientists will have to work out whether or not such an idea makes any sense.

Each of the five main views of death and resurrection can support the *new earth* and the *general resurrection*. Those views that more closely tie our own destinies to that of the earth and its history give more importance to caring for this earth and its history.

Soul-Flight puts less emphasis on the *new earth* and the *general resurrection* since it puts less emphasis on the resurrection. Our souls may get their bodies back at the *general resurrection* and in the *new earth*. But having a redeemed body and visiting a redeemed earth is nice but incidental. Neither our personal identities nor our ultimate bliss depends on having these bodies or having the earth redeemed. For Soul-Flight, as with *immediate resurrection*, the real action happens elsewhere—on a spiritual plane of existence or in some other dimension. Whatever happens to the earth almost seems beside the point.

Soul-Sleep and the *Emergent Dualist* version of Soul-Flight give the resurrection greater import and can thus give greater import to the *general resurrection* and the *new earth*. For the former, resurrection restores our consciousness. For the latter, resurrection places our minds back in brains where they belong. Yet neither of them requires resurrection for the restoration of our personal identities. Thus even these versions of Soul-Flight cannot as greatly emphasize the importance of the *general resurrection* and the *new earth* as much as the other views can.

Reassembly, on the other hand, gives the greatest importance to the *new earth* and the *general resurrection*. It more directly links our own destinies to the earth's destiny, since the restoration of our personal identities depends on the reassembly of particles from this earth. Most Slipstream views also give them importance, since these views are based on the idea that we survive in a diminished capacity in another material dimension until we can be fully restored in *this* material dimension. Unlike Soul-Flight, Slipstream, by definition, is temporary. Some Slipstream views, such as body-hopping and body-splitting, may give less importance to the *new earth* and the *general resurrection* since they may grant us a full existence between death and resurrection.

Re-creation and Re-formation both require resurrection for the restoration of the full person and the latter traditionally adheres to the *general resurrection*. Some Re-creation and Re-formation views may also require that the resurrected body come from matter from this material dimension even if it need not be from the same material particles that made up the original bodies. Re-formation may require this since our souls are so closely linked to our bodies that they may only be able to perfect or complete a body that is of this earth. If so, then it, like the Reassembly view, more closely ties us to this earth.

The issue then is one of degree. Reassembly provides the best support for the *new earth* and the *general resurrection*. But nearly all the other options support them too, although to varying degrees. Soul-Flight and some Slipstream views support them the least. The traditional understanding of *immediate resurrection* is the only one that can't support them.

The last four chapters have shown some of the ways in which the five main views of death and resurrection and their many variations make a difference for other issues that matter to us. Some of these differences are substantial. Others are a matter of degree. At this point, you may wonder how you will decide which view to choose given how much there is to consider. Help is on the way. Turn the page.

Finishing the Puzzle:
Final Reflections

16

Conclusion: Thoughts on Making a Choice

IN SHAKESPEARE'S *HAMLET*, HAMLET picks up the skull of his deceased friend Yorick and says:

> Alas, poor Yorick! I knew him, Horatio, a fellow of infinite jest, of most exquisite fancy. He hath borne me on his back a thousand times. And now how abhorred in my imagination it is! My gorge rises at it. Here hung those lips that I have kissed I know not how oft. Where be your gibes now? Your gambols, your songs, your flashes of merriment that were wont to set the table on a roar?[1]

The skull reminds Hamlet that death is inevitable. The lips he once kissed will someday be gone as will the lips with which he kissed them. Mothers, fathers, sisters, brothers, friends . . . all will die. So will we. We are all on a spaceship set for self-destruct.

Hamlet also wonders where Yorick's "gambols" and "songs" are now. We wonder the same about the Yoricks of our own lives. We also wonder what will become of our own gambols when we are gone. Will Yorick gambol again? Will we?

The scene is a *memento mori*—a reminder of death. It leads us to reflect on both death and the life that will eventually end in death. It changes us, so that we can no longer look on death and life the same as we did before. We cannot reflect on death without also reflecting on life. May this book also be a *memento mori*. It asks us to think hard about what may become of us after we die. It also explores how our understandings of death and resurrection shape the way that we go about our lives here and now.

---

1. Shakespeare, *Hamlet*, 5.1, lines 3515–21.

Finishing the Puzzle: Final Reflections

This book has presented and analyzed the main Christian understandings of what happens to us after we die. It has shown that we have many promising options to choose from to explain how we might live again after we die. We need not believe that death stops us from gamboling now and anon.

The five main options can be subdivided into further options. See appendix A for the full list. Which then should we choose? Here are some things to consider:

1. All five of the main options are defensible. Given enough modification and revision, each one can offer an internally consistent account that accommodates biblical, scientific, and philosophical concerns.

2. Some options are better than others. You may rank them differently depending on how you weigh their respective strengths and weaknesses.

3. If you believe that some of the options are equally strong then also consider their implications for the concerns raised in chapters 12 to 15. Choose the option that best accommodates the implications that matter most to you. If you strongly feel that life is best lived by balancing our inner and outer lives, then you may wish to choose a view like Re-formation that emphasizes both our souls and our bodies. If you strongly feel that at least some animals should enjoy an afterlife, then you will want to choose a view that makes that possible.

4. You can also combine some of these options. Soul-Flight and Reassembly have a long history of going together. Reassembly also combines well with Re-formation, since some understandings of Re-formation require that the person's resurrected body must consist of some of the original body's material particles to be *numerically* the same body as the original body. Slipstream can combine with *emergent dualism*, since the emergent mind can connect with a slipstream brain until the resurrection. Slipstream can also combine with Re-formation's views of the self, since the person's essential pattern may be stored in slipstream matter until the resurrection. But Re-creation cannot combine with any of the other options. The other options each depend on something that exists between death and resurrection that links the resurrected person to the original person. Re-creation denies any such link. Combining options is a good idea when one option's strengths can overcome another option's weaknesses. But it can also make one option weaker by adding new weaknesses to it. Many believe that combining Soul-Flight with Reassembly

conclusion: thoughts on making a choice

tacks on Reassembly's weaknesses without giving Soul-Flight much in return.

5. Also consider when you think the resurrection occurs. There are three options. First, the dead are immediately resurrected in another dimension. Second, the dead are resurrected in the future in this dimension at the end of history. Third, the dead are resurrected immediately but in the future in this dimension at the end of history. This last option requires a warping of the timeline so that the future of this timeline folds back on itself and intersects every moment of the timeline before it, as we saw in chapter 9. Soul-Flight is compatible with all three, although Soul Sleep is only compatible with the second. Reassembly is only compatible with the second option for it requires that the resurrected body consist of some of the same matter as the original body. That matter stays in this dimension, moving through all moments of time between death and resurrection. It cannot jump directly into the future. Re-creation is compatible with the first two options. There is no need to bend time and space to assure the resurrection of the same person since nothing need remain continuous between the original and resurrected persons. Re-formation is consistent with all three. Slipstream best fits future resurrection since it attempts to find a way to preserve at least part of the person *between* death and resurrection. But some of the options within Slipstream can skip the *interim state* altogether. Body-hopping, body-splitting, and body-snatching are compatible with both *immediate resurrection* and immediate/future resurrection.

6. Reassembly is generally considered the weakest option. So you may not want to choose it. While God can orchestrate the universe to make sure we all get enough of our atoms back, there seems to be no non-arbitrary explanation for just how much of our original atoms we need to preserve our identity. Reassembly also may require too much divine intervention in history to keep everyone's atoms sorted out until the resurrection.

7. Soul-Flight is also harder to defend although it still has many defenders today. It draws a sharper line between soul and body than the Bible seems to warrant. It also goes against the growing scientific evidence that our mental lives are deeply connected to our brains and nervous systems. If you are scientifically inclined, you will find Soul-Flight less appealing. Both Soul-Sleep and *emergent dualism* are improvements over *traditional dualism*. But many feel that they still too strongly divide mind from body.

8. Re-creation handles the scientific data well since, according to it, we cannot exist without brains or something like them. It also better fits the Bible's *holistic* view of the human person, although it may still distinguish self from body more than the Bible warrants. Re-creation also has difficulty explaining scriptural passages that suggest an *interim state*. But its biggest problem is philosophical—how is the re-created person a re-creation of the original person and not just a replica of her?

9. Re-formation handles the biblical data well. It is *holistic* and yet allows for an *interim state*. It also acknowledges the reality and evil of death. Re-formation is also more in line with science than the other soul-based views. It acknowledges the close connection between our minds and our brains, since, according to it, almost all our mental activities require our brains. Yet it still, perhaps contrary to the scientific evidence, requires that our souls are conscious between death and resurrection. It also has difficulty explaining how the soul, as the organizing principle of the body, can exist apart from the body. How can organizing patterns exist by themselves without being in some material or other? For that matter, how can a disembodied principle of organization be conscious?

10. Slipstream's strength is that it both allows for an *interim state* and requires that the self is always embodied. It thus satisfies two seemingly contradictory biblical claims. It also satisfies the scientist's demand that all mental activity requires a brain or something like it. It also has no difficulty accounting for personal identity since there is continuity between the resurrected and the original person. But it has difficulty explaining the biblical idea that death is an enemy. It also requires the existence of other dimensions and the ability for at least something of ourselves to jump dimensions at death. Contemporary science is more open to such possibilities. But new scientific evidence may deem it impossible, thus making this view vulnerable to future potential scientific findings.

You may prefer a more systematic approach to making a decision. If so, I offer the following criteria:

Biblical Concerns

1. Has a *holistic* understanding of the human person?
2. Accounts for the *interim state* or otherwise explains those passages which suggest it?
3. Places our hope for the afterlife in the resurrection?
4. Accounts for the *general resurrection* or otherwise explains those passages which suggest it?
5. Explains how death is an enemy?
6. Places our hope for an afterlife in God and not in a *natural immorality*?

Scientific Concerns

1. Handles scientific data concerning the early stages of the embryo?
2. Handles scientific data concerning the evolution of the human species?
3. Handles neuroscientific data concerning the close connection between mind and brain?

Philosophical Concerns

1. Offers a promising account of how the resurrected person can be *numerically the same* person as the original person?
2. Avoids the *problem of duplication*?
3. Has promising answers to objections?

> ### Implications
>
> 1. Preserves the *Communion of the Saints* and its implications for communing with the dead?
> 2. Can emphasize cremation as a good option?
> 3. Views death as both friend and enemy?
> 4. Emphasizes both our inner and outer lives?
> 5. Makes possible the resurrection of at least the higher animals?
> 6. Can emphasize the *general resurrection* and its implications for history, community, and peace?
> 7. Can emphasize the resurrection of the earth and its implications for creation care?

Your list may differ from mine. You may, for example, not worry about the *problem of duplication*. Not all philosophers do. But most do. You may also be less concerned with some of the implications I listed above. You may not, for example, as highly value the *Communion of the Saints* and so you might cross it off the list. Or you might wish to focus on either our inner or our outer lives but not on both. Or you may be less concerned about the fate of animals or the earth and may cross those off the list. Or you may add some things to the list. It may be very important to you that *near-death-experiences* are genuine out-of-this-body experiences and so you may add to the list: "can explain how near-death-experiences are genuine out-of-this-body experiences." That is less important to me because I am satisfied with the idea that *near-death-experiences* happen in our brains before complete brain death. In my mind, those experiences can still be genuine encounters with God and the deceased. You may also want to add: "Makes possible ghostly visitations and communications with the dead via mediums." Such things are not important to me so I left them off my list. Some things need to remain on the list for your view to be rationally defensible. For example, offering a satisfactory account of *personal identity over time* is non-negotiable. So is "having promising answers to objections."

Choose the view that at first looks most promising to you. Then go down the list. I like the Self-as-Ensouled-Body version of Re-formation because I like its ideas of persons as living bodies and of souls as patterns that shape our bodies. How does it stand up to my list? I use the categories "strong," "moderate," and "weak" to quickly show how well the view handles each criterion.

Re-formation

Biblical Concerns:

1. Has a *holistic* understanding of the human person?: strong (The person is an ensouled body.)
2. Accounts for the *interim state*?: moderate (The person in the *interim state* is conscious but is not the full person.)
3. Places our hope for the afterlife in the resurrection?: strong (The resurrection restores the full person.)
4. Accounts for the *general resurrection*?: strong (All are raised at the same time after the *interim state*.)
5. Explains how death is an enemy?: strong (The full person ceases to exist at death.)
6. Places our hope for an afterlife in God and not in a *natural immorality*?: strong (The resurrection restores the full person and depends on God.)

Scientific Concerns:

1. Handles scientific data concerning the early stages of the embryo?: strong (The soul does not arise until later in the embryo's development.)
2. Handles scientific data concerning the evolution of the human species?: moderate (The soul as a pattern can develop gradually through evolution.)
3. Handles neuroscientific data concerning the close connection between mind and brain?: moderate (It still requires some consciousness to occur without the brain.)

Philosophical Concerns:

1. Offers a promising account of how the resurrected person can be *numerically the same* person as the original person?: strong (The same soul restores the same body, which restores the same person.)

2. Avoids the problem of duplication?: moderate (Can patterns be duplicated?)

3. Has promising answers to objections: moderate (It does not completely resolve the problem of whether patterns can exist and be conscious apart from matter.)

Implications:

1. Preserves the *Communion of the Saints* and its implications for communing with the dead?: moderate (The dead are conscious but are not full persons.)

2. Can emphasize cremation as a good option?: strong (Can interpret cremation as emphasizing our bodily connection to the earth.)

3. Views death as both friend and enemy?: strong (Death is enemy because the full person ceases to exist; It is friend because part of the person survives.)

4. Emphasizes both our inner and outer lives?: strong (We are both souls and bodies.)

5. Makes possible the resurrection of at least the higher animals?: weak (It is hard to explain how animal souls can survive death.)

6. Can emphasize the general resurrection and its implications for history, community, and peace?: strong (It is no problem for all to be raised at the same time in history.)

7. Can emphasize the resurrection of the earth and its implications for creation care?: strong (Our restoration to full personhood at the resurrection can coincide with the earth's resurrection.)

Re-formation, for the most part, fares well. Its weakest point is its difficulty accounting for animal resurrection. For me, that is a serious strike against it. I am also concerned about its difficulty explaining how organizing patterns can exist without matter and how they can think and be conscious without brains or something like them.

I might, however, get better results by combining Self-as-Ensouled-Body, which I consider to be Re-formation's greatest appeal, with one of the Slipstream options. That way the person's pattern, or soul, would be connected with some kind of matter between death and resurrection and may also have some kind of brain that would allow it some consciousness. It could also more easily explain how an animal's pattern could survive its death by circumventing the problem of explaining how an animal's soul could function and thus exist without a body.

Let's see what happens when we apply the criteria to Soul Storage. If I allow the soul some minimal consciousness while in storage, then I can upgrade three of my criteria without having to downgrade any of them.

> 1. Handles neuroscientific data concerning the close connection between mind and brain?: strong (It requires something like a brain for thinking and consciousness.)
> 2. Has promising answers to objections?: strong (Patterns neither exist nor are conscious without matter.)
> 3. Makes possible the resurrection of at least the higher animals: strong (Animal patterns can be stored more easily than human patterns.)

Some may quibble with Soul Storage's ability to answer objections. For example, they may question whether consciousness could exist in a storage device. Yet it is conceivable that an omnipotent God could create a storage device from which a minimal consciousness might emerge. Others may object that the soul cannot be stored in anything material other than its own body. But I see no reason why not so long as it is not actively shaping that material into its body. A song has a pattern. We store that pattern in a CD or flash drive where it is not actively shaping sound waves to give "body" to the song. Combining Re-formation with Soul Storage, however, still faces the *problem of duplication*. As noted in chapter 11, something about our organizing patterns would need to be inherently non-duplicable so that multiple copies of it could not, even in theory, be stored. So the combination of Re-formation and Soul Storage still has some work to do in showing what that something is.

Soul Storage gives me nearly all I want. So I choose it. But I might change my mind tomorrow. I might find reasons to reevaluate its handling of my criteria. Or I might find a better understanding of death and resurrection that fits Self-as-Ensouled-Body. I might also opt for Re-formation alone to explain the human person's death and resurrection, but choose Soul Storage to explain the animal's death and resurrection. There is no reason why God cannot use one option for humans and another one for non-human animals as long as a consistent criterion of identity over time is used in both cases.

You may find neither Re-formation nor Soul Storage as appealing or as promising. As this book has shown, you have many other promising options to choose from. Choose one and see how it handles your list of criteria. Or think up an option other than the ones I have explained in this book and then apply your criteria to it. The most important thing is to be consistent in your choice of view and be open to further modifying it as you continue to think about it and improve on it.

If God can get us from death to resurrection, then God can do so whether or not we have figured out how. But, in the meantime, we need to be actively working on developing beliefs about death and resurrection that are rational—that are consistent and can respond to challenges. It's important for dialoguing with those who deny the afterlife. It's also important for how we are to live this present life.

Let's keep thinking then about death and resurrection. Let's loosen our imaginations and ponder new possibilities. Imagining the resurrection is not empty speculation when grounded in careful considerations such as those in this book. Science fiction is the Christian's ally. It opens us up to considering other possibilities that may improve on those we are already familiar with. We need Christian geeks and nerds. Lots of them.

Meanwhile, our ship is set to self-destruct. And we have a button to push . . .

APPENDIX A

Death and Resurrection: The Options

1. Soul-Flight: The soul survives death and joins with a *numerically different* body at the resurrection.

  A. Traditional Dualism: The soul is created separately from the body and can unite with any body. It is also fully conscious when separate from the body.

  Works for: Self-as-Soul.

  B. Soul Sleep: The soul is not conscious when separate from the body because it needs a brain or something like it to be conscious.

  Works for: Self-as-Soul; Self-as-Emergent-Soul.

  C. Emergent Dualism: The soul emerges from the body but can exist and be conscious when separate from it. It can only unite with a body sufficiently similar to the body it first emerged from.

  Works for: Self-as-Emergent-Soul.

2. Reassembly: At the resurrection, God collects enough of *numerically the same* particles that made up the original body at death to form the resurrected body. The resurrected body is thus *numerically the same* body as the original body.

  Works for: Self-as-Body; Self-as-Brain.

3. Re-creation: At the resurrection, God remakes the person from scratch by creating a new body for the person. The body may or may not need to be sufficiently similar to the original body depending on the view of self that Re-creation uses. But most require that the body be sufficiently similar.

> **Works for:** Self-as-Structure; Self-as-Information-Bearing-Pattern; Self-as-Software; Self-as-Psyche; Self-as-First-Person-Perspective.

4. Re-formation: The person's essential pattern, or soul, survives the death of the body. That pattern shapes new matter at the resurrection into a body sufficiently similar to the original body. The soul cannot join with a body that is not sufficiently similar. Depending on the view of self that Re-formation uses, the resurrected body will be *numerically identical* to the original body because it is shaped by *numerically the same* soul as the original body.

> **Works for:** Self-as-Information-Bearing-Pattern; Self-as-Ensouled-Body.

5. Slipstream: At death, the person or the person's soul survives death by joining with matter in another dimension. At the resurrection, the person or the person's soul slips back into this dimension by joining with its resurrected body.

> **A. Body-Hopping:** At death, the person takes a *numerically different* body in the other dimension. That body is likely less substantial than the original body. At the resurrection, the person again takes a *numerically different* body.
>
> **Works for:** Self-as-Soul; Self-as-Emergent-Soul; Self-as-Structure, Self-as-Software; Self-as-Psyche; Self-as-First-Person-Perspective; Self-as-Information-Bearing-Pattern.
>
> **B. Body-Morphing:** At death, the person's soul uses new matter in another dimension to form a body sufficiently similar to the original body. That body though will be less substantial or able than the original body and may take a ghostly or chrysalide form. This temporary body may or may not be *numerically identical* to the original body depending on the view of self that this view uses. At the resurrection,

death and resurrection: the options

the person's soul uses new matter in its original dimension to form a substantial and fully able body that is sufficiently similar to the original body. The resurrected body may or may not be numerically identical to the original body depending on the view of self that this view uses.

Works for: Self-as-Information-Bearing-Pattern; Self-as-Ensouled-Body.

C. Body-Splitting: At death, the ongoing chain of life-processes that occur in our bodies splits in two. One ends in the corpse. Another continues in a less substantial body in another dimension. That body is *numerically identical* to the original body because it is a continuation of the original body's ongoing life-processes. Those ongoing life-processes continue in the resurrected body thus making the resurrected body *numerically identical* to the original body. This view works for views of the self that require having *numerically the same* body. It also works for views of the self that sometimes, but not usually, require sameness of body.

Works for: Self-as-Emergent-Soul; Self-as-Body; Self-as-Brain; Self-as-Psyche; Self-as-First-Person-Perspective; Self-as-Information-Bearing-Pattern; Self-as-Ensouled-Body; Self-as-Living Organism.

D. Body-Snatching: At death, God removes the person's body or brain and stores it in another dimension until the resurrection. God substitutes a fake body in its place, which is the person's corpse. The resurrected body or brain is *numerically identical* to the original body or brain because it was preserved in existence between death and resurrection. It also works for views of the self which may require a continually existing body.

Works for: Self-as-Emergent-Soul; Self-as-Body; Self-as-Brain; Self-as-Structure, Self-as-Software; Self-as-Psyche; Self-as-First-Person-Perspective; Self-as-Information-Bearing-Pattern; Self-as-Ensouled-Body; Self-as-Living-Organism.

E. Soul Storage: At death, God stores the person's essence, whether program or pattern, in some highly complex material storage device in another dimension. At the resurrection, God puts that essence into the resurrected body. The person's program or pattern may or may not be conscious when stored depending on whether or not it is possible.

Works for: Self-as-Software; Self-as-Information-Bearing-Pattern; Self-as-Ensouled-Body.

APPENDIX B

Views of the Self

1. Self-as-Soul: I am my soul. Any future person is the same person as me as long as he is the same soul as I am.

    Works best with: Soul-Flight: Traditional Dualism, Soul Sleep.

    Can work with: Slipstream: Body-Hopping.

2. Self-as-Emergent-Soul: I am my *emergent* soul. Any future person is the same person as me as long as he is the same *emergent* soul as I am.

    Works best with: Soul-Flight: Emergent Dualism.

    Can work with: Soul-Flight: Soul Sleep; Slipstream: Body-Hopping, Body-Splitting, Body-Snatching.

3. Self-as-First-Person-Perspective: I am my *first-person perspective*, or my awareness of being me. A future person is the same person as me as long as he is the type of being that has the possibility of having the same *first-person perspective* as me.

    Works with: Re-creation; Slipstream: Body-Hopping, Body-Splitting, Body-Snatching.

4. Self-as-Psyche: I am my psyche. I am the stream of memories, thoughts, beliefs, desires, emotions, talents, personality traits, moral traits, personal relationships, choices, perceptions, and experiences that make up my psychological life. Any future person is the same person as me as long as he has the same psyche, or consciousness, as me.

Works with: Re-creation; Slipstream: Body-Hopping, Body-Splitting, Body-Snatching.

5. Self-as-Software: I am a highly complex program, much like a computer software program. Any future person is the same person as me as long as he is the same program as I am.

Works with: Re-creation; Slipstream: Body-Hopping, Body-Snatching, Soul Storage.

6. Self-as-Information-Bearing-Pattern: Any future person is the same person as me as long as he is the same *information-bearing pattern* as I am.

Works with: Re-creation; Re-formation; Slipstream: Body-Hopping, Body-Morphing, Body-Splitting, Body-Snatching, Soul Storage.

7. Self-as-Ensouled-Body: Any future person is the same person as me as long as he is the same ensouled body as I am and thus has the same soul and body as I have.

Works with: Re-formation; Slipstream: Body-Morphing, Body-Splitting, Body-Snatching, Soul Storage.

8. Self-as-Structure: I am a bodily structure. Any future person is the same person as me as long as he has the same bodily structure as I have.

Works with: Re-creation; Slipstream: Body-Hopping, Body-Snatching.

9. Self-as-Living-Organism: I am a living organism. Any future person is the same person as me as long as he is part of the same ongoing biological life as I am.

Works with: Slipstream: Body-Splitting, Body-Snatching.

10. Self-as-Body: I am my body. Any future person is the same person as me as long as he is the same body as I am.

Works with: Reassembly; Slipstream: Body-Splitting, Body-Snatching.

11. Self-as-Brain: I am my brain. Any future person is the same person as me as long as he is the same brain as I am.

Works with: Reassembly; Slipstream: Body-Splitting, Body-Snatching.

APPENDIX C

The Timing of the Resurrection

1. Immediate: The person is resurrected immediately in another dimension.

    Works with: Soul-Flight: Traditional Dualism, Emergent Dualism; Re-creation; Re-formation; Slipstream: Body-Hopping, Body-Splitting, Body-Snatching.

2. Future: The person is resurrected in the future of this dimension.

    Works with: all options.

3. Immediate/Future: The person is immediately resurrected in the future of this dimension through the folding of the future back onto the past.

    Works with: Soul-Flight: Traditional Dualism, Emergent Dualism; Re-creation; Re-formation; Slipstream: Body-Hopping, Body-Splitting, Body-Snatching.

APPENDIX D

Glossary

Communion of the Saints: The traditional Christian belief in a spiritual union between living Christians and the Christian dead in Heaven and Purgatory. It is connected with belief in an *Interim State*.

Dualism: The belief that we are made up of two parts, the material body and an invisible immaterial part. Emergent dualism holds that our immaterial part emerges from our brains, whereas traditional dualism denies this.

Emergence: The belief that a property, such as a belief, or a mind can arise from a collection of parts, such as neurons, such that the property or mind is greater than the sum of those parts and can't be fully explained by them.

First-Person Perspective: The way in which I can think of myself as a someone, a self, and a subject. It is my awareness that I am me.

General Resurrection: The traditional Christian belief that all will be raised at the same time at the end of history.

Holism, Holistic Anthropology: The belief that we are integrated wholes with spiritual and material aspects. We do not consist of two or more completely distinct and different substances.

Immediate Resurrection: The belief that we are immediately resurrected after we die. There is no gap in time between the moment we die and the moment we are raised.

Information-Bearing Pattern: An essential pattern or structure that carries information about a person's personality, moral traits, memories, beliefs, desires, habits, relationships, bodily structure, and such.

Interim State: The traditional Christian belief that the dead exist and are conscious in some state between death and resurrection.

Natural Immortality: The belief that we naturally survive our deaths. God does not need to intervene to make our survival possible.

Near-Death Experience: A personal experience, near death, in which a person seems to leave the body and experience another world. It usually includes meeting deceased loved ones.

New Earth: The belief that the Earth will be renewed and somehow preserved at the *General Resurrection*.

Numerical Difference, Numerically Different: Two things are numerically different to each other if they count as two different things in the universe. Numerical difference does not mean that they do not resemble each other, have different characteristics, or are different kinds of things. It means that they are not one and the same thing. A suitcase at 8:45 p.m. is numerically different from a suitcase at 8:30 p.m. if they are not one and the same suitcase, even though the suitcase at 8:45 p.m. may look like the suitcase at 8:30 p.m. and be the same brand of suitcase as the suitcase at 8:30 p.m.

Numerical Identity, Numerically the Same: Two things are numerically identical to each other if they count as one and the same thing in the universe. Numerical sameness does not mean that the two things resemble each other, share many characteristics, or are the same kinds of things. It means that they are the one and the same thing. A suitcase at 8:45 p.m. is numerically identical to a suitcase at 8:30 p.m. if they both count as one and the same suitcase even though the suitcase at 8:45 p.m. may now be painted red.

Non-reductionism: Everything cannot be ultimately explained in terms of elementary particles and the laws of physics.

Only X and Y Principle: The principle that our *personal identity over time* cannot depend on what may or may not happen to some other thing or person.

Personal Identity over Time: The problem of determining what makes a person at a later time *numerically the same* person as a person at an earlier time.

Physicalism: The belief that only physical things exist. Therefore, we have no immaterial parts, such as souls.

Problem of Duplication: Suppose that something can, in principle, be duplicated or split such that the resulting two things have equal claims to being *numerical identical* to the thing that was duplicated or split. If so, then that thing cannot be what determines *personal identity over time* since it would violate the *only X and Y principle*.

Psychological Features: The parts of us that we associate with our minds, such as memories, beliefs, desires, emotions, talents, personality traits, and moral traits.

Reductionism: The belief that everything can ultimately be explained in terms of elementary particles and the laws of physics. Or, regarding the mind, the belief that everything about the mind can ultimately be explained in terms of the activities of the neurons in our brain operating according to the laws of science.

Sheol: The shadowy place of the dead in the Old Testament.

Trichotomism: The belief that we are made up of three parts: body, soul, and spirit.

Bibliography

Adler, Jerry. "Atheists Discuss the Benefits of Faith." *Newsweek*, November 9, 2006. http://www.newsweek.com/atheists-discuss-benefits-faith-106975.
Aquinas, Thomas. "My Soul Is Not Me." In *Aquinas: Selected Philosophical Writings*, edited and translated by Timothy McDermott, 192–93. Oxford: Oxford University Press, 1993.
———. *Summa Theologica*. Translated by Fathers of the English Dominican Province. Westminster, MA: Christian Classics, 1981.
Augustine. *The City of God*. Translated by Marcus Dods. New York: Modern Library, 1950.
———. *Confessions*. Translated by Henry Chadwick. Oxford: Oxford University Press, 2008.
———. *On the Care to Be Had for the Dead*. Translated by H. Browne. http://www.fordham.edu/halsall/source/augustine-onthecareofthgedeadnpnf1-03-39.asp.
Badham, Paul. *Christian Beliefs about Life after Death*. London: Macmillan, 1976.
Bartholomew, Anita. "After Life: The Scientific Case for the Human Soul." *Reader's Digest*, August 2003, 122–27.
Bloesch, Donald. *The Last Things: Resurrection, Judgment, Glory*. Christian Foundations 7. Downers Grove: InterVarsity, 2004.
Brown, Montague. "Aquinas on the Resurrection of the Body." *Thomist* 56 (1991) 165–207.
Brown, Warren S. "Cognitive Contributions to Soul." In Warren S. Brown et al., *Whatever Happened to the Soul?*, 99–125.
———. "Conclusion: Reconciling Scientific and Biblical Portraits of Human Nature." In Warren S. Brown et al., *Whatever Happened to the Soul?*, 213–28.
Brown, Warren, et al., eds. *Whatever Happened to the Soul? Scientific and Theological Portraits of Human Nature*. Minneapolis: Fortress, 1998.
Bynum, Caroline. *The Resurrection of the Body in Western Christianity, 200–1336*. Lectures on the History of Religions, Sponsored by the American Council of Learned Societies, New Series 15. New York: Columbia University Press, 1995.
Cooper, John. *Body, Soul, and Life Everlasting: Biblical Anthropology and the Monism-Dualism Debate*. Grand Rapids: Eerdmans, 1989.
Corcoran, Kevin. "The Constitution View of Persons." In Green and Palmer, *In Search of the Soul*, 153–76.
———. *Rethinking Human Nature: A Christian Materialist Alternative to the Soul*. Grand Rapids: Baker, 2006.

———, ed. *Soul, Body, and Survival: Essays on the Metaphysics of Human Persons*. Ithaca, NY: Cornell University Press, 2001.
Crick, Francis. *The Astonishing Hypothesis: The Scientific Search for the Soul*. New York: Scribner, 1994.
Cullmann, Oscar. *Immortality of the Soul or Resurrection of the Dead? The Witness of the New Testament*. London: Epworth, 1958.
Damasio, Antonio. *Descartes' Error: Emotion, Reason, and the Human Brain*. Rev. ed. New York: Penguin, 1994.
Dante. *The Divine Comedy of Dante Alighieri: Purgatorio*. Translated by Allen Mandelbaum. New York: Random House, 2004.
Davies, Brian. *An Introduction to the Philosophy of Religion*. 3rd ed. Oxford: Oxford University Press, 2004.
———. *The Thought of Thomas Aquinas*. Oxford: Clarendon, 1992.
Dawkins, Richard, and Steven Pinker. "Is Science Killing the Soul?" Interview by John Brockman, the Guardian-Dillons Debate, Westminster Central Hall, London, February 10, 1999. http://edge.org/conversation/is-science-killing-the-soul.
Dennett, Daniel. "The Non-Believer." Interview by Deborah Solomon. *New York Times Magazine*, January 22, 2006. http://www.nytimes.com/2006/01/22/magazine/22wwln_q4.html?_r=0.
———. *Sweet Dreams: Philosophical Obstacles to a Science of Consciousness*. Cambridge: MIT Press, 2005.
Descartes, René. *Meditations on First Philosophy*. 3rd ed. Translated by Donald Cress. Indianapolis: Hackett, 1993.
———. "The Passions of the Soul." In *The Philosophical Writings of Descartes*, edited and translated by John Cottingham et al., 1:325–404. Cambridge: Cambridge University Press, 1985.
Dunn, James. *The Theology of Paul the Apostle*. Grand Rapids: Eerdmans, 1998.
Emerson, Ralph Waldo. "Self-Reliance." In *Ralph Waldo Emerson: Selected Essays, Lectures, and Poems*, edited by Robert Richardson Jr., 148–71. New York: Bantam, 1990.
Evans, Abigail Rian. *Is God Still at the Bedside? The Medical, Ethical, and Pastoral Issues of Death and Dying*. Grand Rapids: Eerdmans, 2010.
Fowler, Shannon. "Why New Atoms Aren't a Fountain of Youth." *NPR.org*, July 14, 2007. http://www.npr.org/templates/story/story.php?storyId=11893583.
Francis of Assisi. "The Canticle of Brother Sun." In *Francis and Clare: The Complete Works*, edited and translated by Regis Armstrong and Ignatius Brady, 38–39. New York: Paulist, 1982.
Geach, Peter. *God and the Soul*. 2nd ed. South Bend, IN: St. Augustine's, 1969.
Goetz, Stewart. "Substance Dualism." In Green and Palmer, *In Search of the Soul*, 33–60.
Green, Joel B. "'Bodies—That Is, Human Lives': A Re-examination of Human Nature in the Bible." In Warren S. Brown et al., *Whatever Happened to the Soul?*, 149–73.
———. *Body, Soul, and Human Life: The Nature of Humanity in the Bible*. Grand Rapids: Baker, 2008.
———. "Resurrection of the Body: New Testament Voices concerning Personal Continuity and the Afterlife." In Green, *What about the Soul?*, 85–100.

———, ed. *What about the Soul? Neuroscience and Christian Anthropology*. Nashville: Abingdon, 2004.

Green, Joel, and Stuart Palmer, eds. *In Search of the Soul: Four Views of the Mind-Body Problem*. Downers Grove: InterVarsity, 2005.

Gundry, Robert. *Sōma in Biblical Theology with Emphasis on Pauline Anthropology*. Society for New Testament Studies Monograph Series 29. Cambridge: Cambridge University Press, 1976.

Hanley, Richard. *The Metaphysics of Star Trek*. New York: HarperCollins, 1997.

Harris, Murray. *Raised Immortal: Resurrection and Immortality in the New Testament*. Grand Rapids: Eerdmans, 1983.

Hasker, William. "Emergent Dualism: Challenge to a Materialist Consensus." In Green, *What about the Soul?*, 101–15.

———. *The Emergent Self*. Ithaca, NY: Cornell University Press, 1999.

———. "On Behalf of Emergent Dualism." In Green and Palmer, *In Search of the Soul*, 75–100.

Hassabis, Demis, et al. "Imagine All the People: How the Brain Creates and Uses Personality Models to Predict Behavior." *Cerebral Cortex*, March 2013. http://cercor.oxfordjournals.org/content/early/2013/03/04/cercor.bht042.full.

Hick, John. *Death and Eternal Life*. Louisville: Westminster John Knox, 1994.

———. *Philosophy of Religion*. 3rd ed. Englewood Cliffs, NJ: Prentice Hall, 1983.

Homer. *The Odyssey: The Story of Odysseus*. Translated by W. H. D. Rouse. New York: Mentor, 1937.

Hyland, J. R. *God's Covenant with Animals: A Biblical Basis for the Humane Treatment of All Creatures*. New York: Lantern, 2000.

James Randi Educational Foundation Staff. "One Million Dollar Paranormal Challenge." http://www.randi.org/site/index.php/1m-challenge/challenge-faq.html.

Jaworski, William. *Philosophy of Mind: A Comprehensive Introduction*. Oxford: Wiley-Blackwell, 2011.

Jeeves, Malcolm. "Brain, Mind, and Behavior." In Warren S. Brown et al., *Whatever Happened to the Soul?*, 73–98.

———. "Human Nature: An Integrated Picture." In Green, *What about the Soul?*, 171–89.

———. "Mind Reading and Soul Searching in the Twenty-First Century: The Scientific Evidence." In Green, *What about the Soul?*, 13–30.

Jones, D. Gareth. "A Neurobiological Portrait of the Human Person: Finding a Context for Approaching the Brain." In Green, *What about the Soul?*, 31–46.

Kafka, Franz. *Metamorphosis*. Translated by David Wyllie. Project Gutenberg, 2002. http://www.gutenberg.org/files/5200/5200-h/5200-h.htm.

Kagan, Shelly. *Death*. New Haven: Yale University Press, 2012.

Kassam, Karim, et al. "Identifying Emotions on the Basis of Neural Activation." *PLoS ONE* 8 (2013) 1–12. http://www.plosone.org/article/fetchObject.action?uri=info%3Adoi%2F10.1371%2Fjournal.pone.0066032&representation=PDF.

Langley, Silas. "Aquinas, Resurrection, and Material Continuity." In *Proceedings of the American Catholic Philosophical Association: Person, Soul, and Immortality*, edited by Michael Baur, 135–47. New York: American Catholic Philosophical Association, 2001.

Lewis, C. S. *The Last Battle*. New York: Macmillan, 1956.
———. *The Problem of Pain*. New York: Collier, 1962.
Linder, Douglas. "The Leopold and Loeb Trial: A Brief Account." University of Missouri-Kansas City, School of Law, 1997. http://law2.umkc.edu/faculty/projects/ftrials/leoploeb/accountoftrial.html.
Lindsay, Ronald. "Thomas Aquinas's Complete Guide to Heaven and Hell." *Free Inquiry* 11 (1990) 38–39.
Linke, Detlef. "God Gives the Memory: Neuroscience and Resurrection." In Peters et al., *Resurrection*, 185–91.
Martin, Raymond, and John Barresi. *The Rise and Fall of Soul and Self: An Intellectual History of Personal Identity*. New York: Columbia University Press, 2006.
McDannell, Colleen, and Bernhard Lang. *Heaven: A History*. New Haven: Yale University Press, 1988.
Meacham, John. "Heaven Can't Wait: Why Rethinking the Hereafter Could Make the World a Better Place." *Time* 179 (2012) 30–36.
Mitchell, Tom, et al. "Predicting Human Brain Activity Associated with the Meanings of Nouns." *Science* 320 (2008), 1191–95. http://www.stanford.edu/class/cs379c/suggested_reading_list/supplements/documents/MitchelletalSCIENCE-08.pdf.
Moltmann, Jürgen. "Is There Life after Death?" In *The End of the World and the Ends of God: Science and Theology on Eschatology*, edited by John Polkinghorne and Michael Welker, 238–55. Harrisburg: Trinity, 2000.
Murphy, Nancey. *Bodies and Souls, or Spirited Bodies?* Cambridge: Cambridge University Press, 2006.
———. "Nonreductive Physicalism." In Green and Palmer, *In Search of the Soul*, 115–38.
———. "Nonreductive Physicalism: Philosophical Issues." In Warren S. Brown et al., *Whatever Happened to the Soul?*, 127–48.
———. "The Resurrection Body and Personal Identity: Possibilities and Limits of Eschatological Knowledge." In Peters et al., *Resurrection*, 202–18.
Murphy, Todd, and Michael Persinger. "Debate Concerning the God Helmet." http://www.innerworlds.50megs.com/The_God_Helmet_Debate.htm.
Nagel, Thomas. *Mind and Cosmos: Why the Materialist Neo-Darwinian Conception of Nature Is Almost Certainly False*. Oxford: Oxford University Press, 2012.
———. *What Does It All Mean? A Very Short Introduction to Philosophy*. Oxford: Oxford University Press, 1987.
———. "What Is It Like to Be a Bat?" *Philosophical Review* 83 (1974) 435–50.
Nichols, Terence. *Death and Afterlife: A Theological Introduction*. Grand Rapids: Brazos, 2010.
Nishimoto, Shinji, et al. "Reconstructing Visual Experiences from Brain Activity Evoked by Natural Movies." *Current Biology* 21 (October 2011), 1641–46. http://gallantlab.org/_downloads/2011a.Nishimoto.etal.pdf.
Nowakowski, Richard. "Stable Neuron Numbers from Cradle to Grave." *Proceedings of the National Academy of Sciences* 103 (2006) 12219–20. http://www.pnas.org/content/103/33/12219.full.
Palmer, Stuart. "Christian Life and Theories of Human Nature." In Green and Palmer, *In Search of the Soul*, 189–215.

———. "Pastoral Care and Counseling Without the 'Soul': A Consideration of Emergent Monism." In Green, *What about the Soul?*, 159–70.

Parfit, Derek. *Reasons and Persons*. Oxford: Oxford University Press, 1984.

Pasnau, Robert. *Thomas Aquinas on Human Nature: A Philosophical Study of Summa Theologiae* 1a, 75–89. Port Chester, NY: Cambridge University Press, 2001.

Perry, John. *A Dialogue on Personal Identity and Immortality*. Indianapolis: Hackett, 1978.

Peters, Ted, et al., eds. *Resurrection: Theological and Scientific Assessments*. Grand Rapids: Eerdmans, 2002.

Pickover, Clifford. *A Beginner's Guide to Immortality: Extraordinary People, Alien Brains, and Quantum Resurrection*. New York: Thunder's Mouth, 2007.

Plato. *Phaedo*. Translated by G. M. A. Grube. Indianapolis: Hackett, 1977.

Polanyi, Michael. *The Tacit Dimension*. Garden City: Anchor, 1967.

Polkinghorne, John. "Eschatological Credibility: Emergent and Teleological Processes." In Peters et al., *Resurrection*, 43–55.

———. *The God of Hope and the End of the World*. New Haven: Yale University Press, 2002.

———. *Quarks, Chaos, and Christianity: Question to Science and Religion*. Rev. ed. New York: Crossroad, 2005.

Ross, James. "Together with the Body I Love." In *Proceedings of the American Catholic Philosophical Association: Person, Soul, and Immortality*, edited by Michael Baur, 1–18. New York: American Catholic Philosophical Association, 2001.

Rowling, J. K. *Harry Potter and the Deathly Hallows*. New York: Scholastic, 2007.

Rynkiewich, Michael. "What about the Dust? Missiological Musings on Anthropology." In Green, *What about the Soul?*, 133–44.

Sample, Ian. "Stephen Hawking: 'There Is No Heaven; It's a Fairy Story.'" *Guardian*, May 15, 2011. http://www.guardian.co.uk/science/2011/may/15/stephen-hawking-interview-there-is-no-heaven.

Shakespeare, William. *Hamlet*. http://www.opensourceshakespeare.org/views/plays/play_view.php?WorkID=hamlet&Scope=entire&pleasewait=1&msg=pl#a5,s1.

Skinner, B. F. *Walden Two*. Indianapolis: Hackett, 2005.

Sommerhoff, Gerd. "The Abstract Characteristics of Living Systems." In *Systems Thinking: Selected Readings*, edited by F. E. Emery, 147–202. Harmondsworth, UK: Penguin, 1969.

Stump, Eleonore. "Non-Cartesian Dualism and Materialism without Reductionism." *Faith and Philosophy* 12 (1995) 505–31.

Swinburne, Richard. *The Evolution of the Soul*. Oxford: Clarendon, 1997.

Thiselton, Anthony. *Life after Death: A New Approach to the Last Things*. Grand Rapids: Eerdmans, 2012.

Van Inwagen, Peter. "The Possibility of Resurrection." *International Journal for Philosophy of Religion* 9 (1978) 114–21.

Wade, Nicholas. "Your Body Is Younger than You Think." *NYTimes.com*, August 2, 2005. http://www.nytimes.com/2005/08/02/science/02cell.html?pagewanted=all&_r=0.

Webb, Stephen. *Good Eating*. Christian Practice of Everyday Life series. Grand Rapids: Brazos, 2001.

Wesley, John. "Sermon 60: The General Deliverance." Preached November 30, 1781. http://www.ccel.org/ccel/wesley/sermons.vi.vii.html#fna_vi.vii-p0.4.

Wright, N. T. *For All the Saints? Remembering the Christian Departed*. London: SPCK, 2003.

———. *Revelation for Everyone*. Louisville: Westminster John Knox, 2011.

———. *Surprised by Hope: Rethinking Heaven, the Resurrection, and the Mission of the Church*. New York: Harper, 2008.

Subject Index

abortion, 41
All Saint's Day, 14, 148, 150
All Soul's Day, 148, 150, 186
animalism, 131
animals
    and resurrection, 178, 183-86, 202, 204-205
    and souls, 73-74, 115-16, 119, 181-83
    in Heaven, 14, 178-86, 198
    treatment of, 185-86, 192
body-hopping, 129, 133-34, 140-41, 143, 185, 199
body-morphing, 129, 135-37, 140-41, 143, 149, 152, 156, 185
body-snatching, 129-32, 140-41, 143, 149, 152, 185, 199
body-splitting, 129, 137-41, 143, 152, 156, 185, 199
brain damage, 33, 62, 67
Buddhist conception of the self, 111
burial, 13, 151-54
care for others, 170-72
commissurotomy. *See* split-brain operation.
communion of the saints, 147-151, 202, 204
community, 23, 25, 168, 170, 191-93, 202, 204
consciousness, 31-32, 36, 42, 57-58, 61, 67, 73-76, 97, 103, 114, 117, 123. 142-43, 183, 203, 205
conservation of energy, law of the, 58-60, 139

creation of the soul, 31-32, 72-74, 123-24
creation, renewing of, 22-25, 187, 190
cremation, 13, 151-54, 202, 204
death
    as enemy, 25-26, 29, 54, 119, 154-56, 201-204
    as friend, 54, 154-56, 202, 204
    as natural, 13, 25, 136-37, 155-56
dualism, 18-19, 53-54, 56-58, 62-64, 67, 73-76, 108-9, 112, 117, 119, 123-24, 171-72, 199
duplication, problem of, 45-47, 83, 86, 102, 104-6, 113, 119, 130, 134, 139, 141, 201-202, 204-205
embryology, 32, 73-75, 124, 201, 203
emergence, 68-69
emergent dualism, 68-76, 109, 114-15, 119, 123, 129, 131, 133, 152, 175, 182-83, 193, 198-99
euthanasia, 41
evangelism, 170
evolution, 31, 72-75, 124, 201, 203
first-person perspective, 102-4, 120, 184-85
forgiveness, 175
free will, 61, 79, 172-75
funerals, 13, 148, 156
general resurrection, 22-25, 29, 104-5, 131, 138, 143, 151, 187-94, 201-203, 204
ghostly bodies, 132-33, 135-36, 140, 160, 164
ghosts, 7, 14, 140, 157, 164-65, 202
"God helmet", 36

"Green" burial, 154
Hamlet, 129, 197
Harry Potter, 27, 97, 119, 140, 190-91
heaven, 6-11, 13-14, 22-27, 41, 52-54, 121-22, 132, 143, 148, 149-50, 155, 159-60, 170, 178-81, 186-91
hell, 132, 191
holistic anthropology, 18-19, 29, 55, 61n7, 93, 105-6, 120, 153, 200-201, 203
identity over time, problem of, 39-40
immediate resurrection, 24-25, 93, 98, 104-5, 143-144, 150, 159, 163-64, 192-94, 199
immortality of the soul, 28-29, 82, 117
information-bearing-patterns, 109-14, 131, 141, 182
interim state, 20-22, 24, 26, 29, 68, 113, 120, 122-23, 136, 144, 148-50, 163, 185, 199-201, 203
Last Judgment, 8, 22-23, 25, 82, 94, 98
Leopold and Loeb Trial, 174
lifestyle, 168-69
mediums, 157, 162-65, 202
memento mori, 197
memory, 6, 11, 26, 32, 34-35, 42-44, 46-47, 61, 67, 76, 96-100, 109, 111, 161, 183
mind-body interaction. *See* soul-body interaction.
moral traits, 33, 96
near-death experiences, 14, 157-62, 165, 202
neuroscience, 11, 32-37, 61-64, 67, 73-74, 76, 93, 101, 105, 119, 123, 160-61, 201, 203, 205
new earth, 23-24, 187-94
non-contradiction, law of, 8-9
non-reductionism, 70
numerical identity, 39-42
omnipotence, 9
only X and Y principle, 45-46, 102
peace, 180, 191-92, 202, 204
personal identity over time, problem of 40-47, 97-98, 102, 120, 201-202, 204

personality, 11, 32-33, 40-42, 44, 46, 61, 63-64, 96, 111-12, 176
physicalism, 57-58, 62, 124
praise/blame, 172-75
praying for the dead, 147-50
pre-existence of the soul, 31
problem of duplication. *See* duplication, problem of.
psychological features, 11, 32, 37, 44, 61, 79, 96-97, 99-101, 173, 184
purgatory, 132, 148-50
quantum resurrection, 28-29
Reassembly, 77-88, 115, 118-20, 130, 138, 150-53, 156, 159, 163-64, 175, 183, 193-94, 198-99
Re-creation, 89-106, 113-14, 119-20, 150-52, 156, 159, 163-64, 175-76, 184, 194, 198-200
reductionism, 70, 101, 113
Re-formation, 107-126, 137, 149-50, 152-53, 156, 159, 163-65, 176, 182-83, 188, 194, 198-200, 202-206
reincarnation, 8, 81, 144
relational view of the self, 19, 97, 112, 120-21, 153, 176
relics, 82, 153
religious experience, 35-36, 169
replication, problem of, 101-104
resurrected body, the, 26-28, 72, 79, 82-84, 86-87, 114, 118, 132, 152, 194, 198-99
resurrection
  as metaphor, 6
  of Christ, 22, 26-27, 29, 56, 60, 81, 154, 164
rich man and Lazarus, story of the, 21, 24-25, 122
salvation, 170
Self-as-Body, 79, 130-31
Self-as-Brain, 80, 130-31
Self-as-Ensouled-Body, 115, 130, 135-37, 141-42, 176, 202, 205-206
Self-as-First-Person-Perspective, 103-4, 130, 139-40, 175-76, 185
Self-as-Information-Bearing-Pattern, 110-14, 130, 133-34, 175
Self-as-Living-Organism, 131

Self-as-Psyche, 96-101, 105, 130, 133-34, 175-76, 184-85
Self-as-Software, 95, 130, 133
Self-as-Soul, 52-65, 69, 72, 79, 82, 100, 105-6, 129, 185
Self-as-Structure, 94, 113, 130
Sheol, 20, 54, 94, 133
ship of Theseus, 84
Slipstream, 127-144, 149, 152-53, 156, 160, 163-65, 176, 185, 188, 193-94, 198-200, 205
soul-body interaction, problem of, 56-58, 74, 119
Soul-Flight, 51-76, 80-82, 98, 119, 148, 152, 155, 159, 163-65, 175, 181-82, 193-94, 198-99

Soul Sleep, 66-68, 113, 119, 129, 141, 148, 159, 163-64, 175, 193, 199
Soul Storage, 129, 140-43, 149, 156, 185, 205-206
spiritual body, 27, 55
split-brain operation, 36, 73-74
Star Trek, 35, 45-47, 96, 103, 128-30, 142, 163
suicide, 171
trichotomism, 18
vegetarianism, 183, 186
well-being, 167-68
worship, 169

Name Index

Aquinas, Thomas. *See* Thomas Aquinas.
Augustine, 81-82, 164, 170
Bynum, Caroline, 28n8, 118n4
Calvin, John, 181
Cooper, John, 19n3, 158n2
Corcoran, Kevin, 126n9, 139-40
Crick, Francis, 79-80
Cullmann, Oscar, 154-55
Damasio, Antonio, 33n2
Dante, 127, 132-33, 135
Darrow, Clarence, 174
Davies, Brian, 101, 118n3
Dawkins, Richard, 61, 65
Dennett, Daniel, 58n5, 61, 65,
Descartes, 28, 56, 62, 64, 181-82
Doyle, Arthur Conan, 163
Dunn, James, 18n1, 20n5,
Emerson, Ralph Waldo, 8
Francis of Assisi, 59, 155
Gage, Phineas, 33, 63, 99, 111
Geach, Peter, 80n2, 88, 118n3
Green, Joel, 18n1, 19n2
Gundry, Robert, 18n1
Harris, Murray, 20n4
Hasker, William, 71n2, 126n9
Hawking, Stephen, 96
Heraclitus, 40
Hick, John, 90-93, 101
Homer, 132-33
Hume, David, 112
Jesus, 20-25, 29, 56, 59-60, 81, 120, 122-23, 151, 154-56, 164, 170, 190
Kafka, Franz, 100
Kagan, Shelly, 179

Laplace, Pierre Simon de, 59
Lewis, C.S., 9, 179, 181, 184
Locke, John, 100
Luther, Martin, 25, 66, 180
Moltmann, Jürgen, 148n1
Murphy, Nancey, 18n1, 35n7
Nagel, Thomas, 57n4, 75n3
Parfit, Derek, 46
Pasnau, Robert, 123n6
Paul, 10, 20, 22-28, 54-55, 80, 87, 94, 104, 122-23, 155, 187
Persinger, Michael, 36
Pickover, Clifford, 28
Pinker, Steven, 61
Plato, 28, 168n2, 171
Polanyi, Michael, 177
Polkinghorne, John, 23n6, 109-16, 120, 125, 154n3, 182
Porco, Carolyn, 9
Randi, James, 164
Ross, James, 135n5
Rowling, J.K., 119, 190n10
Schiavo, Terry, 103
Shakespeare, William, 197
Skinner, B.F., 174
Socrates, 154-56, 168
Stump, Eleonore, 118n4
Swinburne, Richard, 67n1
Thomas Aquinas, 9, 14, 82, 109, 114-21, 123-26, 135, 149, 156, 164, 179-82
Van Inwagen, Peter, 130-31
Virgil, 132-33
Wesley, John, 181
Wright, N.T., 23n6, 150, 180, 189-90

Scripture Index

Genesis
2:7   19

Psalm
25:20   19
36:6   179

Isaiah
11:6-9a   180

Matthew
4:4   122
6:10   23
26:39   155

Luke
23:43   21, 120, 122

Romans
8:19-23   23
8:21   187

1 Corinthians
15   10, 29, 87
15:18-19   22
15:19   26
15:20-22   22
15:20   81
15:26   25, 155
15:42-44   27, 80
15:49   27n7
15:52b   23
15:52b-55   80-81
15:54-55   25-26
15:56-57   25

2 Corinthians
5:2-4   24
5:8   20, 54, 94, 122
12:2-4   20

Philippians
3:21   27n7

Colossians
1:20   187, 191

1 Thessalonians
4:16   23

Revelation
21   187
4:6b-8   180

www.ingramcontent.com/pod-product-compliance
Lightning Source LLC
Chambersburg PA
CBHW052058230426
43662CB00036B/1393